DIFFERENT PEOPLE

DIFFERENT PEOPLE

Conversations on Art, Life
and the Creative Process

Carl Abrahamsson

With 19 photographic portraits by the author.

TRAPART books

Different People
Trapart Books 2021

ISBN 978-91-986243-6-6

Text & Photographs © 2021 Carl Abrahamsson

Trapart Books
P.O. Box 8105
SE-104 20 Stockholm
Sweden

info@trapart.net
www.trapart.net
www.patreon.com/vanessa23carl

Different People

Carl Abrahamsson: Introduction   7

Conrad Rooks   9

Malcolm McLaren   25

Stelarc   39

John Duncan   55

Charles Gatewood   73

Mark McCloud   89

Ralph Metzner   109

Peter Beard   123

Bill Landis   135

Ralph Gibson   145

Maja Elliott   157

Michael Bowen   169

Bob Colacello   183

Dian Hanson   195

Anton Corbijn   207

June Newton   221

Kendell Geers   235

Simeon Coxe III   247

Vicki Bennett   257

Brian Williams   269

DIFFE
RENT

PEOPLE

Different People: Introduction

As a journalist, I am basically a fanzine writer. Always was, always will be. What that means is that I've always been driven by my own desires rather than waiting for an assignment from some editor. I've always chased, retrieved, amassed and written up stories based on my own whims and interests — fairly indifferent as to whether any magazine, newspaper or website would eventually take the piece in question. Somehow it's always worked out, and I cherish that independent spirit. The safety of being employed by a magazine would probably have made greater financial sense, but there's certainly something to be said for the actual freedom of *free*lancers.

I like people who think, feel and will things. And who then create art based on that existential bedrock trio. I know it's an extremely vague and worn-out word, but "passion" can be both endearing and inspiring — even if you're not really super interested in what a certain person is doing. The mere force of passion can definitely be good enough for a great story.

In 2007, I anthologized some interviews in a Swedish book called *Olika Människor* (that's right: "Different People"). It was suggested by an underground publisher, and I thought it was interesting to see how these pieces (basically written between 2000 and 2007) would work as a whole.

The book didn't really do that well. Sweden is, after all, a very small country, and most of the people I like to talk to are under the radar of norm-core reality. I was, however, happy about the fact that many younger journalists liked the book, and found my attitude of allowing people to truly talk engaging and refreshing. Being a journalism college dropout myself, I knew exactly what they meant. I absolutely hated the taught formality of standardized journalism, and decided, at age 23, to just carry on with my own approach, no matter what. I have never regretted that decision.

Returning to this specific material in 2021, I can see it all from a better and wider bird's eye view. When you put loose ends together, you can sometimes see a pattern emerging, and you can — hopefully — tie all these ends up. Are the voices too disparate? Perhaps, but then so is every day of our lives. Are the voices too desperate? Perhaps, but then that just makes them create great things. Are they representing something homogenous? I hope not.

There is one thing that unites them, though: these people create culture, whether we like that culture or not. Personally I do like it, because once upon a time I made it clear that I did want to talk to these very different people. As many current affairs aspects of these talks are already long gone, what remains is hopefully some kind of psychological, intuitive insight into creative minds that experience trials and tribulations just like you and me. Perhaps not of exactly the same nature or essence, but trials and tribulations none the less.

Creators of culture often have a quite problematic relationship with themselves and the inherent aspects of creativity: compensation, narcissism, solipsism, bitterness, etc. It seems to be part of the psychological make-up of most creatives to feel a strong need to be acknowledged. I'm not here to specifically analyze why this is in each specific case, but I am certainly here to acknowledge and appreciate these creatives and their work, as they were and as it was. Whatever is needed to keep them going is all fine by me.

I already more or less knew what these people wanted to say – sometimes even before the meetings and actual conversations. But to see beyond the predictable, and keep asking "why" and "why not" is still my job after some 35 years of talking to creative people. This anthology reflects a mere portion, a segment, a piece of the pie of curiosity that will hopefully remain after we've gobbled it all up.

This book is very different from the Swedish test pilot edition of 2007. Not only because I've added several more interviews (running up until 2011, basically) but also because I've contextualized them through myself; through my own voice. I didn't want to simply display a collection of talks, but rather to tell a story of why all of this happened. Because that makes more sense in that better bird's eye view I mentioned. Seen from this perspective, I have orchestrated the voices rather than merely presented them. The anthology has now become a choral work, if you will, celebrating heterogeneity, integrity and creativity as such.

Does this choral composition sound harmonious enough? Well, that's not really for me to judge, is it?

Carl Abrahamsson, Stockholm, February 2021

Conrad Rooks, 2000

Conrad Rooks

"The best material isn't produced by choice but by chance."

How come this incredibly talented moviemaker, Conrad Rooks (1934-2011), never made any more mind-boggling epics after "Chappaqua" (1966) and "Siddhartha" (1972)? This is surely one of life's little mysteries.

I tried my best to figure some things out though, by going to see Rooks in the year 2000. Then at age 66, he was living a reclusive life in a bungalow on the beach in Pattaya, Thailand. He told me he was indeed working on new projects and there were computers en masse all over the house, indicating some kind of editing process, I guess.

"Chappaqua," Rooks' first and probably most well-known film, is a suggestive psychedelic insight into the very core of drug addiction. And into the fierce and painful battle of trying to regain free will. With astoundingly beautiful cinematography by Robert Frank, music by Ravi Shankar and contributions from Beat icons like William Burroughs and Allen Ginsberg, "Chappaqua" is an underground jewel in film history. It displays, in images typical of the era (both visually and psychologically), an eternal story about human dignity.

"Siddhartha" is a pretty straight recounting of Hermann Hesse's classic novel of illumination. In this film also, there's some exquisite cinematography; this time by Swede Sven Nyqvist. Despite the slow pace of the film, it became a success in India – a feat very few foreign films manage.

Conrad Rooks' life was fascinating in many ways. Partly through the outer life experience in itself – a comfortable financial background, becoming a misfit, an escapist, getting caught in various forms of dependency, inheriting $3 million (in the 1960s – what would that sum be in today's value?), and using that money to make his films. But also partly through the inner journey, with initial restlessness, losing his free will to drugs and drink, later reclaiming it and, even later, the need to tell of his experiences in a very poetic manner.

Through all of these phases, inner as well as outer, Rooks had metaphysical beacons guiding him through the stormy seas of the soul: native American sha-

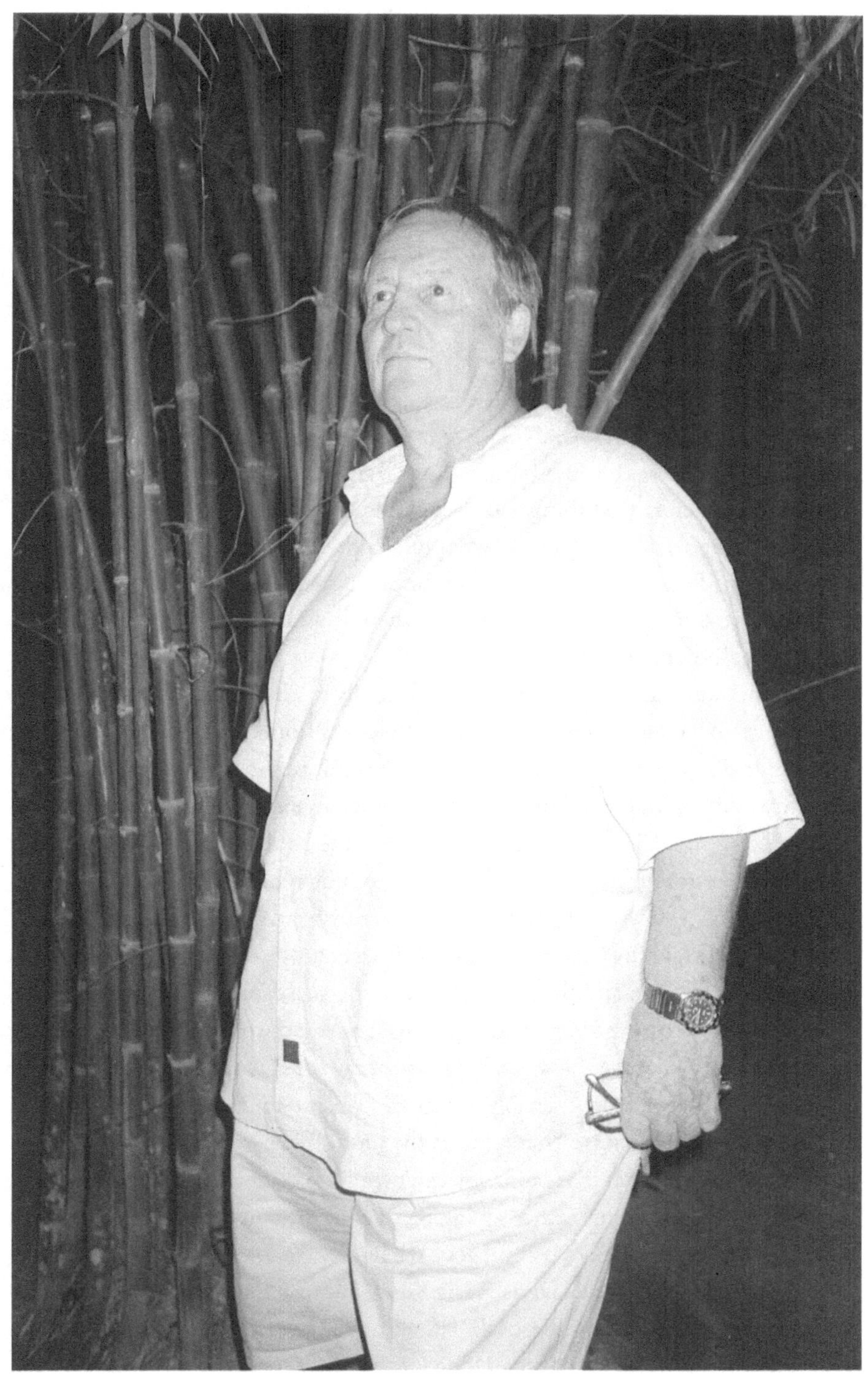

manism, psychedelics, Hinduism and Buddhism. The phenomenon that he has mostly become associated with – the "Beat" culture – is probably what affected him the least.

Conrad Rooks died on December 27th, 2011.

– The Beat scene was a very drug-taking culture, Rooks remembered. Also, New York at that moment, with all the Jazz musicians, was heavily into junk (heroin). So was Bill (Burroughs) and all of that crowd. I was much more into alcohol, but I would take junk to get over a hangover.

But what really got me, I think, was the trip I made with my wife around the world. We left for the East in 1959 and I was heavily addicted to alcohol and anything else I could get my hands on. We came out here because of our interest in Buddhism, of course, but there was a drug trail too, long before there were any hippies. Long before that thing was even going on. There were a few Italian aristocrats who smoked opium. I smoked opium with Cocteau through my wife. This was more of a fluke. They offered me a pipe and I said, "Sure..." That didn't make me an addict, but I had been exposed to it then. It was through the Italian prince Dado Ruspoli that I got hooked.

Ruspoli was also friendly with the Royal Family in Thailand. My first wife was a Russian aristocrat and we came out here with letters from her father. We had those letters of introduction and we stayed with a Thai prince. He had a French wife, and my wife was fluent in French, as that was her first language. There was an automatic connection there. He gave us a Thai house at the back of his house. We stayed there for three or four months until we found our own house. In those days there were no streets. You went practically everywhere by boat. It was really old Siam.

We started smoking opium and got the finest stuff brought to us. We used to start cooking at 9 pm and then went on until the sun came up. We stayed in the dream. This went on for a very long while, maybe six months or so. My wife wasn't into it like I was, because she was taking care of my son. I was into the experiment; she wasn't. As a result I got terribly addicted. I was up to 72 pipes a day, which is an extraordinary addiction. That really is the limit. If you go beyond that, you're a dead man. It's so toxic at that point you can't really go beyond it. In the midst of all this, I got a letter from my father saying he thought he wouldn't be around much longer. It'd be a good idea to try and get back home.

I started, but only got as far as Hong Kong, because I had this horrible addiction. Alcohol wasn't doing the trick. I found out that the rickshaw boys would deliver five grams of heroin for ten Hong Kong dollars. I got every rickshaw boy in

Hong Kong running around. Finally I'm living with the rickshaw boys. I had sent my wife and child back to America and was now living in a hut made of rags and tin, overlooking the glorious Hong Kong harbor. The boys were my source, so I thought, "why not move in?" The rest of the time I spent with a bunch of Australians in the lobby of the Peninsula Hotel.

Finally I got another letter from my dad saying, "This is it... Hurry up..." So I did. When you go back to America, you dread it because you know you can't really continue with the drugs. You have to try and find some way off. I went for alcohol, so I wound up drunk all the time. It's really not a good way to live. Within a year of my getting back, my father had a massive heart attack. His death shocked me so much.

Of course, this meant an extra turbulent period in Rooks' life. Despite the fact that he was existentially at rock bottom, Lady Luck smiled at him and provided the inheritance from his father (who had helped build the cosmetics giant Avon). If this twist of fate hadn't occurred, Rooks claimed he would have most likely died.

— My wife told me about a doctor in New York who knew about addictions; a Viennese doctor. He was treating people like myself with very unorthodox methods. He was giving speed to get me off the alcohol. And he succeeded. But it had to be just the right mixture of speed and vitamins. A pretty massive vitamin shot with the right amount of speed in it. I didn't get addicted to speed and I didn't get drunk. It takes your metabolism and puts it right, almost instantly. Remarkable. That enabled me to stay away from things. All of the crawling up the walls was gone. He then suggested I go for a treatment where I wouldn't get addicted to the shots. It was a method that had saved a lot of French top actor junkies. I went to Zürich and took this treatment. It was pretty horrific. But it certainly did me a lot of good. I stopped everything. I stayed clean and sober for 14-15 years. During that period I made my two films.

With his feet on the ground, a sober mind, and a fortune on his hands, Rooks could seek solace in making films. He had been writing poetry all along but was convinced he could only translate his vision properly through film. For a while, he worked with exploitation master Barry Mahon, who at this time (early 1960s) produced masterpieces like "Violent Women," "Rocket Attack USA," "Hollywood Nudes Report" and "The Adventures of Busty Brown." I asked him what his most important lesson from this era was.

— I learnt we could make a movie for $29.000! That blew my mind. I couldn't believe it. When I realized that, I also realized what an enormous croque de merde Hollywood is, from start to finish. They inflated everything beyond their wildest dreams. And they're all in league together on this. But it's just a great hype. So I woke up when I learned I could make a movie for very little money. Forget Hollywood! Why not make a movie about my own life for a little more and put Moondog in it, put Ornette Coleman in it?

And this was how "Chappaqua" was born, one of the most hallucinatory movies ever made. Rooks plays the lead himself, as alcoholic drug addict Russell Harwick, who reluctantly checks in at a clinic in France to detox and regain normal consciousness. William Burroughs in the role as head of the clinic in this nightmarish environment is priceless, especially considering what a state Burroughs' own metabolism was in at this time.

— I was stone cold sober shooting the film so you can imagine what it was like trying to get back into that state of mind. It wasn't the easiest thing I've ever done. I had to hypnotize myself, saying, "you're stoned again." I couldn't just act it. I wasn't willing to start it all over again so I had to use a form of hypnosis. That triggered all the behavior and emotions from the unconscious; the memory of it all. Even to the point of bringing all the pleasurable aspects out too. The euphoria. It was also a way for me to take that entire thing and throw it out the window. It was a period of my life that was finished. In that sense, it was successful. That's a magic theory.

It was the most horrific thing I could have done to my family, I'm sure. They weren't really thrilled about the film or its publicity. Hollywood of course tried to use it in the worst possible way. I was still young and stupid enough not to realize what they were doing. Everyone actually believed that that's how I was. You become stuck with that. No one could really believe that I'd acted it all. No one was willing to believe that I could act in that way. It was so effective that no one's ever hired me to act because they think I'm not capable of acting. I think that happened to Orson Welles too, to some degree. The only person who realized it was my brother. He even said, "well, it looks like you're another Orson Welles... you're going to end up the same, stuffing yourself at French restaurants..." It's when you get caught in your own mythos. You have to watch the myth.

I might add that there are two "Chappaquas." There's one shot on 16mm, which was the precursor of the final version. We were just warming up in a way, basically learning how to operate all of this equipment. We thought that if we could operate everything on 16mm, we could automatically do it on 35mm too. After we had traveled, shot, edited, traveled, shot, edited and so on, we became quite good at it. I spent 18 months on the road with the first "Chappaqua." It was a long time. I used up five rented cars that I just burnt out.

The insurance paid for it, even though some cars had bullet holes. Because we were shot at quite often by the police. We got arrested in Mississippi and thrown into this redneck jail. That was quite an experience. That experience later on became the Jack Nicholson scene in "Easy Rider." I had told Peter Fonda about it and he used it. Initially he was going to call it "Easy Rider and Captain Marvel." I just told him, "the theme is these guys on the road meeting a lot of stupid redneck Americans and getting damned near killed... and actually killed in the end." I told him about a number of these experiences. He got the message and he did a hell of a job. He had a good writer working with him. He recorded a lot of the stuff I told him. You're lucky... I usually don't open my mouth that often after that experience. Anyway, it doesn't matter. It became a great film. In the final analysis, it's always nice to see something good come out of things.

William Burroughs' novel *The Naked Lunch* was at this time one of the most scandalous and debated books around. Now that Rooks had money to spend he was actually the first one to buy the movie rights for the book. Initially it was that book he wanted to make a movie of, in order to illustrate the state he'd been in during his years of drug abuse. I asked him what he thought of David Cronenberg's film version from 1991.

— Not very good. I don't think he understood what *Naked Lunch* was about at all. And he's certainly never been a junkie. I don't see how anybody who hasn't been a junkie could even conceive that they could shoot *Naked Lunch*. I'm not saying he isn't creative and that the film wasn't pretty and all of that.

I think "Chappaqua" is as close as I can get to *Naked Lunch*. One could never have distributed *Naked Lunch*. No studio would touch it in 1963. So what good would it have done to spend a lot of money and time when you knew that it couldn't be shown? I thought somehow that I could do it but when I really tried to start work on it I realized that it wasn't going to be tolerated. "Chappaqua" was for me almost like the next best thing. Today it's different. I feel I've run out of steam there though. Each film takes six years of your life. We don't have forever here.

In 1966 "Chappaqua" was released and getting good reviews. Surprisingly good reviews if you consider the advanced cinematography and sometimes incoherent narration (if that's the correct word here). The film was nominated for a Golden Lion at the Venice Film Festival in 1966, and was eventually awarded the Special Prize of the jury.

Encouraged by this, and realizing he still had some money left, Rooks now wanted to go for one of the strongest Western interpretations of Eastern thought: Hermann Hesse's *Siddhartha*. As "Chappaqua" had received good reviews in Sweden, and Rooks was an admirer of the work of Ingmar Bergman, it was natural for him to court Bergman's cinematographer Sven Nyqvist. Also, Nyqvist's own love for Hesse's novel was well known (something that is mentioned, for example, in Nyqvist's son's documentary from 2000, "Ljuset håller mig sällskap").

— Yeah, I was in Sweden a lot. But I got so tied up in India, and married an Indian girl. I have a son of 18 there, who's now in art college in America. My life changed totally. I became very Indian in a sense and was very involved with India. That romance lasted a long while. But unfortunately like all good things, it came to an end. I divorced that wife and life changed radically. You find that many of your alliances really aren't your alliances at all. Suddenly you're a stranger in a strange land again. You're not really, of course, but one can get paranoid at times like that. I came back to Thailand, to the place I visited with my first wife 41 years ago: the beach in Pattaya.

The theme of Siddhartha is man's search for answers to the basic existential questions. The answers, if they're to be found at all, lie more in simplifying than complicating. The very same theme applies to "Chappaqua" and, it seemed, to Rooks' own life. I asked him if he looked at himself as someone with a specifically Hindu way of looking at life.

— There's a stronger theme, and that is Buddhism itself, and Eastern thought. It's running so strongly through so many areas of contemporary life. My then wife and I went East 41 years ago. For me, the most severe time trip was when I went to Angkhor a few weeks ago. I walked on the same ground as my wife and I had walked on. There wasn't anyone out here back then. Now, Angkhor is surrounded by thousands of yuppies from all over. It was astounding for me to see this. The forest was in control when we were there and there was only one single place to stay. Over the last 41 years, it's been torn down but the foundation is actually still there.

But it was also built as a scale model of the universe. And a scale model of time, time travel, incarnation, reincarnation, etc. If you go from one end to the other, you have made an entire trip through birth and re-birth. Going through that walk with my Thai wife evoked so many memories. The place was built for that reaction to happen. It's been stripped of all its treasures: the most magnificent Buddhist art in the world. It's in collections and in some museums. Basically, everywhere but there. Those things vibrate. A lot was destroyed during the Vietnamese war. The destruction went on with everybody. You can really see the devastation. There's even carved-in graffiti in those old trees, like "Kilroy was here". It's just disgusting. Gradually, that 75-acre compound is being worn out by all the tourists. It wasn't meant to have millions of tourists climb all over it on a constant basis. There isn't a great deal of money to help the temples. The country itself is struggling to reach some kind of level of civilization. That monster (Pol Pot) did unimaginable things to his own people. It bugs me that he could die in his bed. He should have been put through a meat grinder slowly. His first brother's torture chamber is probably the second most popular tourist attraction in Phnom Pen after the "killing fields."

But perhaps exposure to Buddhist sacred sites and objects can help enlighten Westerners, I suggested. Illumination by inspiration?

— We have Richard Gere running around with the Dalai Lama. There's nothing wrong with that. Let's hope that Richard is sincere and trying hard. Anyone who can do the Dalai Lama some good is very high up in my book. That's the most wonderful man imaginable. Anything that can support him, I'm very much in favor of. Buddhism is after all a serious philosophical, psychological training of the mind. Whoever embarks upon it should do so with trepidation. My wife's brothers entered the monk-hood for four months, and that's how it is. Sometimes it transforms them and sometimes they're no better than when they went in.

It's certainly a very remarkable environment here in Thailand, where something that's 2500 years old is practiced in this modern context, as a phenomenon. It is this thing, amidst these 300,000 whores, that I think is very, very interesting. That this can all be balanced in some way. Amidst of all of this, there is a powerful message about many different things. I can see why Americans are fascinated with Buddhism and other Eastern things.

We have more geriatric men coming to Pattaya than anywhere else, except maybe Florida. I have never seen anything like it in my life. Just take a look on the beach and see all the old men. It's endless, in the thousands. They're pensioners from Europe, Scandinavia, and they're all way over 70.

A woman wrote an interesting piece in the *Pattaya Mail* recently about the symbiotic relationship between these old men and these young girls. Of course, money. Of course, the "father image." Of course, many things. But nevertheless, they truly do enjoy each others' company. It isn't solely some sort of business deal. There are a number of factors involved. It exists and it works.

So this is a theme I find quite interesting for a movie. But I'm working more on the technological aspect than anything else right now. You really shouldn't work with more than one or two actors, to just set the pace. But the more performance you can get out of non-actors, the better off you're going to be with this. Both as far as the girls are concerned, and as far as the older men are concerned. When you start doing that, it starts getting tough because you're with people who don't know all their lines and are not ready all the time to deliver. So it's going to be a lot of shooting. But as it doesn't cost much to shoot on video, and the editing can be done speedily, then it's worthwhile. I'll probably edit on celluloid eventually though, as I think it's still a bit sharper. I'll have to experiment a bit and see what looks best.

One could ask why a driven movie director like Conrad Rooks, with his good self-esteem and good enough reputation to seek out new capital, didn't want to make a new film in his native USA?

— I hate Los Angeles. I can't stand it. I hate the movie industry there and of course that makes it a little hard for me. I will never be on their side.

Well, aren't there other places than Los Angeles he could have handled? Both the American and the international market for "independent" films seems stronger than ever.

— If I take the right route, and that's to go through the festivals, then perhaps... The ones where I was most successful and most popular. If it gets some kind of attention, that immediately gets noticed by distributors. The great secret about this is to keep it in such a low budget area but still have it look so professional that you can't possibly lose. If "Blair Witch Project" can make it, then... I'm also thinking of von Trier and the Dogma-attitude. I was doing "Dogma" before they were even born. The Dogma I was doing grew out of Beat writing. The essence of the Beat was anti-establishment, anti-everything... Just a stream-of-consciousness and let it all roll... Then it would have some kind of symbiotic relationship. That was very much Burroughs' approach to his writing and his basic artistic efforts. These things have a way of wanting to join each other no matter what you do. They have a life of their own. The trick is to find these connections and to find this life.

Another aspect that greatly appealed to Rooks was that the new technologies, with video cameras and digital editing in computers, have made everything both easier and cheaper. In his beach cottage in Pattaya, there were computers all over the place.

— I must get with it. I'm now taking apart and building my own machines. I'm inside the computers now because that's where it's at. When I got involved with cameras, I really got involved with them. I lived with them and slept with them. I shot day and night: thousands of feet just to get a feeling for the light and the camera. You have to do the same thing with computers: to become one with them in some way. The only way you can become one with it is to constantly live with it. That's why I have some eight computers in here right now, and there's even more in my bedroom. I don't know how my wife can live with me, frankly. It's like living with a pack rat who's constantly bringing stuff home.

I work a lot like Bill, from the newspapers. I chop up newspapers. A lot of his lyrics were chopped out of newspapers. The Dadaists too, of course. It's not necessarily a new tradition but it's finding new outlets.

I realized that my collective unconscious knows everything anyway. It's centuries old, millennia... The thing is: How do I get to it? Very often I just scan newspapers and wherever my mind seems to focus on, that's what I cut out. And then you start collecting these things. After a couple of years you have thousands. Then you go back through them and see what the fascination was at the time. What is the connection? And you start moving them around and pasting them up on the wall and studying them. Very soon, patterns will emerge: a mosaic.

And in those patterns Rooks found new ideas?, I wondered.

— Sure, and storyboards and storylines and then, finally, text. It will all be a gigantic mosaic of thousands of items from the past and present. And even the future. Memories that keep drifting and returning when you dream or wake up. I always try and write this stuff down, because you can't really imagine what it's all about. Later on, it'll become clear.

Jack Kerouac was doing a lot of this stuff. He was getting high on speed, Benzedrine, and playing Charlie Parker and various other people; listening to those riffs and those scats and trying to write like that. He only had a beat up old typewriter but he was pasting his papers together on rolls and typing on bits and pieces that just fell to the floor until he had lots of stuff. He was doing it off the top of his head. He was stoned, listened to Charlie, listened to Bop, listened to Jazz and he's trying to keep up with it all by activating his subconscious. Plus his literary background. After all, he was an English major at Columbia. He was involved with a lot of authors that he was fond of, and he was mimicking them. All of these things at the same time. And he was also having intense discussions with Burroughs and Ginsberg and, I might add, Robert Frank, who was around then too. Huncke too, and Neal Cassady.

When I think back, that was what he was trying to make me aware of. I didn't quite understand it at that point in time. I was much more traditionally oriented. I finally just paid Bill to teach me the cut-up technique. That was the best way to do it. I started doing that with him for hours and hours in his little room at the Beat Hotel in Paris. I'd come in and say "How many hours can we put in?" and he'd say, "let's do four or five." Anyway, he was stoned so it didn't matter to him. I wasn't. But he taught me how to do it. He pasted stuff up on the wall too, and I began to understand what it was all about and how it works. It was important to me, because the guy that had been so instrumental in developing the technique was teaching me. He really was like a kind of Harvard professor anyhow. People even called him the "professor." That was one of his nicknames.

Bill was one of the funniest guys I've ever known. A very sardonic, black, insane sense of humor. He was really poking fun at everybody. I hope people realize that. In *Naked Lunch* he's just putting everyone on. Science Fiction, Scientology, whatever... That was Bill's very funny mind at work.

Another central character in the development of the "cut-up" method was Burroughs' friend Brion Gysin. Not entirely unexpectedly, Gysin too was a part of the Rooksian crowd in Paris when Rooks was working on editing "Chappaqua" in the mid-6os.

— Gysin was always into the Dreamachine[1] and I didn't find that particularly exciting. He was always trying to sell me his paintings. I bought hundreds of Gysin

---

1 A spinning cylinder with a light source inside it that Gysin developed together with mathematician Ian Sommerville. Looking at this cylinder with one's eyes closed may trigger psychedelic patterns and hallucinations.

paintings and I bought the original Dreamachine too. When I was working with that, I also started working with Ian Sommerville. Ian was really a super-bright kid and a very interesting guy. He worked with me on the soundtrack for "Chappaqua" for months and months. Bill also worked with me. We shot, took a look at it, shot some more.

I also had Man Ray helping me. He was very much into the same things. He also believed in the same loose approach. He also believed that things have their own relationship, one that we can't really understand until we put them together in new ways. I spent a lot of time with Man Ray, quite often going to lunch. We looked at the material in different screening rooms in Paris. The man who was the CEO of the lab we used had a son and he was friends with my girlfriend. She knew this family very well. The father allowed me the freedom of the lab so that I could do whatever I felt like. The little ladies in there taught me a lot of things. It was a fantastic time. I could experiment with a thousand different things. This was all pre-video of course, so there was no other way but trial and error.

When I look at MTV, I see stuff that we were doing back then, but optically, not digitally. It all started with Harry Smith and then moved onwards. I spent years with Harry too. That was a really unique relationship. If there was ever a true genius, it was Harry Smith. His head was too heavy for him. He was all brains. They should have taken his brain out when he died. It was like possessing several libraries at the same time. Any subject, just push the button. Any question, and he'd pour out a lot of material.

Harry was very much into the Kabbalah and studying that. He'd found a group of Jews in New York, and he was the only outsider to be allowed to sit in in their sessions. They had an electronic Kabbalah board there, with a Tree of Life that could light up. But the only one who could really explain it to them was Harry Smith! I found that very funny. The Rabbis couldn't explain it. He became a leading expert on the Kabbalah for the Jews.

I had so many great times with him. One was when he'd taken over a huge Park Avenue townhouse. It was a palace, and he'd taken the ballroom and turned into his workroom to build a three dimensional camera which shot in 3-D. He did it by taking old RKO cameras from the late 30's and tearing them apart. Then rebuilding them on huge levered stairways that moved up and down and had to be operated by cranks. He shot the most extraordinary film. He invited me over to a couple of screenings. It was just incredible stuff. Very unusual. Very few of the people he showed it to had any idea of what he was doing.

He was issuing Owsley's finest grade-A acid to people as they came in. He had, for the first time, enormous money behind him. He needed three or four projectors to show his work. All of it was based on trances that he had learned from American Indians: mind-patterns... He knew how to trigger these patterns. Activating these patterns, he knew what results would follow. Talk about magic! He was doing some extraordinary magic; he really was. He was definitely a magician.

When I met him, he lived at 300 1/2 East 85th Street. It was a house that belonged to one of the big houses. Harry somehow had a room on the top floor. A poet friend took me over there and we started throwing rocks at the window. Finally, this weird looking thing that looked like he was the assistant to Frankenstein or something; a Quasimodo type, as he was hunchbacked too... He stuck his head out, looking absolutely mad. His beard hadn't been cut for years and he wore really thick glasses. We went up there to find cans and cans of film and sculptures from American Indians and feathers. It looked like he had a part of the Museum of Natural History at home. He was making these films in his bathtub. He did everything himself, even the developing!

He was working with old army surplus cameras. They were used by bombardiers to film where they bombed. You could buy one for five to seven dollars at the time. He bought film stock that was out of date. I started going there and studying with him. I realised immediately that this was an incredible source of information. Bill Burroughs and Harry Smith have been the two biggest inspirations and influences in my life.

The late 1960s and early 70s were undoubtedly a vital time for creative and groundbreaking filmmaking, with detours into mind-expanding experiments and courageous grandeur. Except for Rooks and people like Nicolas Roeg, there was also Chilean Alejandro Jodorowsky, with his epic cult classics "El Topo" (1970) and "Holy Mountain" (1973). I asked Rooks what he thought of those films.

— He got too much into Black Magic for me. I think "El Topo" was a very interesting film. But I think the Devil got him, finally. Roman Polanski is an example of that too. The Devil will come after you if you keep on playing with his themes. I wouldn't want to pay the price that Roman has had to pay. If you're playing with these things, you're playing with fire. Jodorowsky made "Holy Mountain" as an adaption of Thomas Mann, and then there was the other one where he was butchering elephants. That's a huge sin. That will condemn you forever. He's lucky he's still alive.

I'm thinking also of the guy who made "Mondo Cane" and movies like that.

You're treading on very dangerous ground. If you keep peering into the abyss, you can fall into it. That's exactly what I'm talking about. You're allowing the audience to peer into the abyss. Also, it's the same with "The Exorcist." He's asking for trouble again. At a certain point the abyss peers back.

I wondered if film, like any art form, isn't a useable channel when wanting to understand man's own dark side, in order to create a better balance?

— Sure, but are you prepared to pay the price? You're not a Saddhu, you don't have the protection of the gods, you don't know how to call on the supreme force… So who's going to protect you? Tell me. What are you going to do when all the Siddhi come after you? Are you prepared to take all your clothes off and wander for 20 years? And put up with everything? The nature, the atmosphere, the mountains…? I don't think so. So that's why I say you shouldn't fool with it unless you're willing to take to the road. You're playing with some heavy stuff. That's the great danger in my opinion. You can be fascinated with it and you can even write about it and be like Colin Wilson who makes his living out of writing about the occult. It's dangerous stuff. Of course the public is fascinated.

Conrad Rooks seemed to be doing OK in Thailand. But sometimes it seemed obvious as we talked that his own story was like a two-edged sword. On one hand I clearly noticed that he would have liked to make more movies. And who can blame him? His sense of moviemaking was sublime and he could really tell a story in a unique way, whether it's fast-paced and experimental in "Chappaqua" or slow-paced and conventional in "Siddhartha." On the other hand there was a part of him that knew what $3 million in 1963 could have meant to if he hadn't invested it in his movies.

— It's like 30 years of poverty when I could have been enormously wealthy and never have had to worry about anything at all. That was a sacrifice.

I wondered what inspired him as a child. Was it obvious to him all along that he wanted to work with film?

— Actually, I wanted to be a poet. I was often booted out of schools but the one thing that kept me going was that I got poems printed. The English teachers felt I had talent but they didn't know how to develop it. They were always very close to me. The English teachers were always my best friends. I knew that I had some talent.

I've written thousands of letters and I've kept many. You chop them up and keep the really good parts. That becomes your book. Then you couple that with the thousands of newspaper articles. There are people that I've spent time with who suddenly appear in a newspaper. That's something you should write about.

I spent four days getting drunk with Ernest Hemingway. That's an experience. He and I were dancing with the gypsies and drinking. Have you ever seen that wonderful painting by John Singer Sargent, where he shows the flamenco dancers and the girl with her castanets...? That's exactly how it was. They were dressed in exactly the same way. Hemingway loved that stuff and so did I. If you get stoned enough, you can dance with them. You have to reach a certain level of high. The same is true in Cuba. You can dance with Cubans if you can reach a certain level of high. My brother and I used to take on all the Blacks, all the Puerto Ricans, everybody in New York City... And we were both blond white kids. It got to the point where Tito Puente used to take his hat off to us because occasionally we did win.

Our interview came to an end in the infernal Thai heat. Conrad Rooks wanted to take me to dinner at the best seafood restaurant in Pattaya, and who could say no? Before we finished, I asked him which his all-time favorite movie was.

— "The Treasure of the Sierra Madre." That had everything for me. Location work, real people mixed in with actors, shot under very difficult conditions, and it had some of the most gifted people in the business involved. It's almost a surrealist piece of work when you think about it. It's a great novel and a great theme. There's a bio on Bogart that goes into great detail about the shooting of that movie. It's very interesting. The penultimate scene of scenes is when Walter Huston dances his Pan dance when they discover the gold. That's evoking everything back to the Greeks. An act of genius. It's the great god Pan dancing. Cinema at its best. A magical confluence of talent, you could say. A lot of the best material isn't produced by choice but by chance. That was Burroughs' theory, anyway.

Malcolm McLaren, 2001

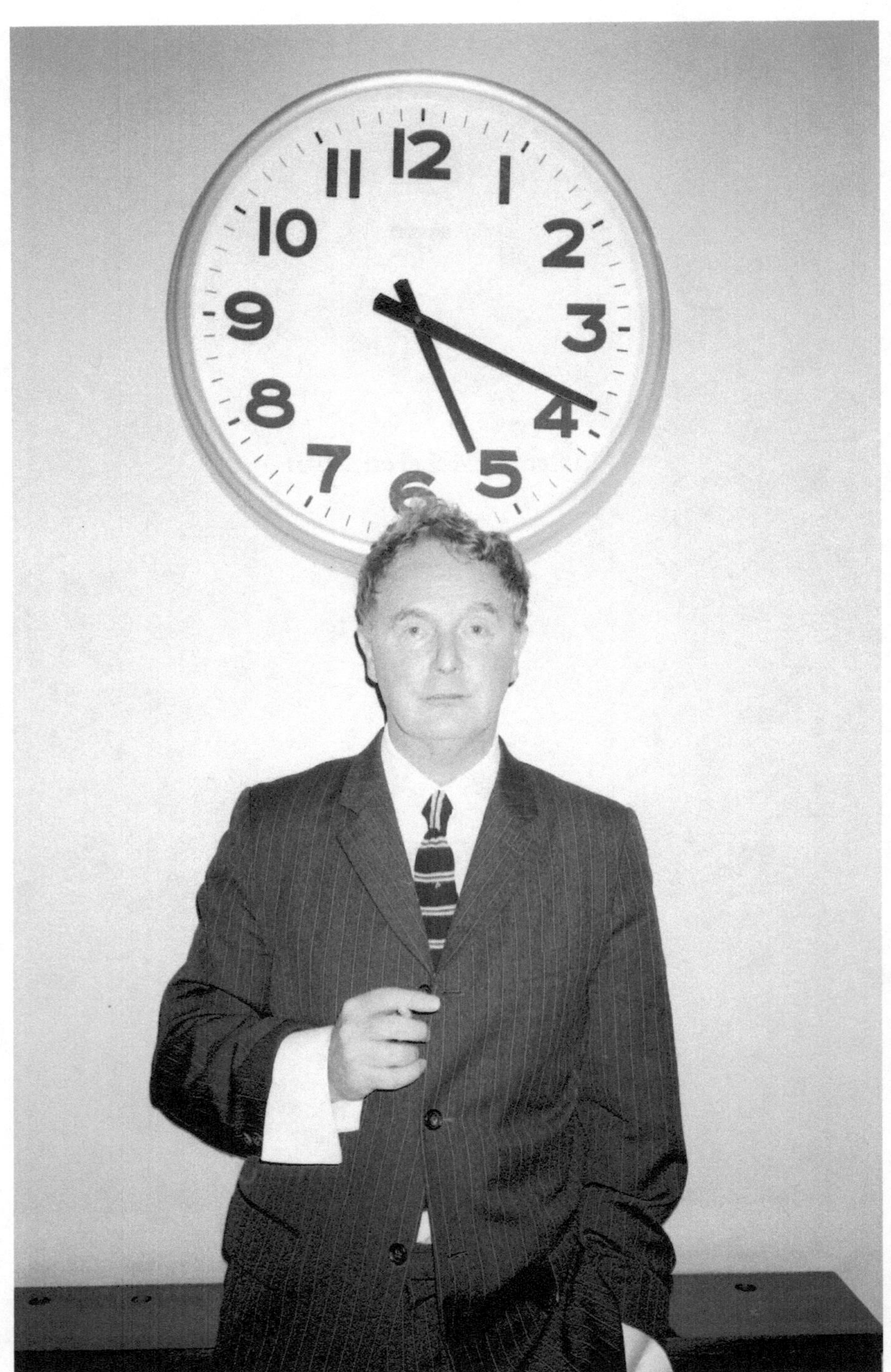

Malcolm McLaren

"I adore living in chaos."

Back in 2001, I had the good fortune to sit down with legendary entrepreneur and thinker/talker Malcolm McLaren (1946-2010) as he visited Stockholm. McLaren was a truly charming man: intelligent, cultured, eloquent, and, needless to say, a real cultural prime mover. He was also a man completely aware of his own faults and errors, but he seemed to rather enjoy them than regret anything he'd ever done. And he definitely did a lot!

There is a great number of people who owe a lot of things — and careers — to Malcolm McLaren. Although he will always mainly be associated with the Sex Pistols (as their manager) and the punk movement, there were many, many other claims to fame, or infamy. Before the Sex Pistols, he had managed sordid glam rock pioneers New York Dolls, and run a clothing shop in London (called "Sex") with his partner, designer Vivienne Westwood. After the first punk tsunami had rolled on back into the ocean of commercial infinity, he mentored/styled more ephemeral acts like Adam and the Ants and Bow Wow Wow; always stressing the surface and weird outfits that were, or became, "trendy," more than the quality of the music itself.

Then he gradually focussed on his own musical career. Creating assemblage music with whatever was looming in the Zeitgeist (ethnic, hip-hop, opera, etc), he managed to have a few hits (remember "Buffalo Gals" or "Double Dutch"?) before moving on into other media explorations (film, TV, theater, and more).

He was, without a doubt, a brilliant theorist and agent provocateur (incidentally the name of his son Joseph Corré's lingerie/clothing brand — how Freudian is that? Or simply an apple fallen from a powerful tree?) who bravely not only presented new mutations but was also more than willing to explain at length why these were relevant.

In many cases, McLaren literally shot from the Hip, and this can be both a blessing and a curse. If you're addicted to always being in the now, and to celebrating it in a commercialized way, there will always be a harsh backlash stemming from the future. Regardless of how well you can describe a theory in, say, 1976 or 1993, the future Today is always a stern judge. Where some few expressions of pop culture manage to transcend, survive and even become mythic (mainly because of going straight for the emotional jugular vein), others will simply be mercilessly relegated to cruel mirthful mockery and sadistic glee. There is undoubtedly a brutal difference between an impact and a fad. The legacy of the Sex Pistols rests solidly on the powerful music they made and the attitude they conveyed; not so much on how they were "styled" by Westwood or managed by McLaren. They have become timeless and culturally significant. But can that really be said for "Adam Ant?"

McLaren's striving to be constantly hip actually ostracized him from the sphere that I perceive he was constantly longing for: Art. Malcolm McLaren definitely wanted to be an artist, and also be regarded as an artist. A scandalous one; one that made dents and created ripples on the surface of the status quo of British/Western inertia.

No-one can ever deny that McLaren was ultra-creative, and art can certainly include whatever elements you see fit (especially in post-surrealism and post-modernism). But the creations in themselves are unfortunately seldom enough in the psychological make-up. There also needs to be acclaim and acknowledgment for most artistic minds to be happy.

However, McLaren's connections to the world and psychology of fashion sort of ruined this. There is nothing more dangerous to an artist seeking more than fleeting recognition than to be associated with a specific time period, and/or the fashion of that day. You can certainly make a quick buck or impression by being hot or hip today. But then what?

As the shenanigans of Malcolm McLaren became more and more verbal and conceptual, he took on the persona of an intellectual jester in a rapidly developing internet-based media landscape. But there was less and less focus on his own actual creations, as they increasingly merged with already existing power structures (Hollywood, Broadway, "Reality" TV, etc.) far too controlled, greedy and ruthless to allow free rein for punk primadonnas with too much integrity.

Where McLaren often claimed that "I adore living in chaos," I think that this was an attempt at making a virtue out of necessity. If you have been successfully formatted as a satirical motormouth who is always a great go-to source for scandalous quotes, then you will very likely stick to that persona. Especially as the years pass by, and no-one seems to give any real credence to your attempts at, for instance, pushing musical boundaries.

McLaren was taught by an art school teacher that, "It is better to be a flamboyant failure than any kind of benign success." This evokes an attitude that explains a lot, and the quote has even been paraphrased on his tombstone at Highgate Cemetery in London as, "Better a spectacular failure, than a benign success." The tombstone makes perfect sense when you look at McLaren's life. He certainly lived life to its fullest, its most spectacular; raking in what he could, but also leaving behind many unfinished projects and plenty of scandalous debris — as if that were indeed part of a conceived "modus operandi." In a way, always running towards the next project while spraying semi-memorable Zeitgeist stardust along the way — mainly for his own acknowledgment needs.

This is, of course, all speculation on my side. But I genuinely wish he could have lived longer and perhaps matured into a focus that would have shown even more of his intelligent versatility than being caught up in comments on the fickle present and the sometimes quite desperate attempts to be "fashionable."

— What's currently on your mind, Mr McLaren?

I think it's unquestionable that the war that's going on is not a war about who survives in Afghanistan. It's more about a war about the New World Order. It's a war that is now being subjected to a debate about its genuine future and sense of culture. It's a war in which we'll all debate about how useless or how important we are. How we actually look at our culture and the future. We'll debate what's good and what's bad about it. It's extraordinary that this idea of Islam has actually provoked it; provoked us all into thinking that. In bookstores in New York, since September 11th, I've seen people at the Middle East sections sitting on the floor crosslegged reading about Islam. For the first time! They have now discovered another part of the world and it intrigues them and confuses them. They definitely want to find out more about it. That's interesting because people have found another idea. There are other cultures out there that don't necessarily want to belong to the idea that we call America. America is confusing for Europeans because America is a concept. It's not really a country. It's a concept based on a lot of people who escaped from Europe over the past two centuries. They came and tried to create another idea. They're still squabbling about what that idea is... America is filled with a melting pot of cultures. Within it are many disenfranchised people who are not directly in sync with the nebulous, most complex organisation called Washington. If someone were to say to me "I don't understand Islam...," I would say "I have no idea what Washington is... Why they do what they do and the reasons they have..." It's a difficult thing because in essence it's a concept that isn't alien to the rest of the world but it's very convoluted, full of immense contradictions. It's very difficult to comprehend. If you live in the Islamic world I would say it's even more difficult to understand. For instance, if you are, supposedly, a superpower with all the things that go with a superpower, why would you need anyone else to help you fight your battles? I wonder just that, as a question. Does that mean that America is somewhat vulnerable? Does it necessarily believe in its own self? Does it understand its own self? Its own concept? It's so full of contradiction and yet we've all got to join in, rally round the flag without even thinking twice... All under the word America seems to have coopted: "freedom"...

This is the problem we all face now: Who owns the language? Why is your interpretation of freedom better than ours? That's the problem and that gets right down into the root of the culture itself. I think that's what we're undergoing now. What is globalization? In one word, people in America say globalization means fast food. That's globalization right there. Coca-Cola, the hamburger, Hollywood, fast film, fast art... All of this is in some sense a contradiction or in direct opposition to the culture under the heading Islam. Islam does not necessarily understand or have in its dictionary the word "marketing." This word is alien to their culture. Maybe also "entertainment." If you went to France, they would have a difficult time understanding the word "marketing." It's a word equally alien to them in some sense. It's alien to their culture. They can't see what entertainment is. It isn't showgirls, it isn't John Wayne... And it isn't about fast food. Yet we're all supposed to rally round this culture... This is the real debate that's going on in the 21st century and it will define what we think in the next 25 years. That's why this war was probably inevitable and probably a long time coming. It came in a welter of mad tragedies... But life is an opera. It's full of love and it's full of death. It's a journey and the journey is now reaching a point where there are serious obstacles that we have to come to terms with. Before, we were all under this immense cloud created by globalization. It was a false premise that was sold to us. It can best be described with one word: Shopping.

Shopping is the new cultural ideal of the Western world. They've managed to incorporate in that word "Entertainment." A new word today is "Shopatainment." It's about the satisfaction you get when you go shopping. Shopping for anything. Once the entire culture comes under that umbrella, perhaps that has replaced what was once the Church, where we acquired some form of salvation, some form of self knowledge. When the conquests of that civilisation happened, we had the Museum that we looked up to. There were ideas about society that we were supposed to believe in and allow to ennoble us. It started with the renaissance which was, in essence, a very Islamic idea. The renaissance owes itself to Islam. To then take it further we can say that the super department store has replaced the museum like the museum replaced the church. This is the culture we've built up. This culture has enabled the commodification of the planet to be the noble pursuit. Shopping is the way to enjoy it. The satisfaction you get. But, invariably, when we get home after having been shopping, we look at these things that are supposed to have quenched our thirsts, fulfilled our desires, acquired some sort of semi-salvation, and we realize it all doesn't. So we go back to the department store the next day and buy more. That has reduced us to people who are constantly confused. It's the quest now to decide how to move forward. Do we strip our culture bare, do we look for alternatives? Is the department store physically going to become more like a church? Is it physically going to be more like a museum? Can we incorporate all those things in it? Or is it just going to crumble? Is America as a concept on its way out? Is the World Trade Center disaster a kind of sign of a crumbling empire? This is the real debate.

— The rational processing through media, journalism, etc., is obviously very, very controlled. Do you think that maybe non-rational processes like art could help creating a clearer image?

I think you have to define what it is. That word has changed so much now that you could say that fashion is art, as art is fashion. Before, it was some sort of ac-quiring self knowledge, critique, finding out some kind of salvation, some kind of knowledge that will help you change life, and to look at life in another way. Art today is a fashionable commodity that can be purchased with relative ease. Per-haps just as decoration or as "keeping up with the Joneses." Part of one's attempt to look fashionable. Looking fashionable today means having power. If you have the look, you have the power of God and government both. Fashion seems to be the driving force, the engine. Fifth Avenue in New York is the powerhouse. It's in-teresting to note that Rudolph Giuliani literally came on TV a few hours after the World Trade Center disaster and told all New Yorkers: "Please, take a holiday... Go shopping. Please support your local store. Please don't forget... I'm a baseball fan but Broadway is the heart and soul of New York and we must buy a ticket. Please go out, spend the money in the restaurants, fill them up, show that you believe in freedom... Show you have no fear... Show them that you continue to shop!" I was staggered, because all my polemic, all my thoughts came startingly true. In this one simple statement three hours after this huge disaster... Thousands of people have just died and all he's concerned about is shopping... That said everything to me.

– Speaking of politics and speaking of mayors... How did your own mayoral campaign in London go?

My mayoral campaign was set up... I was, to some extent, cajoled. When the mayoral elections came about in London, everyone was absolutely furious... Looking at this supposed position given to us by this Karaoke Prime Minister, Tony Blair, saying that this was something that London should have. London had the mayoral function taken away by Thatcher. This was now given back for us in order to feel that London might have some autonomy. Nevertheless it was going to be autonomy ruled by the government. In other words, they were going to select who they thought should be our Mayor. My own, and many other people's anger and frustration at such audacity decided that, as Londoners, we wanted something else than Tony Blair Fleetwood Mac. He wasn't even a "townie." He was a country boy. It all provoked us into thinking "We can't have that..." So I decided to write an article that I was asked to for the *New Statesman*, which is a political magazine in London and services every politician, writer and collegiate professor. It's an important current affairs magazine. I wrote an article for them some three months before the actual election and I realized I was being set up by this magazine whose owner, a man called Jefferey Robinson, actually had to step down for corruption... He was at the head of the Treasury. I think he wanted to get back at Tony Blair and I was like the court jester set up to do this. To fire a few arrows like some old fashioned Luddite... I accepted it because I thought that it was good at least to fire an arrow.

So I went on television together with the Minister of Education and talked about the various issues involved. Like, "Why do we need a politician as Mayor? Surely it's time that we didn't have a politician..." Politicians today seem more like management consultants. They're all in league with the big corporations and therefore they don't act independently. I decided we needed an independent voice. Not to think that I wanted to be the Mayor at all, but the only way I could get on the platform was to suggest I would be. Once I had managed to air all my views, from anti-Starbucks, anti-globalization to basically wishing to be able to have a beer while reading Charles Dickens in the library... Thinking about how London could suddenly become a different place. Less serving the corporations and big businesses and more serving the community as a creative force. London cared about that, as I think any community does. There was a sense at that time that one's freedom... That the expense in London, the economy, had grown out of all proportions. It was booming but no-one could afford to do anything other than the tourists or big business handled by the City. There was a desire that we needed to enforce... London for Londoners. Before London gets taken over by corporations from foreign sources. So it was a kind of mad anarchic adventure, just to plug in to those values. I was able to criticize in a way that I think many people enjoyed. At one point a man who was once a Labour party MP decided to cross that rubicon and become an independent... I think I helped him do that. He sailed on the winds of my machinations, and of course his own, and became Mayor. But by becoming the Mayor he was seriously shackled and I haven't heard more about him since. That isn't at all surprising...

— Some of the ideas that you presented certainly have a substance. I'm thinking about the fact that Germany will soon have legal brothels and legal prostitution to a much greater extent than before. That was one of things that you presented. Do you think that your ideas will be the inspiration for actual politics in the future?

I think they already have been. Some candidates took up parts of my manifesto. They were literally being peeled off. I'm talking to a guy in opposition and he's using my own words... It was very funny to see that. Suddenly everyone was saying that "I am independent! I might represent the Conservative party but I don't listen to head office... I'm an independent person... I believe in London..." It was funny that I did actually set the cat among the pigeons, as we say in England.

— Do you see it as a blessing or a curse to be this kind of instigator? A sower of seeds? At many times, you don't get to reap the fruits...

That's the curse of any artist. You never set out to reap the benefits. It's your job. You're there to provoke and change life. An artist's life is a failure, but in the most beautiful sense of the word. Ever since I went to art school I was taught that it means to fail... In a way, that allows you not to have any fear; it allows you the ability and genuine freedom to express yourself... But to fail miserably is not the point. The point is to fail magnificently! Rather to be a flamboyant failure than any form of benign success. That's the job of any artist.

— What would you say is your greatest strength?

My greatest strength is to have little fear and perhaps be less concerned with that world of "career" and more concerned with that world of "adventure." It really is just a question of staying creatively in a position where you are never for sale. I think that if someone stood up in England and said, "I'm not for sale!" it would be a change in that society. Today we are all working under this dreadful umbrella that Tony Blair created but that he now speaks very little about. The word "Cool Britannia..." We all had to serve under that word. He had tried to turn the country into a commodity. If you didn't serve under Cool Britannia and didn't believe in it, you really weren't wanted on the island. This idea was something that you can't ever go along with, because it meant that everything in it was for sale. The idea of not being for sale is something that I think artists have somewhat lost the plot about. Today art is merely fashion as fashion is art. We, probably more than anyone else at the moment, have turned ourselves into commodity brokers in terms of culture. The godfather of that was perhaps that Catholic Andy Warhol. He is, inadvertently in some ways, responsible for the children of Andy Warhol that you could call the "britpop" artists. New York would deny that and say that Andy Warhol wasn't about that at all; it was much deeper and far more profound than any of these britpop artists. I have gotten in many arguments about that. To some extent I understand it but the facts are always that people peel off what they want from a work of art, even other artists. You take from a source and you take certain aspects. The aspects of Andy Warhol were very simple. You took this idea of the artifact, this multiple, this idea of concept, this idea of making art by the telephone, this thought of producing objects of desire, objects that appear glamorous. Living your life in a very fashionable world where you yourself become part of the media. Damien Hirst is a prime example of someone who basically is a marketing phenomenon. Not unlike Madonna who you could best describe as one big, fat dollar bill. That in itself has caused us to think about culture in a way that really doesn't serve the purpose of trying to discover the authentic. Quite the opposite. It serves the purpose of authenticating the Karaoke. Most artists today do that. You often hear in the film world, "I want this film to feel authentic..." The very notion of feeling authentic sets up this idea that it isn't authentic at all; they just want it to feel authentic. They want to authenticate something that is Karaoke. I think that's what most artists do today.

— What is your greatest weakness?

I adore living in chaos. I find chaos incredibly comfortable. Because in chaos one always assumes that surprises can happen. Things go inevitably wrong. One always loves to be at that point of disaster. It's exciting. It inevitably leads to extraordinary confrontation, and in a world that is very corporate based and serious in concern of making everything uniform, your weakness is not appearing to be a part of that endeavor. People tend to see you coming. You are already coming with a set of precedence and people have already formed opinions about you. For instance, some people say "You're a manager... How could you be an artist? A manager... That means you're a schemer, a manipulator, a Svengali, a trickster... That means you're very clever." To think of me as an artist... People can't see those two worlds match... They feel they have to be very skeptical about me. They feel they have to hide the silver when I come into the building. "We don't know what game you're at, but you're not taking our money! You're a swindler... We saw the movie! We know exactly where you're coming from..." I found myself to be someone who had great difficulty in explaining that I was the manager, I was the architect, I am responsible for the chaos and disorder that the Sex Pistols presented: what media termed "punk rock." But what they have to understand is that I wasn't a manager per se. I was someone acting like a manager. My true objective underneath it all was to utterly mismanage... I was a great mis-manager! For them to sit back and look at me when I said these things... They thought I had messed everything up by changing the words. They said I'd reinvented new meanings. It's the same way when I turn around and say to you, "Failure is a more interesting and more noble pursuit than success." Why? Because I think failure has much more creativity in the word than success does. Success I always think of as someone who's a member of the golf club. Failure I always think of as that person with mud in his hand, throwing it at the neck of the golfer who was the prefect at school and who you always inevitably hated, who you knew was completely bought, ambitious and horrible. But, in effect, that's the world.

I'll never forget when I saw a movie recently called "Election," directed by Alexander Payne. It was about politics but politics taken inside the school; politics seen from the point of view of high school. You could see how certain people would become extremely ambitious and be the ones who would define and conform and really use and abuse you. But for all intents and purposes, they seemed incredibly noble. It was a beautiful way of describing America and its concept. One couldn't help but be somewhat sympathetic but also hate the liberal school teacher who didn't want this girl to succeed and therefore fraudulently messed up the local school election by manipulating the votes. In essence, he didn't like this girl. She was too ambitious. He ended up being thrown out. At the end of the movie he was thrown out, he was on the street. Once a noble professor but now throwing mud at a car, virtually a limousine, carrying this girl who was now looking towards the White House. That was a complete metaphor for America itself. Things like that imbued me with terror as I suddenly felt my weakness. I realized it could have been me on the street, throwing mud at the car of someone similar in my life.

— Will there be any more Malcolm McLaren records? Any new musical projects?

It's so difficult to make records… I'm defined as someone who's smart, who's not a real artist, who doesn't sing, who doesn't play any real instruments… The record companies are constantly subjected to thinking if I am for real or not. I'm like an enigma. I make records like a film director without a camera. I've got to make my movie but I don't have a camera to make it with, I just have a recorder. If I explain it that way, they ask, "How on earth can you make records if you don't play and sing?" I draw a map on a wall. Not a geographical map but a map of feelings. I denote the ideas and I get a bunch of musicians, I infect them, seduce them, manipulate them to do my bidding on this wall. Somehow I come up with these albums that sometimes look conceited, pretentious, difficult, contrived… But that's the way I work. I try to support it with as much chaos as I can and that's usually me trying to sing but inevitably failing to do so… That's the piece of work in the end. It lives or dies on that basis. The people in the industry usually look at me as if I'm insane, saying that this is not the way they make music… You're supposed to hurt your fingers as you play Chuck Berry 50 000 times and you're supposed to swallow what he's done and manipulate it and regurgitate it and turn it into your own work. All under the Karaoke guise of looking authentic. It's just natural; it's not an outlawed activity anymore. It plays perfectly into the hands of an industry that has co-opted this disenfranchised musical form and turned it into a business. So you're coming along and trying to upset the bandwagon and it's very difficult to try and convince anyone that that's a good idea.

Occasionally the French understand it. They understand it because the words "entertainment" and "marketing" don't quite fit in. An artist who has a polemic, a philosophy, tends to be looked upon as intriguing and fascinating in their ever growing existential outlook in culture itself. Therefore they have managed to survive by believing in this auteur spirit and not allowing themselves to be constantly subjugated to turning everything into a commodity. In that pool, I've often found solace and the ability to work. I think that's the reason I was given that freedom to work for French television. About a year ago, I made a series of small films and was given a carte blanche to say and do what I wanted. It's leading me back to Paris to do further films. The conceptual values in America, as nebulous and contradictory as I think they often are, also allows me to be a cultural warrior. In that sense, we can still fight.

— If you had immediate access and unlimited funds, what kind of a record would you make?

I'm intrigued by the authentic. I look to the origins, to the music, the phenomenon that was to be known as rock'n'roll. A music that I have to say probably became a phenomenon due to organized crime. Just after the war, by the Mafia. It was basically through the rise of the jukebox business... It was a kind of culture that wasn't considered important or worthy. It was left by the roadside and picked up by those that see a niche in business. The Mafia after the war saw this booming business: the jukebox. A machine that could replace the live act in every bar in Southern United States. They needed stuff to put in those machines. They saw these raggedy old swing bands, top heavy, unwieldy, not economically viable. They broke it down to a bass player, a drummer, a saxophonist... Throw them into a little studio, give them 20 minutes to cut a record and keep it short. The saxophone plays the riff, the others play the rhythm... Take the guy on the street corner who writes the filthiest lyrics, really rude... The word rock'n'roll had been a currency since the 1920s inside black music. "My baby rocks me with one steady roll..." Rock'n'roll was merely an analogy for sex. They put this together and gave it a boot. Before you knew it, these mafiosi had tons of this new stuff pumped into the jukeboxes, which acted almost as a messenger. This messenger was sent all across Europe through the US Army Camps during the Marshall Plan after the war. It filtered through and a new generation desperate to express itself sought that out as a counterpoint to the establishment and before you knew it, the Mafia had discovered and inadvertently caused the success of this phenomenon that later became known as rock'n'roll. That's the true story! But a story that's never talked about... As the Mafia grew, they swallowed up profits and they found their way into laundering money and taking over and becoming part of a much bigger industry. Towards the end of the 1950s, they were almost in control. The American establishment, not wanting to deal with this Southern white trash with these black illiterates... Chuck Berry in prison on rape charges, Buddy Holly dying in a plane crash, Jerry Lee Lewis fucking his 13 year old cousin, Eddie Cochran and Gene Vincent thrown out of America and ending up in a car crash outside London. The man that seemed to be the lean desperado, also constantly imitating the black man, Elvis Presley, had to go in the

Army. In 1958, the whole notion of this music with filthy lyrics, this rock'n'roll, this Mafia driven industry was stopped and moved to a fine little port town on the edge of Europe called Hamburg; run by villains, run by gangsters... Anarchy reigned... Here, they had to serve the black GI, the white GI... Merchant seamen and all the roughnecks... Here, rock'n'roll could be held in a holding pattern for a new generation that wouldn't know what the older generation listened to. No-one knew the origins, the authentic... The same people who would play Chuck Berry came back in the early 1960s and played in London to a whole new generation and suddenly, without America not even knowing about it, these English groups were going to export back to the US what had already been written, coded and played in the 1940s. For all intents and purposes, it was being played by ragged-haired white kids. It was English, so they thought that maybe it was acceptable. They were playing to college audiences. Mick Jagger would run back to England and say to Jeff Beck, "Don't tell them it's anything to do with their music... Just keep your mouth shut and we're going to make millions..." That's what happened and that's the end of the story of rock'n'roll really.

Stelarc, 2002

Stelarc

"We have always been zombies,
and we have already become cyborgs."

Stelarc (originally Stelios Arcadiou, born 1946) is an Australian gentleman-artist who's gone to great lengths to experiment with the fundamental facts of human perception, physiology and even of life itself. As contemporary art continues to become more and more evanescent and ephemeral, it's always refreshing to encounter someone who not only has genuinely weird and wonderful ideas but also the courage to throw himself into the maelstrom of hardcore psycho-physical causality. This civilized and highly sympathetic Dr. Frankenstein of the art world should, in the best of all worlds, receive the Nobel prize (exactly for what is not as relevant). But, as has been stated elsewhere many times, this is not the best of all possible worlds. Instead, struggling on in his grandiose trans-physical machinations, Stelarc remains an eclectic enigma to the world. I sat down with him in Stockholm in 2002 to chat for a while about his truly challenging ideas. Not even my half-hearted attempts at playing the "proto-natural" Devil's Advocate could make him change his humble attitude and will to thoroughly explain. His warm and bellowing laughter, guaranteed to silence an entire café, could probably, in its strangeness, be seen/heard as symptomatic of someone who is either extremely human or an artificial avatar. Stelarc, I think, is a bit of both.

— How did your interest in art arise?

I was always interested in being an artist but at first this was a very naive idea. I thought that art was just about being good at drawing and painting. In art school my ideas changed a lot. I discovered that I wasn't a good painter (laughs). But I was always interested in the human body, not only as a medium of expression but also as a mode of experience. In performance you not only represent the body as an image or as a symbol or metaphor but you experience the body directly, in all its possibilities and limitations. You take the physical consequences of your per-

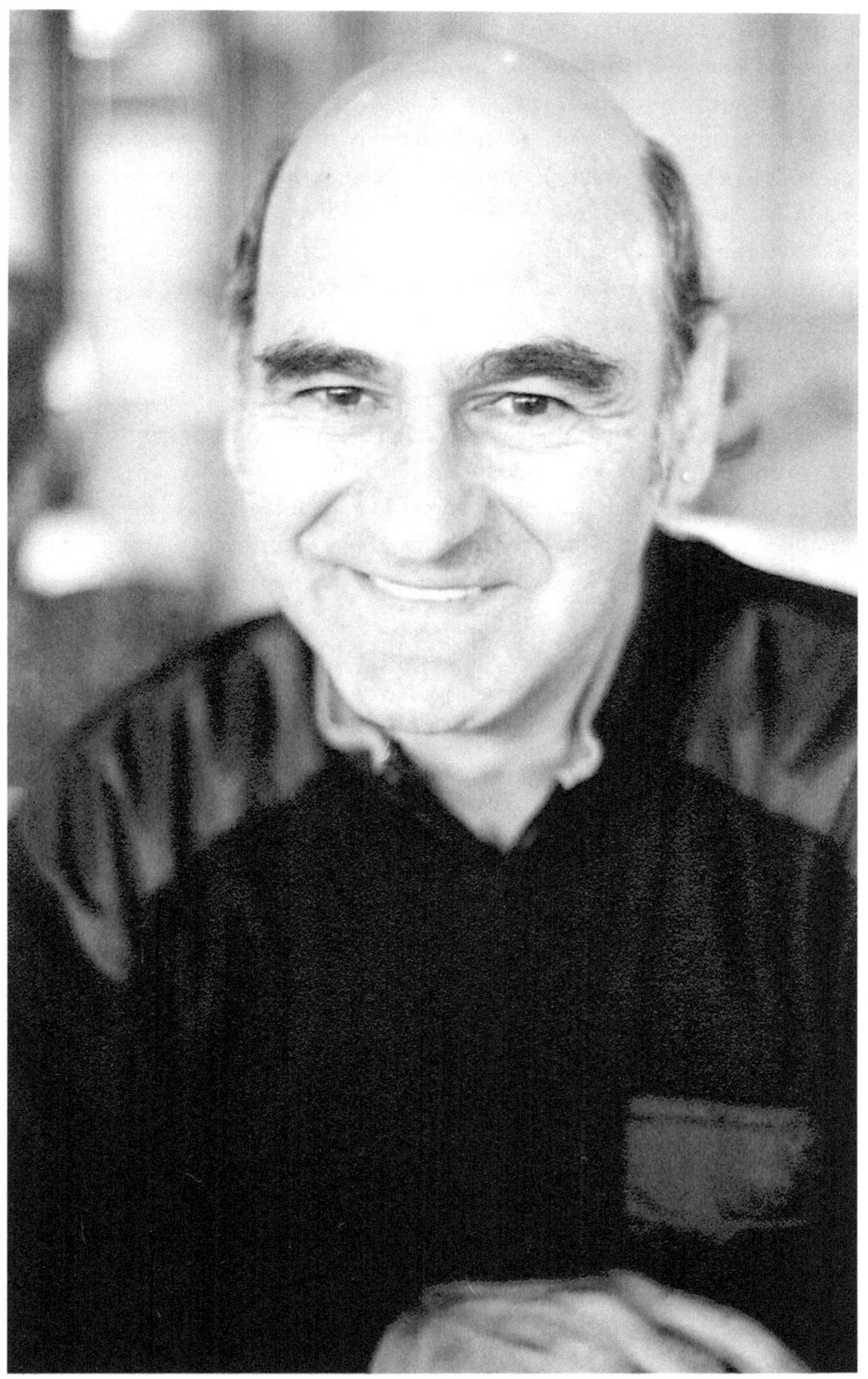

formances. If you want to suspend your body or put something inside your body or extend your body, these are not easy things to do. The body has to experience and articulate the interface. That was really the beginning of my interest in the body and performance. I had a general interest in the evolution of the body; to see the body as a kind of evolutionary architecture for operation and awareness in the world. If we alter the architecture of the body, we adjust its awareness. Just as when we add technological extensions, the body can perform remotely or can project its physical presence, transmit its image and its voice, extruding its sense of self... These are bits of technology that alter the biological architecture and enable us to perform in very alternate ways.

— Is it correct to say that there was a Zeitgeistish focus on this in the mid- to late 1960s and into the 70s, with the body in active performance? I'm thinking of Hermann Nitsch, C.O.U.M. Transmissions, Chris Burden, yo, and many others... In different places but at the same time, there were occurrences of using the body as an almost primordial tool. Why do you think that happened at about the same time?

I think there were various reasons. If we have an historical overview, we can see that there were performances connected to Bauhaus, with Oskar Schlemmer; sort of futuristic body performances, body ballets... And of course, later the more extreme Viennese Actionists. In the early 70s we had performance art as we know it in the visual arts, with people like Chris Burden, Vito Acconci, the Kipper Kids... In the late 60s, you had an increasing etherealization of the art object. Art became more and more minimal, and also art became more and more conceptual. When you reach the end of minimal and conceptual art, there's nothing for the body to play with except itself. In a way, the body turns to itself after the modernist direction of minimalist and conceptual art. In a way, this was my beginning point. It also had a lot to do with my individual concerns, my individual inabilities to use other kinds of media. I was always very interested in and envious of athletes, gymnasts, dancers, and singers who'd use their own bodies in their artistic expression.

— Before you started with the machinery and external gadgetry, you started simply with altering your perceptions, with the sensory deprivation and body suspensions. During these, did you have any illuminations or insights that took you further?

The first things I did were in fact based on technology. The first things I made were helmets and goggles that altered you binocular perceptions. And a compartment that the body was inserted in and which had a revolving dome with electronic sounds and changing light. This idea of something modifying the body's perception and experience were really the first objects that I made very soon after art school. Between 1973 and 1975, I made three films of the inside of my body, inside my stomach, my lungs, and my colon. At that point I guess there was already an exploration of the physical parameters of the body — both the internal and the external. The suspension events were part of a series of performances which also involved sensory deprivation and physically difficult actions. The first suspensions were in fact with ropes and harnesses. It wasn't a linear progression from the physical to the technological; it was more like an oscillation between on the one hand determining the physical parameters of the body and on the other hand exploring extensions of the human body. The realization that these performances generated was not an empowering of the body or a kind of shamanistic experience or a yogic kind of transcendence. The realization was rather that the body was obsolete. We're at the limits of being biological bodies. Our perception and our philosophy is largely determined by our biological structure, by our physiology.

— Isn't there a difference between using external things like helmets and goggles which generate, one could say, a creative distortion, and the hooks which must surely work through pain?

They also create a destabilizing of the body, and a stretching of the body. In a way, that was a physical analogue to extending the body in other ways. You extend the body's form by stretching the skin. There was no methodical or modernist logic about this. It was really an oscillation of concerns...

— When we talk about the body being or becoming obsolete, how do you look upon concepts like soul or spirit?

The more and more performances I do, the less and less I think I have a mind of my own; nor any mind at all in the traditional metaphysical sense. In other words, one of the consequences of filming the inside of the body was the experience of a hollow body. One of the experiences of inserting a sculpture inside the stomach was that the body was no longer a host for a psyche or a soul but simply for a sculpture, an internal esthetic adornment. I think that the words "mind" or "self" or "soul" are really are just words that describe certain sophisticated and subtle behaviors. In other words, I don't think these are actual entities but rather categories of behavior. If you're a spiritual person, you behave in a certain way. You might practice a religion, you might fast, you might be concerned about life after death and so on. If we say you're intelligent, it means that you act in a certain rational way, in a certain appropriate way in certain circumstances. What our language does is to allow us to categorize the world to help to clarify our experiences. But in doing so it often confuses us philosophically. We mistake a category for an entity. Profoundly, we do not have a mind. Profoundly, we do not have a self or a soul, because these are not things we possess. These are ways of describing and explaining our behavior and our conditioned social and cultural responses. For example: When one person says "I go here" or "I make a sculpture" or "I give a lecture in Stockholm," "I" means only this body. "I" only designates this. It's a huge leap of metaphysical imagination to say that "I" is in fact something inside the body. The word "I" is only a word and it refers to this, the body. "You" refers to that body. To say that "you" refers to a spiritual entity or a self or a mind or a platonic homunculus is a huge leap of imagination.

— But wouldn't you in a way agree that your work is in fact very metaphysical, although not in a traditional way? It deals with the physical and tries to clear away illusions.

Again, it depends on the definition one uses in language. Certainly, there is an exploration of the physical and physiological in an alternate way. Metaphysics has an extensive agenda of investigation, not immune to historical, cultural and religious views. The interest is not in metaphysics in that general sense.

— We were talking yesterday slightly about the idea that time is moving faster or at least the human perception of time is that it's moving faster. Information overflow and technological inventions that allow faster communication... The means are certainly there. What would you say will be the result of this? A good thing or a bad thing?

It's difficult to evaluate this experience of time speeded up in either a good or a bad way. I think it's happening because of our instruments and machines. What we really need to do is develop strategies for managing this kind of situation rather than to attribute a value to it. If you measure time in smaller and smaller increments, and if the meditative or the reflective moment between intention and action collapses, then the body becomes more and more a stimulus response machine. In other words, things are happening to it faster, and it has to respond faster. The brain is relatively slow. And the body's metabolism is relatively slow compared to the precision and speed of machines and instruments. I think this is one of the problems: to try to develop new interfaces between the body and its machines, to cope with the slow metabolism of the body and the acceleration in speed of our technology.

— Do you see the technological development as just a very natural development, as a stage in evolution?

It depends where we want to arbitrarily draw the boundaries. If we have evolved, obviously it's as biological creatures. The human body can be seen as a part of natural evolution. If the human body develops techniques and constructs technologies, then by definition technology is just as natural as the body. But we can make some kind of distinction. Some of the materials and some of the machines and instruments that we fabricate and construct aren't available in the natural environment. In this sense it's a kind of post-evolutionary stage. If we augment the biological apparatus of the human body with technological components, then we are constructing an extended architecture for operation and awareness of the world, where the body can perform beyond the boundaries of the skin, beyond the local space that it occupies.

— Kids who've grown up with fast-paced editing on TV and computer games... They seem to be able to integrate more information, and faster. From a Darwinian point of view, the survivors are those with the strongest will to power and the greatest capacity to adapt...

I think this is a relatively small period of evolutionary time to imagine what kinds of lasting effects technology is having specifically on the body. We can't at this time claim that technology is actually improving the capabilities of the biological body. An answer to this question is problematic. What we're seeing at the moment are relatively trivial effects. If people are using their thumbs more in sending SMS's, that doesn't mean it'll be very significant. Developments are happening so quickly that a skill today is obsolete tomorrow. If we played with our thumbs for a few million years then we might see a selective effect in a Darwinian sense. The dynamics of cultural and technological change have superseded and are speedier than any evolutionary changes.

— Do you think that science today has any other value than as a possible profit-maker?

I think that's a simplistic way of looking at science. There are lots of human activities driven by economic and consumerist-capitalist desires. One can argue that a lot of the miniaturization in computer technology for instance, has been capitalist and consumerist-driven. But the final result is that we all have very small and powerful machines where we can be subversive, where we can hack into government systems, where we can construct new kinds of communication. One can argue that there's an economics of art as well as one of science. What's interesting about the scientific community is that it generates information that always has to be tested by a community of other scientists. This is a very rigorous and methodical kind of system. The quality of scientific research always remains high because of this testing and investigative process. Art functions in a totally different way. With art it's not about the factual or the predicted or the provable but rather that it generates contestable possibilities.

— Considering your project "Movatar" as a potential soldier, and other commercial uses of prosthetics...

You have to consider that there are political and military technologies that are being especially developed for these sorts of things. My "inverse motion-capture system," the idea of an avatar performing with a physical body... This is an alternate possibility. The "Third Hand" or the "Extended Arm" don't have utilitarian functions. If they were to have utilitarian functions you would design them in a somewhat different way. The Movatar is not good military technology. It would have to be designed in a much different way. The military is doing all sorts of malicious things. Recently they've turned creatures like cockroaches and fish into surveillance objects by implanting an 8-bit processor controlling the direction in which the cockroach or fish moves, with alternating electrical currents and then having pin-size cameras mounted on their backs. They've even now done this with mice. So you can actually direct a mouse with electrical stimulation and you can turn it into an object of surveillance, but also as a consequence endangering it. It could be useful for exploring earthquake ruins, but it might also be used for military purposes. With all of these technologies, it's in the detail and in its specific use. I don't think any art projects ever really become military or political technologies.

— Have you ever been approached?

No. All of my projects and performances are a little too edgy... They're never in the actual realm of pure research or done for utilitarian use. In that way, it's very unlikely that any of these projects would be engineered for any of those kinds of uses. Look at the six-legged walking robot... This is a very big robot. It weighs 600 kilograms. It's probably the largest six-legged walking robot with a human on board. It selects the leg movements by its arm gestures. It's jerky, it's relatively slow, it can only function on flat ground. There wouldn't really be any utilitarian use for it. It's interesting for me because it explores the idea of navigating spaces. Not with a human bipedal gait but with an insect-like six-legged machine locomotion. By translating arm gestures into movements. All of these are esthetic explorations and make conceptual gestures.

— In terms of your own creative process, how do you come up with ideas? Can you find a creative pattern?

I've never really been interested in observing the creative process. What we call being creative is a process which explores the alternate, the ambiguous, the surprising, sometimes the shocking and certainly the unpredictable... I'm not so interested in the obvious or the utilitarian use of technology, so then I think of other ways of using it, other ways of constructing and creating it. One idea leads to another. A kind of iterative process. There's a new project called "The Prosthetic Head." Artificial Intelligence has been around for a while. There's the famous Eliza program but now there's a perfecting of 3D-modeling. Taking all of these possibilities and then combining them into this project of a prosthetic head. The head will somewhat look like my head. It will be an installation of a very large head. It will make different sorts of expressions. It will have lip synching and speech synthesis and a chatbot database where someone who interrogates the head will elicit a verbal and a behavioral response. It will speak to the person who asks it questions. Hopefully it will also be able to learn from the conversations it has. Any new words or situations will be added to its database. This can be another way of exploring prosthetic augmentation or prosthetic distinction, which includes a virtual actual interface, just as Movatar did. But Movatar was an inverse motion capture system primarily having to do with the movement of limbs. Here, it's more to do with verbal and facial communications. The idea that the human body can converse in a seemingly meaningful way with a virtual entity. This installation will be completed for "Transcinema," a festival in San Francisco in the middle of October. I'm interested in the ambiguity between intention and action or the physical and the imaginary or the actual and the virtual. And the slippages that occur in-between. This prosthetic head project will play on all of these things. You see it, and it looks like my head but it doesn't exactly look like me or speak like me or make my exact behavioral gestures. It approximates them and it's seemingly intelligent and seemingly responds meaningfully but it really isn't. These sorts of things interest me. How convincing must an intelligent pageant agent have to be before one accepts it as a living entity? In other words: If this head looks like me, speaks like me, has my laugh, it becomes a seductive surrogate of my head. It has the advantage that it doesn't have to be in one place. It can be situated on a website for instance. It can be somewhere for everyone or it can proliferate in physical spaces where you can have a kind of physical exchange, a physical experience. It's a project that further explores the idea of a distributed and universal prosthesis. In Movatar the body itself becomes a prosthesis for manipulating the behavior of an avatar. Before that, I had bits of technology attached to my body or inside my body. I've had prosthetic attachments or insertions. Here, the body itself becomes a prosthesis for an intelligent avatar.

— Are you familiar with the company in America called "Real Dolls"?

No.

— It started out as an advanced form of sex doll. But the customers seem to want the dolls for much more — as other kinds of company — as they are so well done, so accurate.

What's intriguing is not so much how totally convincing these automatons are but rather that they're convincing enough to create a disruption between the actual and the virtual. They're approximate enough, so that they focus your attention on what makes them real or seemingly real. I'm very fascinated by these kinds of automatons, whether they're mechanical or virtual. In the realm of ambiguity and the uncanny. These automatons are becoming, in effect, so convincingly real that they focus your attention on why they are not real at all and why they fail as responsive entities. What is missing, in fact, is any kind of intelligent disobedience.

— When one looks at your textual explanations, one comes across terms like "Absent," "Obsolete," "Invaded," "Involuntary"… Can one perceive here almost a hatred for the human body?

Absolutely not. Quite the contrary. It's neither a hatred nor a simplistic acceptance of the biological status quo of the body. When people see the body suspended by hooks or they see you inserting things into your body or when you hear me asserting that the body is obsolete, often people assume that there's a kind of loathing for the body. It's really quite the opposite. They think there's a yearning for disembodiment. But again, it is not about that at all. It's not transcendental yearnings or somehow bypassing the body. When I say that the body is obsolete, what I really mean is that this body, with these functions, has proved to be inadequate in a technological terrain of fast, precise and powerful machines. Information now measured in nanoseconds and light years, where it's beyond our subjective experience. Can we construct bodies that can subjectively experience these extended informational spaces? Can we construct bodies that have an extended longevity? Why should a body arbitrarily be in good health for only 75 years? This has nothing to do with a spiritual yearning for transcendence or an extropian sci-fi yearning for disembodiment. It's simply that if you examine the architecture, engineering and operation of the body, it's very deficient. We can only do minutes without air, maybe a week without water, maybe a month without food. If our internal temperature varies only a few degrees, we're in deep trouble. If we lose 10% of our body fluids, we're dead. Our survival parameters are very, very slim. We're very vulnerable to bacteria and viruses in the environment that are invisible. I'm not about bigger and better bodies in the medical or military sense but rather speculating and tentatively exploring alternate possibilities, alternate structures, alternate interfaces.

— Have you come across any interesting findings in terms of longevity?

Not really. Not in the medical sense. You read theories about the genetic clocks and also the relationship between metabolism and longevity. Generally speaking, creatures with a higher metabolism have shorter lifespans. There's also a theory that all mammals have approximately the same number of heartbeats in any lifespan. It's not really conclusive or convincing in describing our human existence. One interesting thing philosophically is that if we fertilize the egg outside of the human body and we go a step further and we nurture the embryo, the fetus, totally outside of the womb, then technically life begins without a birth. If we can replace malfunctioning organs of the body with replaceable artificial components or transplants, then technically the body need not die, except accidentally or through some catastrophe. We can't eliminate the unpredictable. There is a necessity then to redefine existence as neither beginning with birth nor ending with death. This analogue birth, maturing, declining and dying is no longer what we mean by existence. Perhaps existence then becomes only effective operation. You are effectively operational in the world or you're not. This is a more digital definition. I think there are some interesting conceptual and philosophical implications. Furthermore, what of the idea of developing an alternate kind of synthetic skin? A skin with only a couple of additional capabilities. Firstly being permeable to oxygen so the skin can breathe through its pores. Secondly it might have a sophisticated photosynthetic capability that can convert light and moisture in the air into chemical nutrients for the body. Our skin already does this somewhat in producing vitamin K for the body, through the skin, with sunlight. Imagine if this were a sophisticated photosynthetic skin that was permeable to oxygen. Then you would literally hollow out the human body with just a change of skin. You would not need lungs to breathe, you would not need gastro-intestinal tracts for nourishment, you would not need a circulatory system to convey oxygen throughout the body. Oxygen would already be distributed throughout the body. By constructing a synthetic skin one could totally hollow out the human body. It would be a very seductive strategy because a hollow body would be a better host for the technology one can pack into it (laughs)...

– You've always been the protagonist in your own projects. Have you ever considered taking everything one step further and actually making a transplant, a genetically improved organ?

As an artist, what I'm really interested in is not some kind of sci-fi speculation but rather to see what's plausible at the moment. In other words: what can be constructed now? What kind of interfaces can you experience? And then you can meaningfully articulate this. It's not enough to simply have ideas. Maybe in 50 years' time, with stem cell technology, we'll be able to grow an organ; not only eyes and ears and noses but perhaps a complete heart with all its complexities. A lot of this is intelligent speculation. But the extra ear project is plausible right now. There are already surgical and reconstructive techniques to engineer it. These techniques are available. What is the problem is the kind of conservatism that prevails in the medical community: the ethical considerations for them. Cosmetic surgery is now accepted. If you just wanted to change the shape of your nose or make your lips larger, then that's OK. But if you want to construct an extra feature, an extra part on your body, this crosses over from the cosmetic to the monstrous. For the medical community, at least. Our cyborgs today are experiments made by the medical community on the ill, the injured and aged. I hope some time in the future they will allow artists as well to be experimented on (laughs...)

— Is your work often met by dystopian criticism?

Yes, but I think it's something stemming from the mass media and from our science fiction mentality. There is a kind of dystopian discourse that accompanies the popular press and science fiction writing and is expressed in the movies because it's more provocative. I'm neither interested in utopian blueprints for a perfect world nor dystopian scenarios of computers and robots taking over. There are multiple and very different cyborgian constructs. The most obvious one is a medical, military cyborg: a body that has undergone some dramatic traumatic accident and some of its organs and limbs are replaced, becoming part human, part machine. The increasing micro-miniaturization of technology, resulting in nano-technology, introduce another possibility. All technology in the future might be invisible because it'll be inside the body. The body becomes a host for its machines. The internal landscape of the body becomes the new space for micro-miniaturized and nanotech robots. A future cyborg may not look different externally at all but it will be recolonized and augmented by these micro-machines. This should not be daunting. We already have colonies of microbes, bacteria and viruses inside the body. To introduce nano-machines would mean to augment the bacterial environment and to construct surveillance systems for the body that at the moment it doesn't have. It doesn't have adequate surveillance for pathological changes in chemistry, temperature or blockages in the circulation system. Generally speaking, when the symptoms surface and it can be detected, it is far too late. If you have symptoms, then the pathological condition has advanced too far. I see nano-machines as necessary surveillance and for maintaining and even repairing the internal functioning of the body. A cyborg might become then a biological body with all its machinery inside instead of outside. Another possibility is that machines and bodies generate images that are increasingly imbued with an artificial intelligence. An image is a kind of skin to make that code visible. Imagine that the posthuman will not be determined by the realm of biological bodies or the realm of computers and robots but rather by the realm of intelligent avatars in the medium of the electronic media and internet. As intelligent images, avatars will replicate, proliferate and operate literally at the speed of light. One of the problems will be how can we interface to these avatars whose operations far exceed our subjective experience and the metabolic operations of our bodies? That's another scenario of what a cyborg might be. It may not be a body or a machine. It might be an intelligent avatar.

— Concerning artificial intelligence... Do you think it would be a good thing to go in and program a thing like "will"?

A word like "will," a word like "desire," a word like "curiosity," these are words that describe certain kinds of behaviors in certain situations. It's not really a matter of programming will or desire or intention but rather, in a sense, constructing entities that can generate and perform these kinds of behaviors. The effect will occur. The action is the intent. Curiosity was said to have evolved because creatures were mobile. Being mobile, they explore the world. They search, they navigate and they move through the world due to the promptings of light, heat, smells and tactile sensations. A mobile creature gains different points of view and constructs the world in a three-dimensional and dynamic way. One evolutionary explanation of what we call a curious creature is one that is moving, one that is mobile. What's been interesting recently is a shift from the idea of artificial intelligence, which in a sense focuses attention on so called mental processes, to artificial life. I don't see artificial life as a kind of alternative to artificial intelligence but rather a superseding of an initial approach that was not successful. Initially, artificial life was examined by constructing virtual entities in the medium of computer and electronic space; constructing a virtual world for a virtual entity and then observing any emergent behavior. How it interacts, how it socializes, and if any learning occurs. This way of examining artificial life was not very successful because you could never create a very complex artificial world. We already inhabit a complex world. Why not make simple little robots, release them in the wild and then see what happens? Now, artificial life is explored more and more by making insect-like robots and inserting them into the environment. Why should we be interested in insect-like architectures? We observe insects and see that they form complicated individual and social roles and collaborations. Why do insects do this? An ant has a small brain. But an ant's behavior seems rather sophisticated. Why is that? Because the world is complex. It's the interaction of a simple entity with a complex world that generates interesting behavior. We construct simple robots, put them in a complex world and see what kinds of behaviors can be generated. In humans, we have a genetic repertoire for moving in the world but we have all sorts of social and cultural constraints and colorings and modulations of our repertoire. One could argue that our behavior and largely all of our actions are externally driven or modulated. In some ways then, we can be considered as being simultaneously both zombies and cyborgs. A zombie body is a body that has no mind of its own, that performs involuntarily. We have never had free will, free agency in the romantic and nostalgic way that we believe we had. Most of our behavior is involuntary, is habitual, is automatic. Ever since we evolved as hominids with bipedal locomotion, two limbs became manipulators and we began to construct our artifacts, instruments and machines. Technology from the very beginning determines what it means to be human. We have never been biological bodies, really. We have always been prosthetically augmented bodies. What it means to be human is to make artifacts and to use language. In a way then, we have always been cyborgs. We fear the involuntary, we fear the automatic but we fear what we have always been and what we have already become. We have always been zombies and we have already become cyborgs.

— We've seen a lot of body modifications of lighter kinds these past two decades. You yourself have made an internal sculpture. Do you think that this kind of more substantial body modification will become more generally prevalent in the future?

Body modification and body piercing can be seen as neo-primitive affirmations of the physical body in an increasing video, vicarious and virtual world. On the other hand one can see these modifications and piercings as a cyborgian impulse, of meshing metal with meat. At present, most of what is happening is more cosmetic and decorative, happening on the surface. Increasingly though it is becoming the sub-dermal sculpturing of the body. It is simultaneously a primal and cyborgian gesture.

— I was thinking of the Sherman gallery that represents you... What exactly is sold?

It's a problem. My artwork is managed by the Sherman Gallery in Sydney but it's difficult as a performance artist to earn a living from your artwork. On the one hand museums reward you with a limited fee because a performance is ephemeral. But photographic or video documentation is not valued enough because it's not the actual performance. Performance art as a mainstream art activity came and went in the 70s. This was not enough time for museums to come up with a strategy of sustaining performance artists. It's a problem. I guess in the last five or six years I've done lots of projects and performances with robots. These objects might be sold to museums. But I haven't been successful in selling my Third Hand because I haven't yet received the value I think it deserves. The Prosthetic Head is an interactive installation that could also be exhibited in a museum or a gallery. Jean Sherman has tried very hard. She initially made a portfolio of prints of my suspension performances. She'll have an exhibition of these prints in her gallery. But all this doesn't suffice. I do get an occasional grant. But I barely break even. I've been a full time artist for 14-15 years but it's been a real struggle financially. Just as I need special training to understand what a subatomic particle physicist is talking about or to understand some of the cosmological models of the beginning of the universe, so does a scientist require a knowledge of postmodern discourse and a knowledge of contemporary art practice to understand what art is. I've been to seminars where famous scientists have had their ideas of contemporary art really exposed. Their idea of contemporary art went as far as expressionism. They had no idea what contemporary art practice is, as I had no idea of some of the mathematical modeling they were talking about. Being a specialist is necessary in a world of information overload. It's also an effective strategy for doing pattern recognition, as Marshall McLuhan indicated. Which is necessary to cope with all this information. Collaboration between specialists is necessary to understand what's going on. If you're only a philosopher of metaphysics, I think that's become somewhat irrelevant. The most interesting philosophers are those who take into account recent findings in the cognitive sciences.

John Duncan, 2002

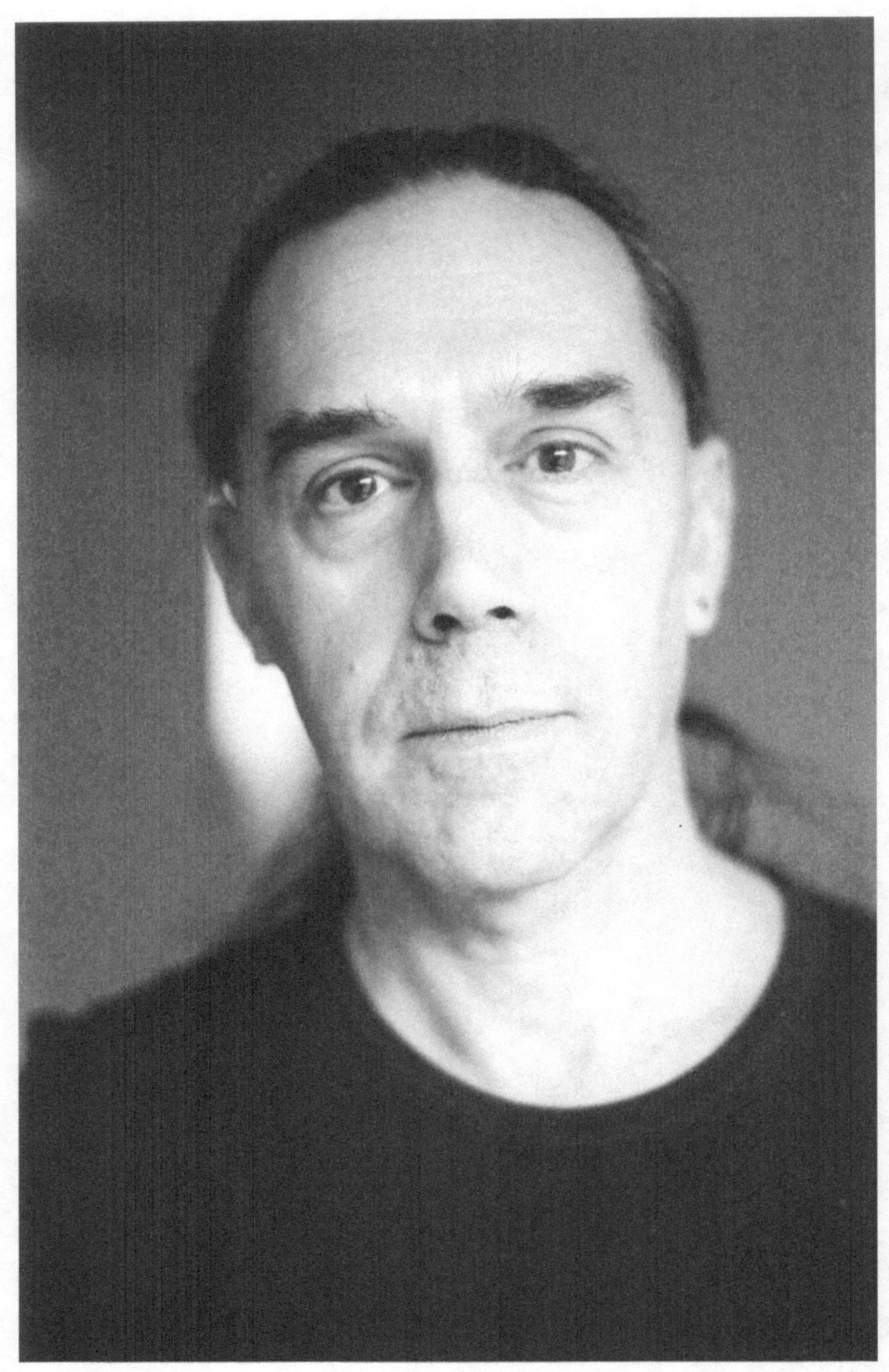

John Duncan

"Power is something I try very hard to avoid."

"The doorbell rings
I open the door
There stands the masked ranger
Slumped shoulders
He raises his right arm
In his hand is a small revolver
He pulls the trigger and fires
Right between my eyes."[1]
(Paul McCarthy)

Does an artist need to be "plagued" or "haunted" by deeply rooted inner demons in order to make interesting art? Of course not. But it certainly helps. If inner drives, anxiety and traumas are filtered via neurosis — and let's absolutely not forget creative talent! — then really interesting things can happen. There's a great and deep abyss between the merely sweet-smelling, ironic, decorative and that which punches you right in the face, and from which you will never fully recover.

It wasn't the visual strength of Andy Warhol's works (nor the business sense of his epiphyte-acolytes) that made him a great artist; it was mainly his own exploiting his sliding position on the autism spectrum. It wasn't Francis Bacon's stark display of anxiety and nightmare visions that made him a great artist; it was mainly his desire to be beaten up by "rough trade" in a feverish mix of Catholic guilt and longing for absolved release. It certainly wasn't the photographic skills of Diane Arbus that turned her portraits into iconic masterworks; it was merely the presence of her own Angst-ridden outsider-ship suffering. Et cetera.

It would be too harsh to claim that there is an absolute equation between the deeply traumatized psyche and great art, but the more you scrape the surface of

---

1 From Paul McCarthy, "Law and Order," in John Duncan, *WORK: 1975-2005*, Errant Bodies Press, Copenhagen/Los Angeles, 2006, p 12.

commodified art history (especially of the contemporary, ironic kind) the more you see there is a very distinct correlation.

American artist John Duncan is definitely plagued and haunted, and has spent his entire life dealing with it through his art. I have a great respect for him. He is without a doubt someone I regard as "genuine," and I've written about his works on numerous occasions. I have even made a documentary film about him in my seemingly never-ending series of portraits, "An Art Apart."

The conversation in this book took place in Stockholm in 2002, when Duncan was present as "artist in residence" at Iaspis (the Swedish Arts Grants Committee's International Program). We had basically just gotten to know each other, and I found him very soft-spoken, sympathetic, and highly intelligent. I knew of his past, with dramatic performance and audio works like "Blind date" (1980, in which sexual sounds were recorded in a morgue), and "Scare" (1976), in which a masked John Duncan fired a gun with blanks in unsuspecting people's faces.

These were violent works, provocative to say the least, not only transgressing the politically correct assumptions of what art "should" be (even in the liberal 1970s). They also transgressed the safety and comfort zone of Duncan himself. Whether for personal, emotional, cathartic reasons or for shock value, his early works signal deep distress and a desire to be acknowledged not only for whatever trauma there was itself, but also for the loud willingness to deal with it.

What could have been an extremely private experience in a morgue, or a cruel prank among friends was contextualized by Duncan himself as works of art, and were thereby entered into the annals of "experimental" and "transgressive" art. Not as cheap justifications or desperate alibis, but because that was the only language that could deal with, and express, the intensity of what he felt on the inside: art isn't a commodity or a career — it is a tool.

As for the controversy that had always existed regarding "Blind Date," he later on even issued a statement that included, "Since Blind Date, all forms of my work are created to raise questions, to find out everything I can about who I am without fear or judgement, and to encourage you to do the same. Think of me as you will."

Inside this pool of sincerity is basically where these works (and others) have remained and gathered strength as parts of a body of work by an artist who has consistently pushed the boundaries for almost 50 years now, and more or less always woven in deeply-rooted emotions in his various expressions (performance, sound art, music, visual art, etc).

For some reason the curators at Iaspis weren't aware of his early work when they provided Duncan with a place in Stockholm and funds. But when someone so graciously "informed" them (that is, "snitched"), time was immediately up, and Duncan was kicked out.

What could have ended as a sad footnote fable of ill-informed cry-babies trying to bully someone who's never made any kind of apologetic secret of anything (maybe that was actually one of the problems involved?) actually morphed into a sunshine fairytale.

When the news broke, several Swedish and international artists spoke up, saying this was a revolting turn of events. In solidarity, alternative residence was set up so that Duncan could continue with the audio projects he was working on at the time. In order to raise awareness and also funds, a support evening was organized at legendary experimental art haven Fylkingen in Stockholm in March, 2002. When asked if my band/project Cotton Ferox (together with Thomas Tibert) would be willing to play, I immediately said yes. As did many others. It turned out to be a beautiful evening not only in support of an artist whose honesty is absolutely commendable, and whose work is always interesting, but also as a stand against this kind of petty curator fascism.

It also gave us a lot to talk about, and it seems to be a conversation that in some ways has been ongoing since then.

— You've been working in many disciplines. Why do you think you've specifically worked so much with audio?

It's a perceptive sense that I wasn't really trained to develop. I don't have a musical background. I don't have a formal training. At a certain point I started imagining what it would be like to be blind; to be more aware of what sound was doing — the properties of sound. That's when I started getting interested in it. The other thing that spurred me on was that I wasn't interested in painting anymore. The basis as my training as a painter was the relationship between the frequencies of light, i.e. color, and our emotional response to those frequencies. I figured the same thing would work with sound, and that there'd be a correlation. I got interested in developing it in that direction, developing audio in the same way I had with images.

— How did you get started with the actual experimentation? What did you use first?

Voice. This was in the early to mid 1970s. I used sounds of breathing. The first thing that I remember recording was the sound of a group of people breathing, and treating that as a chorus. I took that to a guy called Charles Amirkhanian, and he got me on the air on his radio show. That was the very first time I really made what I consider music now. It was also the first time it was put out in public.

— Was your own response to the finished result approximately the same as you had expected?

I didn't know what to expect.

— Were there any other people experimenting with the same kinds of things at the time: using voices and organic sounds?

Now I know there were. At the time, I thought that I worked in a vacuum. I was going along according to whims and didn't know anything about the history of music, or what other people were doing at the time. The closest people I knew who were experimenting with sound were people like Tom Recchion, Fredrik Nilsen, Joe Potts and his brothers, Chip Chapman. I realized later on that they were actually a very loose organisation called LAFMS.[2] All of these people were introduced through a man named Harold Schroeder. Harold and I were driving school-buses; one afternoon after work he started talking about this weird music he was listening to. He introduced me to a record by someone named Lady June, called "Linguistic Leprosy."

— So you found some people who were doing similar things?

Through him, yes. Whether it's by circumstance or fate or the movings of the world, I don't know, but this sort of offbeat guy at this job had heard that I was listening to "strange things." We talked and found out that we had interests in common. He started introducing me to LAFMS people and that's where I went.

— What did your paintings actually look like?

They looked like blocks of color, the size of a wall. It would look like one color. As you sat in front of it and looked at it, you'd start seeing other layers underneath. These layers were other colors, decided by the psychological response they evoked, some of which some were compatible and some were not. They were washes, thin layers of color on top of one another. The more you looked at

---

2 The Los Angeles Free Music Society

the entire surface, the more and deeper you were drawn into it.

— That corresponds very well to the pieces of music you make.

It's the same source.

— Do you regard all of your work as cathartic?

I'm not quite sure how you mean that. What I do is basically to let a sound source work on me, and see where that goes. And then find something complementary to that or find a way to treat that sound. To build an atmosphere that has a psychological effect. I don't know what it's going to be. I'm just trying things. At a certain point, the audio, the composition, starts to indicate directions. It almost makes demands as to what should be added; what will work and what will not. What kind of effect it will have. That it won't contradict itself. And then I just go on. I'm more an operator than anything else. I'm an equal partner with the project itself. I'm not a maker per se.

— Would you call "Blind Date" a cathartic project?

It's now so many different things... The original motive for doing it was cathartic. The motive for making it public was more about giving a personal gesture a universal reference or relevance. At least hopefully. To do something that many people could understand as something fundamentally human. But of course it turned into something more complex than that. It turned all my work into something much more complex than I'd initially intended.

— Was that because you had learnt so much or because you felt elevated to a new level of understanding?

Absolutely. It expanded my head so far beyond what I'd imagined was actually there. I understood my existence as being a very linear process. After that, it was very, very different. It's been very different ever since then.

— Have you consciously tried with other experiences to try and reach a similar kind of breakthrough or elevation?

Yes, absolutely. But they're all private. One of the things that I learned from the original response to "Blind Date" and something that was reinforced by the recent experiences here in Stockholm, was that it's not good enough to do something in front of an audience if they're simply sitting there. They have to meet me half way. They have to demand. The work has to have some kind of structure that demands something from each member of the audience, to pull out of themselves. Otherwise I'm just like a carnival act — basically an entertainer. I'm not interested in that. I don't have enough of a sense of humor to succeed with that. It's essential now that each member of the audience is included. It's difficult for me to see a mass. I see individuals. I always see individual responses. I know that the crowd mentality exists and that crowds have their own psychological structures. It's very difficult for me to see that, but I do understand individual people. That's why the work I've been doing, especially recently, involves getting people to confront a decision within themselves. To participate further or not. That decision is the art. The art begins with that decision. If they decide to go on and continue and go along with the process, then the art continues. If they decide to stop there and refuse this experience, then the art basically stops there for them. Then that's the only thing they walk away with and live with.

— My reaction to that is that it's a very magical view of art, in the sense that it's not in any way made to please or to externalize just for the sake of it. It's there to change something. It's all done with a specific purpose to change something in you or in the participating audience.

That's my hope, at least. If it works or not depends on the participants.

— One could throw oneself into the sea of challenges, and one could learn from very positive and pleasurable as well as from negative and painful things. A quote: "You learn most from what you want least"... To what extent do you push yourself to experience negative emotions or negative experiences?

I've learned that it's not necessary to push myself into bad experiences... They come anyway! For me, the issue is to be prepared to ride them, to be responsive to them. To accept the experience, to accept how I feel about it and, at the extreme, to avoid continuing or spreading it further. I'll give an example... If you do something to me that hurts me, I have a choice to retaliate or to absorb it. Most of the time I choose to absorb it because if I retaliate, then that's my responsibility. It's something I create; however justified I may feel. If I hit you back or get revenge, the revenge is an illusion. On a global scale, I think the things that are happening in Afghanistan are a very, very big mistake. That's not the solution to this. It's not the way to solve the problem. It's just a way to make it much worse. What's going on right now in the West Bank in Israel is another good example. What I mean by absorption is not just holding on to it, but also seeing to it that it goes no further. Just riding the wave, if you will. And understand that it is a wave. It's not something you own, unless you attack or do something deliberately, to act as an instrument of fate.

— On an instinctual level, one naturally reacts to threats. Usually though, most reactions lie on the emotional level...

I saw this in a situation that's the closest I've been to a war situation, in South Central Los Angeles. I was a driving a city bus. All the other drivers who were driving that line or driving in that general area at the same time, which was midnight to six in the morning, had weapons of some kind. They carried guns, they carried knives, they carried meter-long chains that they could use as a whip. I didn't carry anything at all. They were always getting into trouble. The most extreme example was a driver on a line that was parallel to mine. He got cut in half by barbed wire. Someone came on the bus and sort of came up behind him, looped the barbed wire around him and used it like a saw. People were threatening me all the time, every 15-20 minutes, all night, every night, all through the year. I learned that if I ever carried something, I would attract someone who was more desperate than I was and wanted me to test him. By not having anything, by not carrying a weapon, I managed... I carried psychology. I would listen to people, show them respect, and be ready to move out of the way as best I could if they lunged at me. It turned out that in just about every case, that was what they really needed most. This was the most effective tool for dealing with these situations.

— If you don't have any fear, you don't show any fear. And then you don't get attacked.

I always had the idea that it's possible that this would be my last night on the planet. This may be the last thing I do. I had in mind that I felt pretty good about what I'd done. If that should be the case, then I can accept that. I still feel that way. It worked out that way.

Different People

– You transcended the primal fear...

We'll see. It seems that way now. You never know...

– What originally made you interested in art? What made you want to become a painter?

That takes me back to Kansas as a teenager. What I remember is feeling a kind of resonance with certain images and with a way of life. Reading van Gogh's letters... I read his letters more than I looked at the paintings. I became interested in his paintings after reading those letters. You heard all these myths about this crazy guy who lobbed his ear off... It was like a cliché of what an artist is: someone who is crazy and completely out of control emotionally, and beyond reason. Beyond any kind of sense of social balance. Reading his letters, it was absolutely clear that that was not the case. He was extremely clear, extremely articulate in describing what he was trying to do. What he was trying to do was actually to be precise and empirical and at the same time open to his spiritual self. I was really, really impressed with this. This kind of dedication, this kind of focus he had was something that I really identified with a lot. I wanted that in my life. I must have started to paint and draw before that, because I remember a teacher told me about these books: a three volume set of his letters. By that time, I must have already gotten into painting. The only thing I can remember before that is that people in my family helped me start doing that, when they saw that I wasn't responding to school. I found school very boring. The teachers were tedious, they were cut off from the students, they were honing their lessons to the slowest of the students. I didn't know what to do. I didn't even know if I would finish school at all. My family pushed me into doing this instead as a way of at least giving me something to do. I wasn't interested in sports and I hated the people involved. No one knew what to do with me...

– You've lived in in Los Angeles, Japan, Holland and Italy. Four distinct periods... What differences can you see between these different periods? Did the moving create the differences or did the new directions demand your moving?

The atmospheres of these different places shaped the work I did at the time, and also shaped who I became in these places. In the case of Italy, the process is still going on. But it's not just Italy. Being in Stockholm has had an influence and, I have to say, a really positive influence. Especially after the event of March 9th.[3] That night was such a rewarding experience, I don't know how to put that in words. It was very inspiring.

— How would you define the different periods?

LA was concentrated on a sense of myself as a member of society. One in a social order; trying to understand myself as a member of this larger society. Japan was a deliberate move to be completely cut off from society. For me, Japan represents an atmosphere where you can develop yourself inwardly and not show what you feel to anyone. Very often when you meet Japanese people, they don't seem to be like you expected. This essence that they were showing me in letters and in communications, the stuff that's cut off from physical contact, they didn't show that in the way they acted, the way they dressed, in the daily life choices they made. Everyone looked very homogenous... I'm thinking of the people who look like they could work in an office, and very often do. They can interact with other people in an office who would never, ever have an idea that this person has this other life. That's true for nearly everyone there. They keep this other life entirely separate. There was a guy that I met named N. Nakayama, who had run an amusement park construction company. He built ferris wheels and things like that. When the company went bankrupt, he went to prison for several years. When he got out of prison, he lived on the streets for about seven years. He told me that the Japanese are very much like lizards or crocodiles. That made a lot of sense to me, especially in regard to the experiences on the subway trains. They sit there checking on each other but you never see the other's eyes. The eyes are always narrowed, slit, moving back and forth, watching people around them, but unless it's deliberate no one ever really makes eye contact. He saw them as a nation of lizards. This encouragement to develop myself inwardly and not show it to other people turned out to be invaluable. It's been very, very worthwhile to me. In Holland, I started getting that into in my art. Looking for ways to encourage other people to do that. But they usually involved some kind of confrontation with an audience. Usually a confrontation that took the form of me in front of an audience. Usually me doing something nude in front of the audience. Or getting the audience to volunteer to go nude into a situation. I'm thinking of the project "Maze."[4] People didn't know what to expect. Now,

---

3 The date of the John Duncan support evening at Stockholm's legendary experimental haven/ venue Fylkingen.

4 1995. A performance in which Duncan invited naked people into a completely dark room.

in Italy, it's changing. The music is changing, the events, the installations change. Now, they're more like a seduction. The music is more like a seduction. The events are more like promises that something will happen but you don't know what. If you agree to do X, if you do X, you will find out more. If you do not, you will have the fact that you refused to go further as something you take home with you.

— What has X been so far?

A variety of things. Here in Stockholm, it was taking your clothes off and going into a completely dark room with strangers, something that disrupted your sense of space. You couldn't really get an idea of how big or small the room was.

— Would you say that the first three phases make up a kind of thesis, antithesis and synthesis, in the sense that you were involuntarily exposed to the reaction of "Blind Date" in the US? You went inside instead in Japan, and in Holland went both ways, demanding an interaction?

Yes, very much so. Following that line of thought, one could say that the experiences in Italy and Stockholm are those of transcendence. It's in the past. The shock that anyone might feel is not my problem anymore. I'm not interested in all these things anymore. People always come up to me and want to discuss things like "the value of a body," "the value of a human being before and after death," the way that society treats women and so on… already judging me as a representative of that. It doesn't work. I'm not interested in these issues. I didn't care about all this then and I don't now. If I were watching a television documentary about it, then I might continue to watch it. But discussion of these "issues" is really important to others, not me. Why should I care?

— You mentioned that you're meditating…

That's part of my discipline. I started doing that in LA. Then I stopped doing it in Japan and started again in Holland. In fact, I went to Thailand to a Buddhist monastery outside of Chiang Mai; I stayed there about a month and went through a meditation training program they had. The training has nothing to do with religion. It's a way of teaching the discipline of sitting down and practicing and accepting what will happen. The practice I'm doing now is developed from that. It was a very useful base to start from. In LA, it was basically Zen that I practiced. In the end it wasn't enough, although I took that as far as I thought I could. I was not in any way interested in any religion; that's never worked for me. The discipline of practice I translated to the one of the Reichian breath exercise; especially in Japan.

— What's the next step in the experiments with sensual impressions or deprivations? You did this at Lydmar[5] and in Tokyo and in Canada. But that was basically a visual thing.

Visual in the sense that there was a complete absence of anything to see. Audio in the sense that the sound was overwhelming. I was in the room, also nude, responding to each person according to what I felt from them without being able to see them.

— Have you thought of taking it any steps further? There are other senses and things that could be deprived. Movement, agility, having people have earplugs...

There are a couple of projects that I may or may not realize in my lifetime. One of them is an amusement park based on laboratory experiments; based on the experiments on rats. Right now it's important to offer people the chance to leave at any time. So binding people, tying them up or down, limiting their freedom is something that I'm not really interested in.

— The video work in Japan had nothing to do with similar ideas of deprivation?

The idea was simply to make commercial pornography and to see if it could be subverted. The ideas about deprivation came much later, in Amsterdam.

— So, did you manage to subvert commercial pornography?

Certainly not then. If I've subverted anything, I've subverted my own ideas on what it was. In making commercial pornography, there's an interesting labyrinth you get into. Similar to making Hollywood films, I imagine. The producers want to make money on their investment. In order to do that, they pay close attention to what distributors are willing to distribute, who in turn pay close attention to what their customers want to buy. It's a very strict, rigid formula that's very hard to break. Audiences expect to have a storyline. In Japan, the censors demand a

---

5 A performance at Hotel Lydmar in Stockholm in 2002; a development of the "Maze" idea.

storyline with redeeming social value. There's got to be a narrative, there's got to be a reason for all these people doing these strange things in the films. It's not just action and then 60 minutes later, the tape ends. There has to be a beginning, a narrative development and an end in Japan. It's a very rigid structure. You can't really do anything abstract with that. Even if you're interested in doing something outside of this full-on 90 minutes of sex, you still have to conform to these demands. It's much more limiting that I'd expected. The situation in Japan made it more interesting than I'd expected. People who get into it are very often people who are not professional sex workers. They're students, they're people at film school or people who have just graduated from film school. They have ideas and techniques and special effects and camera techniques and script ideas... All of these techniques that are taught in film school, but that they can't use in the commercial industry because it's so hard to get in there in the first place. They have to pay their dues to the union for several years before they can even get into the building. They were so frustrated with that, and at the same time the adult video industry was so open, always looking for people who can do new things. The people I met and worked with could apply what they'd learned in film school and make money out of having fun. And making a sex film was part of it. It was a different situation from what I'd seen in Europe. The films show this. They show that there's a very different way of thinking about them among the staff.

— The pseudonym you used, "John See," was that meant as an anthropological imperative? John... See!

Yeah. It was a message to myself to wake up. By using that name, I don't feel I was hiding; it was a way to try and get out of myself but at the same time give myself a push all the time.

— Do you think that breaking taboos has a value in itself?

That depends on the taboos. It can.

— Do you think it's a prerequisite of the concept "artist" that they need to push the limits? Could someone be an artist and just be fine in the middle?

There are plenty of artists who've done incredible work, really inspiring work, and where they don't push the limits. But please don't ask me to think of who they are... The idea of deliberately breaking a taboo is not something I've really thought about. It's just ended up that way. It's something I've needed to do; I've never considered it in terms of breaking rules and taboos. This is an issue that I actually think about a lot, because it's important to me to avoid inspiring people to cause trouble, just for the sake of doing it. But at the same time... If you're really going to explore who you are and what your life is and really look into your existence, that in itself is very often seen as threatening by people who are not prepared to do that. You have to be ready to deal with the fact that you're going to threaten these people. The research is going to threaten some people. And those people are going to react, out of fear of themselves, out of fear of their own lack of information.

— Wouldn't you agree with the suggestion that the same act can be looked upon differently, depending on if it's done in a pursuit of soul searching or creating shock value? The soul searching is always more threatening...

A lot of people avoid looking into themselves. Someone who's compelled to do that is threatening. If you are compelled to do that, you have to be ready to accept this kind of kick back and this sort of hostile reaction. When this happens, when this resistance comes, it's very, very tempting to look at the people who give this to you as weak, as shallow, as pretentious and spiritually lazy... Any kind of number of negative judgments. All of these things may be true. But none of them really matter. The way I see it now is that, as hard and discouraging as it can be sometimes, ultimately it's a kind of test. If you see this resistance as a test, you come out of it stronger. The alternative is to accept that they are right and to shut up, and to just get back in line. Whether that's good or bad I don't know, but it's not for me. I couldn't do that even if I wanted to.

— What are your thoughts about all of this after the support evening?

The night at Fylkingen on March 9th was a kind of culmination of what I can only describe as a wave of support that I got after Iaspis got into the scandal of kicking me out and their arrogance and cowardice behind their actions. I thought I was completely alone. The day it happened, it just seemed like something that would never end. I thought that no one cared, that my role on this planet was to suffer for other people's stupidity. Starting the next day, Annika von Hausswolff called and asked if it was really true and that she couldn't believe it. Her call was the first time I felt someone had cared about what had happened. After that, the phone didn't stop ringing for two weeks... I felt everything but alone. On March 9th, all of these people... Cotton Ferox, Carl Michael von Hausswolff, the Sons of God, all of these people... All of the things that were done on that night, from the machine that generated sound from fire, to Ingrid Engarås' performance using the space of Fylkingen itself... Very subtle, incredibly beautiful. Everything was of an incredibly high calibre, such as I'd suspected Swedish art would be but hadn't seen. Fetish 23's videos... It was an honor to be included in the night. It was an honor to be there, an inspiration. Amazing work, all on one night, and at short notice. It was a real inspiration to be there. To have this done as a gesture of support, to make it possible for me to stay here longer, I will never, ever forget... I do not feel alone anymore.

— When you're performing a piece, are you all focused in the moment or do you allow yourself to drift away with the sounds?

I'm listening to what's going on and I'm playing the mixing table as a participant. In the beginning, I can say that it's deliberate. I impose what I want to happen onto the instrument and the sound it's making. But after a while I just feel like I'm a part of it.

— Have you ever experienced any kinds of communication in these states of mind?

If I'm simply listening to it, Yes. If I'm part of it, I feel that I have to keep a certain distance: an objectivity. I have to stay conscious enough to work the controls. It's a different thing to be responsible for what happens than being a participant as a listener. I used to get out of control when doing the Reichian exercises. The idea of these breath exercises is to lose physical control, and when I did that I didn't really remember what was happening. I couldn't feel what was happening. I felt like a conduit. The performances would change considerably, depending on the kind of energy I felt coming through me from the audience and out, or from wherever... There were times when it was incredibly beneficent and positive. There were other times when it was openly hostile, especially when it was coming from outside through me and into the audience. The last performance was on the altar of the Parochialkirche in Berlin. There is something in that building — I don't know what it is — that's very strange. It was very strange at the time at least. Definitely hostile. I don't think it's used as a church any longer. From what I heard, there was a crypt underneath the altar. I don't know how to explain it. That was an experience when I needed some kind of defense. There was something happening there, and I didn't know if the audience was aware of it. And it wasn't necessarily a positive thing to open this. It's one of the few times I can remember that I've been really frightened. I was in touch with something and was being used by something that I didn't and don't want to be a part of. It wasn't worth it.

— You once wrote, "When your dreams become flesh, can there be anything but trouble?" I'd say that's a distinctly dystopian view... Some would argue that when dreams become flesh, it's a moment of joy and power and pleasure... Do you still ascribe to this view?

If you're dreaming about pleasure, joy and particularly power, you're going to get them. And they're going to use you. Power is something I try very hard to avoid. If somebody tries to give me power, I try hard to give it back. It can be a distraction. If you get pleasure, you want to hang on to it. If you achieve joy, you want to hang on to it. If you're seeking power, you do everything you can to hang on to it, maintain it, increase it.

— So you see it as a matter of detachment versus attachment?

I see it as a trap. If you try and hang on to these things, you're going to get stuck in a series of illusions, and in trying to maintain the illusions. If you want to understand them as parts of a process and appreciate them for what they are but don't try to hang on to them, then there are things that are beyond that. If you're ready to let go of these pleasurable things, you can go further. If you're not, the growth process stops and the illusions become a kind of hell. Dreams become real. You get what you imagine — and how. So you'd better aim high, impossibly high, because it's going to happen...

— Speaking of dreams... I think that's actually where that quote comes from: your project "The Error"... One thing that seems to be clear is that it's based on dreams. These textual and image fragments make a whole, just like dreams. Would it be correct to define your work as an externalization of inner experiences through a specifically philosophical grid or matrix?

Frankly, I hadn't considered that, and I don't usually try to define things. Basically I write these things down; when they come to me, I write them down. "The Error" is simply a collection of these phrases, and of images that in some way complement them. The two usually don't have any connection at all. They're supposed to add up to, or suggest, something beyond either of them. As for the philosophical structures, I don't have anything fixed in my mind to follow. Perhaps something emerges, but it's not something I consciously use as an architecture.

— In Thomas's film,[6] you mention an abusive father and a desire to interrupt what seems to be a lineage. Spirals become spirals and the victim becomes the victimizer. What do you think would have happened if you hadn't had art as a valve or a focusing point?

I don't know. I can't really imagine. It's difficult for me to deal with the issue of 'what if...?' I have no idea.

---

6 Thomas Nordanstad, "Think of me as you will" (Sweden, 2002). An interview film in which Duncan talks at length about "Blind Date" and other works.

Charles Gatewood, 2002

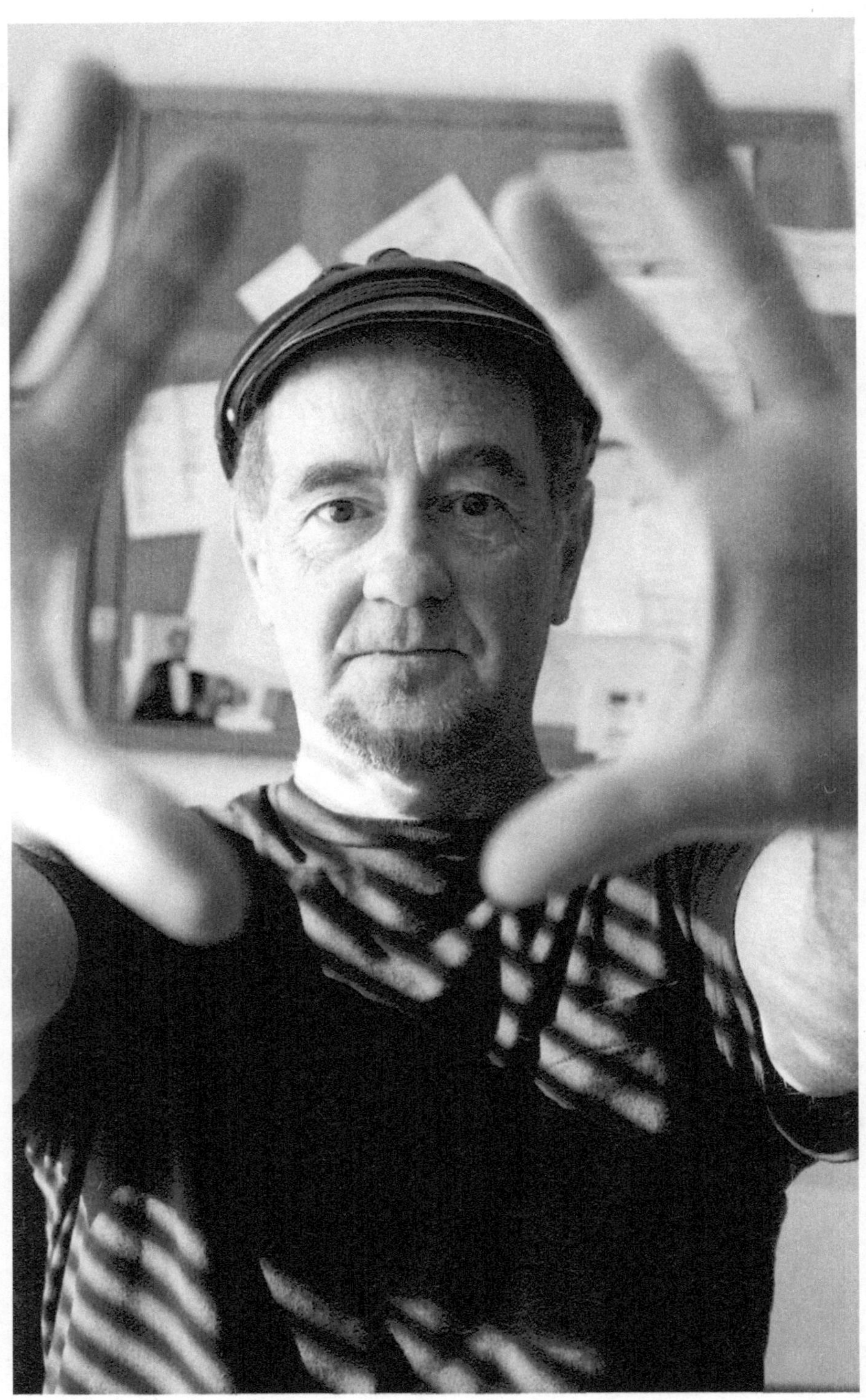

Charles Gatewood

"It's my job to go out and take tough pictures."

I got to know San Francisco-based photographer Charles Gatewood in the early 2000s. He used to be (and still remains) a household name in the underground (so called); shooting iconic portraits of sexual and body-modification pioneers, but also of counter-cultural iconoclasts during the 1960s and onwards. But there was another connection for me, too, that always made me love his images even more. During the mid-1960s, Gatewood tried to evade the American Vietnam draft and spent two years studying in Stockholm, Sweden — my very own hometown.

His favorite hang-out was the Jazz club that my father ran at the time: "The Golden Circle." In my mind's eye, I can see him snapping away cool Jazz people in the dark and sweaty club, and perhaps at some point (or several) talking to my father about this or that. Eventually, my father put together a book about the club, and I brought it as a gift for Gatewood on one of my visits to his wonderful apartment in Bernal Heights. It almost brought tears to his eyes to see the live photos from the club and other evocative ephemera in the book.

Charles Gatewood was a genuinely nice man. He was always friendly and supportive of my own photography — especially the material I used to shoot at San Francisco's annual "Folsom Street Fair." When he died in 2016, it was certainly unexpected to me. I had last met him in 2014, when we worked on the documentary film "Once the toothpaste is out of the tube — An Art Apart: Charles Gatewood" together. He complained about back pains then, but also about the pain medications that made him so tired. No matter what, I finished the film in Sweden, and looked forward to seeing him soon again. When the film was released on DVD, I immediately sent him copies. Then suddenly there was news that he had fallen out from his balcony and was badly injured. He died in a hospital some days later. And a few weeks later, the package of DVDs came back to me, unclaimed. It was indeed a sad day.

The following conversation is from 2002.

– So, lets's start at the very beginning...

I was born in Chicago in 1942, and I grew up in the Ozarks, South Missouri, which is a real primitive hillbilly area. My parents were drunks and party animals, so I grew up pretty fast. When I was ten years old I was sitting in on the family poker games, and pretty good at it. By the time I was 11 or 12 I was having all kinds of adventures. And I discovered pretty early that I like to watch... I remember, I guess I was about nine, crawling under public swimming pool dressing rooms. Did I tell you that story?

– No.

Well, I noticed when I was dressing that coins fell out of a man's pocket and went through the cracks in the floor. I thought, "Hey, I'm going to get that money." And I crawled under the dressing rooms and got a whole bunch of coins. And I crawled under the women's part and got the coins there too. I was there under the women's floor, and when I looked up I saw naked women. I was nine or ten years old. And a woman saw me and screamed, and I got really scared, and I crawled out really fast. It was just a little crawlspace, and I skinned my head and I skinned my back. And I crawled out. I was bleeding, I was dirty, it was muddy, I was filthy, I had a handful of money, and I was scared shitless, and excited at the same time. So, thats when it all came together: sex, money, guilt, dirt, voyeurism, fear... And then, all through high school and college I had raging hormones, you know. Basically all I could do about it was look. I like to watch and look, and especially at girls. At college I lived right across the street from the girls' dorm. Every night the girls would undress, and I got a free show. I was really close. So I invited a photographer to come over and take voyeur pictures. And we started looking at his prints and started talking, but we never did take those pictures. We just talked all night. But I saw what he had done with art photography, and I saw what I could do. All of a sudden I knew that's what I wanted to do. It was just clear in one instant, you know. So my work came from a voyeuristic place. It's still like that but now I think it's much deeper than just voyeurism. But it definitely started in that tradition.

– When you picked up photography, was that immediately after this revelation?

I was in my second year of graduate school in anthropology. I didn't know what

I wanted to do. You can't really work in anthropology without a PhD. And even then, there's museum work, there's field work, and there's teaching. And I just couldn't see myself doing that. I had also been taking a lot of classes in art history, and I was really interested in art. So I was interested in combining my interest in art with my interest in behavior. And that's what I saw in this guy's work. He was a fellow anthropology student. He also was a photographer. He was shooting relationships and social issues and... you know, social interactions and public events. It was the early 1960s, and the 60s was starting to happen. Demonstrations and civil rights all that. And I was on my way to Stockholm. At that point I had been accepted at the Wennergren Center school. They had an English speaking, college graduate level program, with classes in social science. So I went to Wennergrens, and they wrote a letter to the draft board. It was during Vietnam. So I got a student exemption to study there. But I liked the Swedish classes, and actually I worked really hard to learn Swedish. By the time I left Sweden after two years I spoke pretty good Swedish. But except for the Swedish classes I hated the school. The people were nice but Swedish social science was really statistical and extremely boring. And meanwhile the 60s were happening, even in Sweden. There were hippies sitting on the steps of Hötorget every day, you know: protests, scenes. Everybody hung out at a café downtown called "Ringbaren." There was a scene there. There was a party boat that we all used to go to. You know, there were scenes. I stopped going to classes after a couple of months, and just started hanging out with people in the streets; truly freaks and protesters. I decided to be a photographer at that point. I just couldn't see myself doing any more boring graduate work in sociology. I wrote letters to all the photographers in the Swedish phone book asking for an apprenticeship. I was accepted by a group called Visum: Svante Hedin, Jörgen Lundberg and two or three others. I think Svante is still a pretty well known guy. They accepted me as an apprentice so, you know, they taught me the basics of photography. I did darkroom work for them, and when I got good enough, they let me do all the film developing and printing. I did that for almost a year. Then I travelled for a while, and then I came back and got a job as a dark room boy at a company called AB Text & Bilder. I did that for another year. I was the dark room guy and all around, you know, assistant, whatever. Well, mostly dark room. They had press passes, and they let me use the press passes whenever somebody wasn't using them. So if there was a Bob Dylan concert or an Ornette Coleman concert, I got to shoot that because nobody else was interested. I could also borrow their equipment and the press cards so I could get in at almost anything I wanted. By then my

Swedish was pretty good so I was the roving reporter and man about town, and just shooting for myself. Sometimes Text & Bilder would use what I shot. But sometimes I didn't even show it to them. I was just learning, developing my craft, learning my trade. I spent two years in Stockholm. It was hard. I was lonely and broke and alienated. Most of my class mates who were sent over to Vietnam got killed or got fucked up one way or another. That was looking right at me. And I knew the minute I went back they were going to draft me and send me to war. So I was really alienated; I was pretty angry about it. It was a hard time. I lived in a rented room and ate at a worker café, and drank the cheapest red wine that you could buy. Anyway, they did draft me. After two years they drafted me. I went back and I failed the physical test. I managed to fail the physical by doing some very strong acting and lying. I couldn't believe it. I immediately I headed for New York. That was 1966. And the 60s were exploding in New York. I started photographing what I saw in the streets. And my work still has a very strong alternative direction. It's pretty much a straight line.

— In your luggage, you also had a picture that helped you become more famous: the Bob Dylan one.

The Bob Dylan photo, yes. I took that with the Text & Bilder press pass at a press conference, spring of 1966. He had just played that famous London concert, The Royal Albert Hall Concert. He was traveling with The Band. They had just done "Blonde on Blonde." I took that at the press conference. Text & Bilder bought it and syndicated it actually. And that was later a very big selling poster in the States.

— Do you think that that actually helped you while you were in New York; the fact that the poster became so successful?

Well, it didn't hurt. Posters were big sellers in those days. At one point I had eight or ten posters going. That was the bestseller, absolutely. Every college kid in the States had that picture on his wall.

— So while you were working as an apprentice and learning the craft and the trade, did you also study photography in the sense that you checked other photographers and international photography out; things that were going on at the time?

I never took a class in photography, but I looked at every book in the bookstore. Every time the *Popular Photography Annual* would come out I would buy it. I remember I had no money so it was a big deal to buy the *Photography Annual* for, I don't know whatever it was, six crowns or something, or more than that. And I would take it home like gold and study it and look at every page and dream about the day when I would have pictures in the *Popular Photography Annual.* That was a big deal.

— Was there anyone doing photography that immediately inspired you?

Well, I always liked the old guys, especially Robert Frank, Brassaï, Cartier-Bresson... The hip photo journalist, you know, W Eugene Smith. The really good photo journalist who made art from journalism. That's who I admired and that's what I set out to do. I never took a class in photography so I was learning on the job. I worked for a year first in a professional studio so I could learn studio techniques, and more dark room, you know. Learned a little bit more about what I was doing. After three years of apprenticing and assisting and so on, I quit. That was the last time I ever had what you could call a job. I started being a photographer, and New York was cheap in those days. My first apartment was only 52 dollars a month. And photographs in those days sold for at least 35 dollars each. So if I could sell three or four photographs a month, I could pay for my apartment and live. And actually, within a year I moved to a better place. You know, it wasn't that hard to... because I worked my butt off. Yeah, very quickly I was working for *Harpers, New York Times, Saturday Review,* lots of text books also. Lots of text books bought my pictures because I was shooting sociology, basically.

— Do you think that your original interest in anthropology has definitely colored your work?

Oh, sure, I mean, to this day. I was trained to go into the field and bring back information.

— That's exactly what you do.

That's exactly what I do.

— Can you see a dividing line when you move from the recording work, the more classical reporting photography in a sense, and get more into sexual themes? Is there something specific that happened or was it on-going development?

Well, I was pretty much a twisted photo journalist until mid 1970s. I did *Sidetripping*[1] and at the same time I shot all the work on *Wall Street*.[2] Those are still two of my favorite books. I mean it's all candid on the street; very authentic, real photo journalism with social commentary. And then after that I wanted to try something different. I was tired of confrontation in the streets. I was also tired of the pushed Tri-X, grainy look, you know, the look of someone who was in the *Sidetripping* pictures. I wanted to do something more formal, more private, with better quality. I guess I did shift about that time to observe sort of more private realities. I was still shooting in the streets. I shifted from Tri-X to Pan-X, which is a very slow film. I also used more contrast. If you shoot in an apartment, the background gets dark in a nicer way. And you just get the person with a black background. I started using that technique a lot, like flash in the face, and letting the background go black, as black as possible. I started doing ·a lot more portraits of strange people, and fewer candids. That work was published in my book *Forbidden Photographs*.[3] It has a very different feeling. That was a major shift. I still do both. I still do candids, I still do portraits. Probably, since that time I've done more portraits, either posed or conceptual. And at the same time, it's that early candid work that has that real energy, the nitty gritty authenticity that everybody likes. Street photography is a young man's game. Now I go to the Folsom Street Fair for two hours, and my feet hurt and I have to pee. And I stay another hour and then I'm wrecked. The next day I have to take a hot bath and rest.

– You live in San Francisco which is a very interesting place in terms of subcultures and sexual things going on. Do you have something in you, like a driving force, that makes you want to discover new extreme things all the time?

I'm always trying new things. And I'm always interested in finding new subject matter, sure. I try new styles every now and then. Right now I'm making collages. I've never done collages in my life. But I'm having a lot of fun with it. I can show you some. Anytime I have a chance to shoot something that I haven't shot before, of course it's a big deal.

---

1 Charles Gatewood, *Sidetripping*, Strawberry Hills, New York 1975
2 Charles Gatewood, *Wall Street*, R Mutt Press, New York 1984
3 Charles Gatewood, *Forbidden Photographs*, Flash Productions, San Francisco, 1981

— What is there urge-wise for you today except for the collages? Is there anything specific going on that you haven't touched yet?

I've never really gotten into hardcore erotica. Not very much. A little bit. I've always shot a few for myself that I haven't published. But I've done everything else that I want to do. Right now I'm working on this new book called *Dirty*. It's going to be personal art porn from real life experiences of me and my friends and other people. It's very much a San Francisco book. It's going to have some hardcore pictures in it. I want to make some hardcore art. And it'll also contain narrative stories. Little chapters, little stories about each scene. There was a gang bang at a big hotel the other day that I shot. I'll do a little chapter about that. I've been doing X-rated self portraits. There will be some chapters about that. Some groupies. And so on. I have a lot of fun with it. It feels very fresh; it feels kind of forbidden and it's something that I've danced around but haven't really explored yet. Also, it's all color. Even the black and white pictures: I paint them, color them.

— When did you start doing video work also?

About the time the first VCR came out; it was the mid-1980s. I remember getting a VCR and renting my first cassette, and holding the cassette and thinking; I wonder how hard it is to make one of these — it can't be that hard. But I had no idea. I was artist in residence in Florida, at the Daytona Beach Community College. They had me down during a giant motor cycle festival called "Bike Week." A hundred thousand Harley Davidson guys in the streets. So I asked them if they had a video department. And they said, yeah we have a big video department. That's what I want to do for my project. I want to make a video about "Bike Week." And they said, sure you can do that. And I said, well, I don't have any idea how to do it. You're going to have to give me a teacher and a good camera. And they said, "no problem!" I made an hour video documentary with music from the scenes. I started making videos. People laughed at me; they said I was crazy to make videos with that little camera and try to sell them. I made a whole bunch really fast. I spent the summer in Amsterdam and made the video "Weird Amsterdam." I had my Biker video. I started making videos about tattoo and piercing, which was very hot at the time. It was just about to explode, the whole scene. I came to San Fransisco and I made "Weird San Francisco" and "Tattoo San Francisco." I went to Mardi Gras and made "Weird Mardi Gras."

Went back to Florida and made "Weird Spring Break." And many more. Many, many more about, as fast as I could, mostly about body modification. There was no competition. Nobody really understood video. Nobody had alternative video. And I did very well. Within a few years I did very well. The video money was my main source of income from about 1985 until… Well, it probably still is today. Although, starting around the mid 90s the internet started to really change all that. But I got into video in a big way and for a time there I was doing a lot more videos than photography. It's fun. It moves, it sings, it dances, it talks and it's in color. You know, I always wanted to make movies, but I never in a million years thought that I could make a film.

— How do you usually find models? Are you advertising, or do they seek you?

Today they mostly contact me. I do have some ads running always but mostly my work is pretty well known. Girls see my books and want be in my next book. It's fun to get sexy emails from all these people. I work with girls 18 to 25, kinky, you know, in the scene. I should do a book just of the emails I get because it's so fascinating and it's so exciting to hear from a new girl who wants to become a model. I photograph older people too. Some couples. But really my fascination is for, you know, fetish girls.

— In the *Modern Pagans* book you express a strong sense of awareness of your own spirituality. Has that always been there in your life?[4]

I got spiritual in the 1980s when I was trying to, sort of, recover from alcohol and hard drugs, which had devastated my family and was about to devastate me. I left New York and moved to Woodstock and lived the country. I met a girl who was a spiritual seeker, moved in with her, quit hard drugs, quit alcohol for a while, started meditating and chanting Buddhist texts, reading spiritual books by the fire, and so on. Because I knew that I was going to die if I didn't change my life. I always hated the Church when I was a kid, and my parents certainly didn't have anything to do with the church and neither did I. My spirituality came kind of late in life but it came at a good time. I did a lot of meditation in Woodstock and a lot of work there. It took me longer than I thought to kick; especially alcohol. I didn't finally kick alcohol until 1987. But when I came out of the woods and moved to San Fransisco in 1988 I was clean. I mean, I still

---

4 Gatewood was interviewed in *RE/Search Magazine: Modern Pagans*, San Francisco, 2001.

smoked pot but no alcohol and no hard drugs in 15 years. And I also quit coffee, tobacco, you know, most of it. Thank goodness, I'm still here! That was when I really got a clear picture of spirituality and started doing spiritual practices. Since then I've done a lot of inner work. I've taken a lot of classes and workshops. In San Fransisco I identify mostly with the pagan community. Now I do a lot of rituals with the pagans and a lot of my best friends are in that community. A lot of the sex people also have a very strong spirituality. It's very interesting, you know: you meet the most spiritual people here, and some of the most spiritual people are into the heavy scenes.

— Did you ever feel that it was hard quitting it all and then coming to San Francisco and getting involved in these heavy scenes, in terms of there being a lot of drugs around and just a fast lifestyle? Did you find it hard to re-integrate with that world?

Well, yeah. There are temptations. You know sometimes that bottle of booze or that saucer of dope is only inches away. And nobody cares whether you do it or not. But I saw pretty clearly the direction that I headed for. It was kind of a life or death matter. I mean, I've got some vodka and some wine in my fridge right now. For guests. I haven't had a drink for 15 years. Not a drop.

— Would you say that form or content is more important for you?

Both. Yeah, not a question. I'd say they're just about equal. You have to go after both at the same time. You're always looking for the form... Trying to put the picture together. You may not get it, but you're always looking for it.

— Are there any current photographers that you like or admire?

Sure. I love Joel Peter Witkin, Michael Rosen, Eric Kroll, and Annie Sprinkle.

— Have you ever run into legal problems because of your photos?

Not often. It's happened. I mean, I was sued once for a million dollars. You know the artist Boris Villejo? Fantasy paintings... Book covers and so on. He sued me for a million dollars once because I did some publicity pictures for another artist friend as a favor. I took pictures of someone's artwork and gave my friend the film. He was going to publicize a gallery show. And one of Boris' pictures ended up on the cover of *Drummer Magazine* which is a hardcore S/M gay magazine. And they gave me the credit for the artwork. "Cover artwork by Gatewood." So, you always think it's going to be some person in the street or some bad girl or something like that which causes trouble. This was just off the wall. He sued me for a million dollars. That was fun. That was quickly dropped. I've been censored a few times. I've been yelled at a few times. I think the hardest problem has been just figuring out ways to get the work out. Publisher after publisher said no. You know, the heavy work. To do that I self-published several books. I don't do that anymore. I self-published *Forbidden*,[5] *The Body and Beyond*,[6] *Primitives*,[7] and I'm glad I did. I got the books out, I got a lot of attention. At that time, there was no other way to get a quality edition of good books out. I self-published *Wall Street* too. There was no way to get those books out, in quality editions without doing it myself. That was the hardest thing. And it's still hard, getting published.

— Do you think that your work over the years has been an integral part of sexual liberation or liberation in terms of self expression?

Many people have told me that my photographs have changed their thinking and a lot of them say it has changed their behavior. Especially with the "Modern Primitives" stuff. A lot of people don't know I've done a lot of textbooks. I probably have pictures in literally hundreds of text books. And some of those pictures are very tough. They may not be sexual but they show some very tough facts and ideas. So I'm actually changing people's thinking in school. The last time I was in France a student told me that they studied my work in their school. Some of the heavier stuff. I know my work is changing the world little by little. Especially the body modification work. And a lot of that has to do with sexual evolution, personal change, personal growth, reclaiming the body and so on.

— Do you think that there could be any other expression except for art that has the same kind of heavy potential of change?

Music. Politics. There are some people in this country who are into politics but it's not such an age for radical social changes as it is in some other countries.

---

5 Charles Gatewood, *Forbidden Photographs*, San Francisco, 1995
6 Charles Gatewood, *Photographs: The Body and Beyond*, San Francisco 1993
7 Charles Gatewood, *Primitives*, San Francisco 1992

Certainly politics is one vehicle for change.

— Don't you find it strange that as we can see a general liberalization of self expression, yet at the same time there seems to be a very repressive or almost oppressive political force?

That's always been the paradox in America. There's always been that battle going on between radicals and the conservatives here. And it's a funny kind of game because both sides can win or lose. It changes but the constant battle is still the same battle really. "No, you can't!" "Yes, I can!"

— Have you ever shot anything or anyone that you wished that you hadn't, afterwards?

Well, I can think of a couple of times when I didn't take the picture that I had intended to take. Like last time I saw Tim Leary I wanted to take a picture because he was dying of cancer, but he looked so bad I couldn't do it. Basically I have no regrets except for the Boris Villejo picture. I remember once at Mardi Gras I saw this black kid with a really crazy mask on. I asked him if I could photograph him and just as I took the picture I realized it wasn't a mask. He was a burn victim. And I felt a little stupid at that moment, you know. I felt kind of embarrassed. I probably wouldn't have taken that one again. There are a few times, but not many. It's my job to go out and take tough pictures. And now, these days I even set them up.

— What do you think is the thing or the agent that makes photography such a powerful medium?

Well, there's a word called "mimesis." It's the memetic quality. It's so real and believable and lifelike; it has a really incredible power. Paintings can look real but photographs *are* real to most people. And you know the stories about a lot of primitive people feeling that their souls are getting stolen and so on. That kind of magic or whatever you call it is extremely powerful. That's why people are afraid of it.

— Do you have any specific dream projects; something that you haven't started yet, or something that you would really like to do?

Well, my desk is full right now. I have two books under contract I have to finish. *Wet Dreams*[8] and *Messy Girls*[9] are coming out next month. I have two more under contract, *Wet Dreams* and *Photography for Perverts*[10] and I'm going to put together my big body art book. It'll be called something like Charles Gatewood's Body Art/Body Play Source Book, or something like that. It'll be all my best body art pictures and writings in one book. Sort of my career book about that subject. I've been photographing that subject for about 25 years. I'm really well known for that work. I want to get that out in one big book. After that, who knows? It'll probably have more to do with BDSM and fetish. But, who knows? I just got a Lomo camera. It takes four pictures at a time. I haven't used it yet; just got it yesterday. It cost 12 dollars, and it's made out of plastic. It's four pictures together and each one is a different focal length and different framing. It's got a cool format. I can't wait to shoot with it. So you know, who knows, I may be doing a Lomo book or something, next week. I don't know. A lot of my work is very visceral. It sort of comes through me as not really conceptual, theoretical... It's just like, "hey, this looks like fun, I'll do a book about this." And boom, I'm off for two more years, whatever that is? I'm probably working more than I ever have worked in my life. I'm more productive and I have more projects going on. I'm really cooking these days. And it's all good. Three books are coming out, I've done five books in the last year. And a film.

— Would you say that you have a very distinct philosophy of life that you try to live by?

Yeah. It's really important for me to be really free and independent. I live alone and I think I like it. Because I spend a lot of time in my own space, doing my own thing. I work at home. If I put something down I need to know that it's going to be there next week in the same place. And I don't work very well when there's a lot of noise or distractions. I need peace and quiet. Also, being an addict, you know, all I've ever known are extremes, and more and more and more, you know, faster, faster, more and more. I've learnt how to seek a balance; a moderation. I never thought that I would be Mr Moderate, believe me. But it works for me to try to pace myself and not get too crazy, not get too burned out, not overdo anything. Just move ahead and get the work done. Try to be a good

---

8 Charles Gatewood, *Wet Dreams*, San Francisco 2002
9 Charles Gatewood, *Messy Girls*, San Francisco 2002
10 Charles Gatewood, *Photography for Perverts*, San Francisco 2015

guy. Hang out with my friends and do my work and stay out of trouble.

– That's a pretty good philosophy.

I was dangerous when I was younger. I was really dangerous on many different levels. But today I'm probably only dangerous through my work.

– You shouldn't underestimate that!

No, that's good, but I used to be dangerous personally.

– How important would you say that the area and ambience and just the city of San Fransisco has been?

Tremendously important. I did really interesting work in New York. There's plenty to photograph in the New York area. I've also done work all over the world in different places. But San Francisco is special because it's such a liberal and radical home for so many intelligent sophisticated freaks. The scenes here are big and deep and very sophisticated. And the people here, the top people in the field, are very smart, very talented, very skilled and very hot. There's no end of subjects. I run into subjects every day. They call me. For what I do, I don't think that there's any place in the world that could top this. Even New York. I mean, New York has its share of radical people and artistic freaks, but San Fransisco... that's kind of what it's known for. And to me it's the best place I've ever lived. It's casual but it's intense at the same time. Things just flow along. I don't have to look too hard to have fun or to find models, or be creative. Every couple of days another person or another situation pops up. And that's just perfect. It's just better than what I expected. And I don't even have to look for it. It just comes along. How can you top that? Not to mention, you know, this town is famous for being so beautiful and picturesque and having good weather. This is my last stop. You know, I still like to travel but I'm sitting up here on a hill in a beautiful place with a great view, in peace and quiet, and I'm only minutes from the action down in the Mission. I've never had a studio. I shoot at home with natural light on location. Models come here, we have tea, we shoot here or we go in the street, they come back and bring their friends and I work with their friends. Sometimes their friends come back and bring their friends. If you're part of the community and you behave yourself and you do good work and you have fun ideas, yeah, people will call their friends and come back and do it again and that's a big part of it. I'm not an outsider; I'm part of the scene. So people know that I don't have any ulterior motives; I'm not out to exploit them. I'm not out to distort anything or cause trouble. I'm really fascinated about what they're doing. I want to show everybody else.

Mark McCloud, 2002

Mark McCloud

"When you meet telepathically you can't lie."

Mark McCloud, the artist, archivist, and psychonaut par excellence of San Francisco's Mission district, has created a kind of timeless zone inside his literally wonderful Victorian house. The house is jam packed with Mark's various collections; most of them relating to psychedelic culture (and often called "The Institute of Illegal Images").

Starting out as a young American-Argentine numismatist, and then heading into collecting the colorful and perforated blotter paper that LSD is distributed on, McCloud has created an enigmatic approach to LSD in general and blotter in particular. What is art and what is psychedelic experience? Can they be one and the same? What is cause and what is effect? What is potentially healing and what is simply a very arbitrary felony?

Mark McCloud's complete embracing of his own psychedelic experiences, and his desire to publicly "pay back" to the chemical agent itself, and to its many-headed staff of creators (chemists, blotter artists, promoters, distributors, psychonauts, etc), has placed him in a position that has at times been threatening and downright dangerous — to say the least. It's not all groovy colors and cosmic insights when your house is raided by the FBI and DEA.

This had just been the case when I visited Mark McCloud the first time, in 2002. The year before, he was on troublesome trial, charged with "conspiracy to distribute LSD" after some of his colorful blotter paper had been found in "active" mode in a large LSD bust. He was basically facing a life sentence in prison, hadn't a number of cultural bigwigs stepped forward and testified that this is more a question of making blotter paper art, and not one of manufacture and distribution of the illicit drug per se.

Mark McCloud was enlightened, lucky, blessed, and eventually acquitted. In many ways, his fervor simply increased after this trauma. Since then, his own "Blotter Barn" business — producing psychedelic art on blotter paper, in books, exhibitions, etc. — has been featured in many articles and documentaries. In many

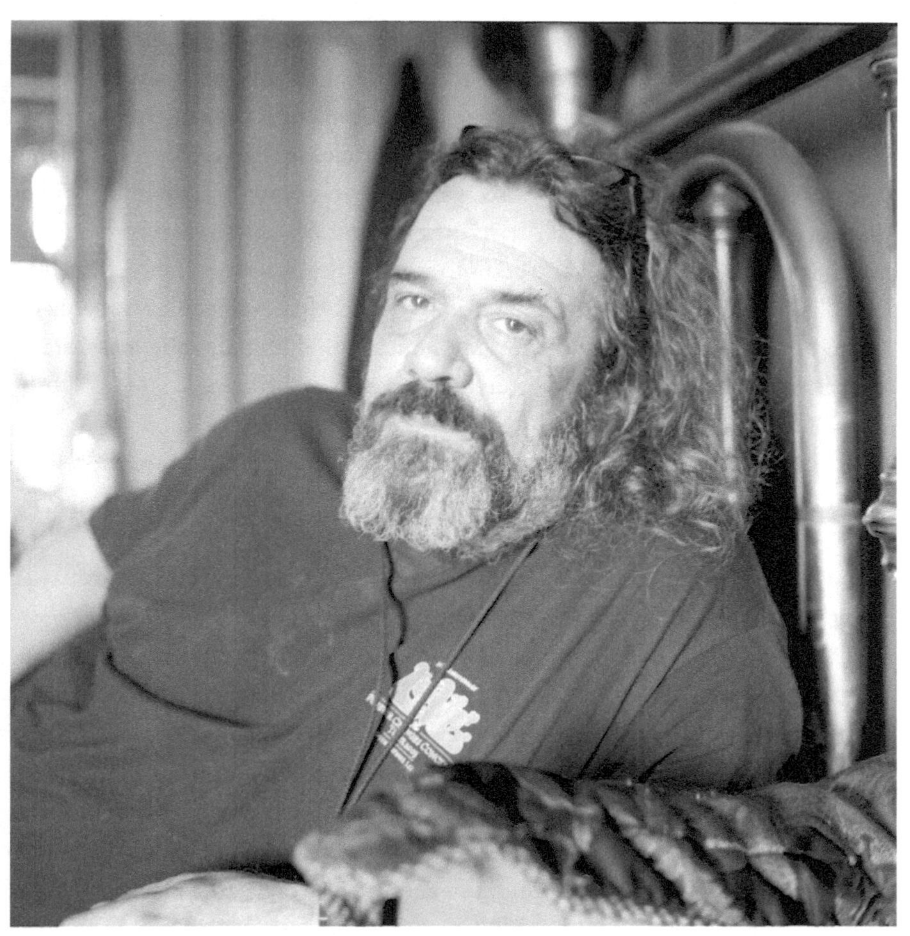

ways, the slightly humorous initial concept of a museum of "illegal images" has gradually morphed into the real thing. Mark McCloud has been a founder, curator and archivist who more and more also took the place of a creative artist of brand new works.

Since my visit in 2002, I have returned many times to McCloud's magic castle. He is a psychedelic sage, whose collections and stories not only entertain but also provide real insights into how counter-cultural developments have very often been chemically induced, and how the psychedelic movement is perhaps stronger than ever, as it's diligently merged with other environments (like ecology, civil rights, philosophy, the arts, technology... to mention but a few). Whatever makes you think critically is dangerous to the status quo, and it's not at all surprising that LSD has been held in special awe on both sides of the existential fence. Mark Mc-Cloud's diligent and visible work has undoubtedly help de-demonize not only the chemical key itself and its effects on the human mind, but also the massive and important cultural impact it has brought, and keeps on bringing.

– OK, let's start in the beginning. When did you have your first psychedelic illumination?

I came to the US when I was 12 from Argentina, and that was in 1966. Of course I'd read *Heaven and Hell*, and all the other Huxley that came out... *The Doors of Perception*. I read that first, and in 1967 I tried mescaline. And then from that, I tried the "Orange Sunshine" LSD. And I'd say I must have tripped maybe a hundred times before I had the "whopper." And the whopper was a "Christmas edition" Owsley did.[1] It made you absorb the entire 1500 micrograms in about three minutes. So, like three minutes later you're on a different planet. That was my big trip. It was right before Hendrix's death. It took me about ten years to integrate that experience. At the end of that integration was when I started collecting blotter.

I got sent to a boarding school in Los Angeles. I started in eighth grade and I went up to senior year so I spent five years in a boarding school in Los Angeles. Every sixth week they let us out for three days. I couldn't go back to Argentina, so I would check in with this family here in San Fransisco. That's how I turned on to the Fillmore and all of that. I was out of it... I could barely speak English. I ended up at the floor of the Fillmore before I could really tell what was going on. Where I'd come from we were hoods, you know. We were like 1950s hoods, like in "The

---

1 Owsley Stanley III (1935-2011) was an American audio engineer and (in)famous LSD chemist working close to the entourage of the band The Grateful Dead.

West Side Story." And so then I ended up in the middle of a hippie scene, you know. And I converted fast. I went back a couple of years later and I tried to tell my old gang in Argentina about peace and love. They beat the shit out of me and called me a faggot.

— How did you come up with the idea of starting to collect blotter?

Blotter has a really interesting history. Dr John Beresford, whose gram of acid turned The Beatles on, thought of putting it on a sugar cube in around 1962. The problem with that, although it was very good for hand to hand distribution, was that you couldn't mail it easily. It would crumble up in your pocket. And so then that's when people started thinking of loading it on other things. And one of the things they came up with was just blotter papers. Like the blotter paper you would use to blot ink. And instead of dipping the entire sheet, they would just hand-load little drops on it. The way the substance would actually effect the papers, you could actually see where the acid was. So you would cut around it and take as much as you could. It wasn't until Owsley's bust in 1971, when they took his micro-tabber and his Orange Sunshine pill press that the need for blotter arose. Until then it was pills and cubes. Once the pill presses were gone in the US, the need for blotter paper arose. Richard Kemp, for example, didn't get busted in England until 1974. And that's when the English pill presses went down. So they were a little behind us in the blotter efforts for that reason. We needed it first. So then, in the early 70s it started appearing, but it was usually no image at all, and it was usually hand-loaded on paper, a drop at a time, instead of dipping the whole sheet of paper. And you know, that concept of dipping the entire sheet was a very radical concept. Because you could actually get very, very even distribution, by judging the absorption rate of the paper and then calibrating the solution to that. Then as the images got better, I started getting into it. But of course, the first great ones I saw, I ate. I made a lot of effort to try to re-find those again. And in many ways that's been impossible. But unusually enough, some of that imagery has ended up floating around in other media. Roky Erickson did a picture disc, in which he collaged one of the first hits I ever took. So I've been able to, thanks to my memory, retrieve a lot of stuff like that. Then I'd say when the flying saucers image came out is when I first was able to score enough of that so that I could save some for the museum. After I learned all about it I learned how to get a good print, take the acid off of it without hurting the print. And so then as I got more educated I stopped eating it and I started saving it. But for a long time it lived in the freezer, because of my uncertainty whether I was going to frame it or eat it. Then, as I started framing them, I noticed that they had that kind of magic to them where a little group of them was enough to get trippers very excited. So as the prints got better and as my connections got better I was able to get more and more un-dipped sheets. Then after my first show in 1987 at the SF Art Institute, the word in the underground was, "Hey OK, there's a guy trying to save examples without implicating anyone." So that's kind of how it snowballed. But there was a lot mistrust when I first started this... And the dealers would just freak at the idea that someone was saving examples of their work. They thought, for sure, it was to implicate that rather than to absolve them. I had that distrust I'd say for a good five years until I noticed the big paper shortage of 1988. And I said, why don't I get into it and try to fill this gap with some of my own ideas, you know, what should be on blotter. And so that's kind of how I got into it. To do that I "apprenticeshipped." I actually did an apprenticeship with a blotter guy whose outfit had just been busted, and he had taken an eight year federal term. I went in there and I took that little outfit over and I started making just paper. And distributing it. At first I started by giving it away. Then I started charging two bucks a sheet. There was such a paper shortage that slowly people started pouring in looking for paper. Then as I had a portfolio of multiples, it was easier for me to meet other blotter artists and trade my folio for an example of their folio. I had a 10-1 ratio going at that time, where you could bring me one sheet and I would give you ten. And it worked well.

— Was it actually offset printed?

No. I'd say the birth of blotter was offset, but the inexperienced beginners noticed that silver and gold inks did not dissolve in an alcohol base. So then, a lot of the first ones were silk-screened. And they were silk-screened by laying down the image either in a silver or gold base. As the color started coming in they started going to offset. Then in about the late 1980s, when I got into it, I switched the whole program, and I took out the silver and gold and went to edible soy-based ink. That was a big deal. Especially when the acid got weaker. Because in the 1970s the grams started off, first step, 2000 hits per gram, which made each hit 500 micrograms. And then it switched to 4000, which made them 250s. And then it went to 8000. Not until the early 1980s the 10.000 came into fashion. And those were called "disco hits" because they were down on 100 "mikes." And if you were still in silver and gold inks, the old heads, to get the old result, were eating this huge amount of paper. And so then I said, why don't we go to soy based inks? They had just started getting sophisticated at that time... And that's the kind of contribution I wanted to make. I wanted to make it more artistic. That slowly took on. I would say that a lot of them now are soy based but not all. I see a lot of vanity prints that are, you know, offset prints. They haven't caught on to the soy based ink yet.

— Over this past decade there's been a lot of what you could call designer psychedelics. Would you say that LSD has kept its number one position?

In the intelligentia, yes. I'd say not in the youth movement. In the 1990s LSD started getting a fearful reputation. It's a much longer trip than the venue, unless it's a three day rave or something. I think that's what happened. As the venues got more and more restricted, then people noticed MDMA, and even DMT. The commitment of LSD isn't as wide as the venue. It used to be the other way around: where the venue itself was as serious as the substance. I'd say it's lost popularity, not in numbers, not in statistics. In statistics, LSD has grown every year; the LSD consumption now being higher than ever before.

— This idea of a blotter museum, did it stem from your desire to collect or your desire to show?

It came from coin collecting, originally. I was a numismatist for many, many years; it was even synchronized with my blotter collecting. But then in 1981 or so I traded in my coin collection to buy more blotters. To me it was the same kind of thing. Because if you look at US coinage for example, you realize that the first US coins were stamped out illegally in basements across the US. And at the expense of your life! If the English caught you making coins you were dead. And blotter, to me, had that same equivalent significance. No one trusted the government anymore. You'd much rather have a hit of acid than a dollar. To me, it made sense, you know. It was like the same thing. So the actual idea of a museum didn't really occur to me at all. It was just this collection. Then, after I showed it the first time, that kind of idea came up out of it. I was really aware of the Albert Hofmann Foundation whose efforts, even to this day, is to get together an acid museum. I talked to Oscar Janiger, who was heading the foundation back in 1988. I told him that when the museum is finished, I'll donate my collection to decorate the walls. I thought of it more like that. Just the visual aid to the whole thing.

— Could anyone call and come and visit and see this?

Yeah. Something that I noticed right away was that there wasn't a way of putting up an ad and saying, "blotter collectors, come on over!" It's such a serious thing to people that have taken it seriously. That was enough to make them overcome their distrust. I still have people that come in and look around and don't say a word and shake my hand and leave. They don't open up. And so, that's something that I've just had to keep as a policy, although it has been very dangerous for me. Because I've had, you know, federal agents come walking in with wires. But I thought that was just part of it. Part of the risk.

— What do you think has been the main reason for all the trouble? Is it your own adamant attitude or is it the blotter itself?

In the pursuit of what I'm doing, when I started out, there was no such thing as un-dipped blotter sheet. So the criminal element is when I had to be frank. And so that's the thing: If they know, they know I know where all the "bodies are buried." And if they can implicate me in a huge conspiracy, perhaps I would turn all those other guys in. I think that's where the troubles really come from: with the ambivalence of my situation.

— So you're saying that someone paranoid might have tipped someone off?

Many times. I talked to an attorney who told me, ten years ago, that when anyone gets busted for LSD, the first thing the feds ask them is: "Do you know Mark Mc-Cloud?" It's for that reason that the proliferation of it gets blamed on me, when in fact I've done a lot to demystify it. They should be thanking me.

— Absolutely. Especially the city of San Fransisco.

I've never had a problem with the City. On the contrary. They ran a cover story on the museum back in the late 1980s in the *SF Weekly*. And a few months after that I got stopped by the cops a few blocks from here, and they looked at my license and said, "Oh you're Mark McCloud, hey, go ahead!" I don't have any problem with the locals at all. They love it. But it's the feds, you know. Kind of like the marijuana thing. San Franciscans are more than willing to accept marijuana, medical marijuana. It's just the feds. San Francisco, having gone through it, know that as the rate of acid is higher in the city, the rate of heroin goes way down. It has always been a city that behind closed doors advocates LSD psychotherapy. But the feds don't have that venue, although the CIA is more sympathetic. CIA has a great love and respect for LSD since they were all forced to trip. Something the FBI is totally unaware of. I've always had that problem. As an artist you have to decide your level of involvement in it. Should I just do the artwork or should I turn a few million people on? So that's why I'm in trouble. It's because of that dilemma. My debt to LSD is slowly being paid off by this effort. It's not enough, because I get a call every week from a prisoner who's doing 25 years on an acid bust.

— Do you foresee a greater integration of psychedelics in society in general?

Of course. Yeah. That's what's obviously been needed. I have a Roman Catholic background, and there is that problem of Roman Catholicism. The ones that aren't educated don't know that Catholicism itself was a psychedelic cult. The host remains round to imitate the mushroom cap. John Allegro wrote a really great book in the 1950s called *The Mushroom and the Cross*, in which he shows that in the 15th century the paintings depicting Adam and Eve underneath the Amanita Muscaria got changed to the Tree of Life. And Jesus' ancient Hebrew meaning only means the chrysalis of the mushroom...

— What about a about greater integration of psychedelics in society? Can you see it happening?

Yeah. It's happening for sure. And I'd say, you know, not just in Western culture. Japan has been a main consumer.

— They need it.

Yeah, they need it bad. You know, when the Al-Qaida thing happened, I was with a group of old (acid) heads. We were kicking ourselves saying, "why didn't we ever turn those guys on?" That's a mistake. Gang of Four acid, Taliban acid... If that had happened, we wouldn't have had this problem. It's like when the Shamanic information came through from South America. It's a contribution. I think that the nuclear bomb and its relationship to LSD is something very, very important.

— Did you ever feel uncertain about the outcome of your trial?

Always. That's what it's about. Let me tell you what it's like. When you are the guy, you have to be the guy all the way through it. Everyone else will drop you. Your child will deny you, your lawyer will deny you, your mom will deny you. You have to be the guy that goes, "No! This is where it stops..." So, of course, you know, as everyone is dropping off you realize, shit, you're on your own, and it's only exciting if it's uncertain. You know that ticket, that ride is only worth it if you don't know the outcome. I always thought I was a goner. I was always pessimistic, coming from Argentina where you would get "disappeared" for no reason at all. I'm much more in tune with that than with the US legal system, which is much more optimistic than I am. I thought I was a goner for sure. But my job is to be the guy that says, "I'm not a goner." In fact while my jury was out the last time, the feds come in and said, "Would you take a tenner?"[2] And my lawyer says, "Take the god damned tenner!" And the assistants and my girlfriend and everyone says, "Take the tenner"! And you have to be the guy that goes, "No! I don't want the tenner."

— That was very brave.

Well, that's what it is. But it's not really balls; it's as far as it goes. You're the "dude." You're going to be paying with the rest of your life. It's your ballgame. And so then, of course you think you're going to get it because, when you're busted, you think you're busted for what you did, of which I'm very guilty. But it's not actually for what you did — it's for what they think you did. There's a difference. I always assumed they would win. I'd been planning my defense for 20 years, but they'd only been prosecuting me for 10. That's where I had the advantage. I saw this coming a long time ago. Before I ever first showed it I knew they would come at me if I kept on that course.

— So what exactly did you feel, if it's at all possible to describe, when they said that you were not guilty?

It's a dream. You're caught by them. You're in such a tortured state by then that it's just like a dream. You don't even realize it at that point. It takes you about three months in decompression before you even understand it.

— Do you ascribe any specific religious or magical qualities to LSD?

Magical. I think that when magic got split into art and science we lost sight of it;

---

2 A ten year prison sentence.

of what it meant. I think that that's the greatest contribution of it, as it returns the magic to it. Even to religion, you know. You can be very, very religious and still be unaware of the incredible magic going on. But I've always seen it like that. That's why I've had a problem with Eastern religions because I've always understood things in terms of Western occult magic. I'd say that LSD probably is the greatest outside influence of that. Even more than Crowley, you know. Crowley's ambiguity way outweighs his clarity. Something LSD isn't lacking.

— Could that be a reason why LSD specifically is so stigmatized?

That's why. But there's another little thing to magic, and that's telepathy. It's not the magic that's scaring everybody; it's the telepathy of it. I think that the government is extremely aware of that one of the last few places you can meet honestly is telepathically. That's what they're afraid of. That technique of communication will be out of their control. To me, telepathy is just part of magic, but I think that's the specific part of magic they are most afraid of. It's because when you meet telepathically you can't lie. Everyone shows their face. I think that's what they're most afraid of, since they have to keep so much of their enterprise in the dark.

— LSD has always been tightly connected with radical thought and the cultural underground. Do you foresee LSD keeping its position in a new generation of movers and shakers?

Well, that's something that is really doubtful right at this point. We're very short of figure heads right now. Owsley[3] is one of our last remaining figure heads who won't even talk about it. Shulgin[4] wrote the "controlled substances act" before he got busted. It's only after he got busted that he realized the discrepancy of it. So we're short on figure heads right now. But I see more psychedelic individuals every day. That's what's going on. It's not so much that we needed Terry McKenna and that we needed Tim Leary; it's just that when we were developing a psychedelic individual, we needed them. But now, as there are psychedelic individuals everywhere, I think there's less and less need for that type of a figurehead. The DJ will do. For that night, the DJ can be, you know, your guru. And I think that that's something that Tim said a long time ago: "everyone will be your guru for five minutes." That's just part of the psychedelic experience. I think that the death of McKenna

---

3 See previous note on Owsley.
4 Alexander Shulgin (1925-2014), an American chemist, pharmacologist and psychedelic pioneer.

is the one that affected me most, because he was so out of the chronology. These other guys were right on schedule. But Terence was just very cool, and his mind turned on. So that's the one I've had the hardest time with, as far as just being out of contact.

— How did you first come in contact with Hofmann?[5] He wasn't really always that open and accessible.

No, but it was through Michael Horowitz[6] that I first made contact. That's how I got back in touch with Leary and that whole side of it. They already were aware of the blotter collection and what was going on with it. But in my blotter search, I was able to purchase a ton of stolen Tim Leary's notes, including the eagle brief that had been stolen from him at St Quentin.[7] He thought it was stolen by the FBI. I bought it all back and I gave it to Michael Horowitz to return to Tim. And as a thank you, Tim took me out. He came up here; he was doing a comedy act. He said, "Why don't you come to the comedy show, and then I'll take you to dinner." That's how I met Tim Leary. This was around 1989, I would say. And as a thank you for this he started sending me information. As he became more aware of what I was doing, he put me in his last book, *Chaos & Cyberculture*. I involved him in signing blotter when I heard he was dying. I got into Hofmann's world through Horowitz and Tim. And through Dr John Beresford, who was very involved with... not de-criminalizing, but against mandatory sentences... I got involved with him, and he was caught up in the Albert Hofmann foundation. I was always sending Albert my stuff anyway, so by the time I was kind of introduced to him, he was already aware of what I was doing. That type of LSD idolatry is not very interesting to me. There's a lot of back patting and a lot of that going on. If you've had enough LSD you know that it's not about self-aggrandizement.

— It's fascinating with all these old men and women who've been doing great psychedelic things in life. But even that is just a temporary thing. What happens when they disappear?

---

5 Albert Hofmann (1906-2008), the Swiss chemist who discoeverd and developed LSD at the Sandoz Laboratories, from 1938 and onwards.
6 Michael Horowitz, Timothy Leary's archivist and founder of The Fitz Hugh Ludlow Memorial Library. Also the father of actress Winona Ryder.
7 Leary's memo/notes for his appeal to the US Supreme Court, 1970.

Well, yeah, but at the same time you'll never find a finer advocate for LSD than Albert Hofmann. You could look far and wide and you won't find a finer embodiment of its qualities. I think that's why he is so devastating. Tim had that stigma that as he left prison: people accused him of being a "snitch." That definitely alienated the psychedelic community from Tim. You know, even his son spoke out against him, denying him, here in the early 1970s; in 1974 when he and Ginsberg had that press conference on Union Square. They were denouncing Tim as a snitch. So when Tim got out he always had that stigma to deal with. Something that never came up with Hofmann, because you know, Hofmann always avoided the illegal side of it. He shouldn't have. He should have been held as accountable as Tim. But being in the Swiss environment made all the difference. Then McKenna had that stigma, being called the Leary of the 1980s and 1990s, and he really was... He became a teller of tall psychedelic tales.

— Do you know if there are any artists that moved on to great success that actually started out in blotter art, and that aren't secret?

Blotter art is an extremely powerful thing. The average amount of time an individual spends on a painting is fourteen seconds. But on a blotter painting, you get twelve hours of concentration. The artists I've met in blotter have mostly been mad scientists. That's one of the charms of the medium. In the early days the images were being picked by the chemist or his associates, and so in a way they're more interesting than just coming from an artist. But just as the renaissance goes through a rococo and a mannerism stage, the same has kind of happened with blotter. I'd say the best blotter was done by the chemist, and then the artist's hands started showing later in the game. Walt Disney got kicked out of the Kansas City Art Institute for plagiarism. He was expelled. He is still my favorite blotter artist; he's just not aware of it. Then you have Alex Grey for example, and Alex is the reluctant blotter artist. I was the first to involve him. But many, many LSD distributors have involved him since. But he is reluctant, you know. He is a family man, and he doesn't want to stand the heat.

— Who is you favorite psychedelic writer? It doesn't have to be thematic about psychedelics, but just in terms of language...?

Probably Buñuel. I don't know if Buñuel ever talked about tripping, but his autobiography added to his volume of work and makes him my favorite psychedelic writer. That's when I first started seeing it in film reality, rather than in film documentary. I think he has a psychedelic stage, kind of, going in his work. But there are so many I love and enjoy... From Artaud up, you know. They're great. I love Hofmann's writings. I love Shulgin's two masterpieces, *Pikhal* and *Tikhal*. Surely underrated, and his writing ability too. He is a great, great writer. But I'm looking out all the time. I like Tom Robbins a lot, as far as having a psychedelic perspective in the writing.

— What do you think is the most important effect that LSD has had on the American society?

Loss of ego. Especially for the Americans. The main contribution I think is that... There's no greater pleasure than to be shattered into a million pieces and then come back together. It's a very old notion: to have been reborn. That's a magical event; not a social-economic event. That's what's actually going on. It's a renaissance, and as in the old renaissance, a lot of people end up in jail for it. When we are able to measure it, we'll realize that everything from the computer to the atom bomb occurred because of the LSD. There is that argument about that in 1938 Hofmann was a Freemason. Did Hofmann pass it around among the club members before releasing it or not? Many people think so. If you read *Morning of the Magicians*,[8] you will realize that back in the 1920s there was a magician that split the atom, and was warning everybody about radiation — back in the 1920s. When you think of the old renaissance you have to see it the same way. Those people that were part of that, or living in that, could barely distinguish that it was a renaissance at that time, until it went baroque or rococo. So I think there's that same effect. The psychedelic art was very popular for a while, and then it became very distasteful, because of the actual qualities of LSD. They're not all rootie-tootie-happy-go-lucky qualities. Some of them are very angst-ridden and have taken people a long, long time to integrate. I can remember a lot of hippies becoming anti-hippies because of their crisis with the substance. But give it ten years and they'll be scratching at the door again to try it. That's what happens: it's the shock, the absolute shock of the information. It takes a long, long time to assimilate and integrate. We've had that kind of problem with the thing itself. We say, "Tim stole our flashbacks." But it's not true. The reality of my Apple computer shocks me, the "psychedelicness" of my Apple programs shocks me. It's only possible through LSD. The computer problem would still probably have been worked on had the engineers not actually

---

8 Pauwels & Bergier, *The Morning of the Magicians*, originally published in French in 1960.

tripped — the problem-solving psychedelics. As a social group, we only intuit right now. Everyone's into the computers but they just don't know why. But it's really a psychedelic instrument. But I think it's an open thing. That's what it's about: it's about an opening up of visual and intellectual possibilities. I don't think we've determined that or that it's reached a finality. I think we're probably at the beginning of a rococo state with it.

— Why do you think that it was discovered at that specific moment in 1938?

I'd say because of need. Our unawareness of organics. We had become so detached from our organic approach, to achieving that, that it occurred in the magical context of a lab. But it came out, as most magical enterprises, of a great need. I don't have any problems with the dates, you know '38, '43, it doesn't matter to me. I've had enough acid to know that it doesn't really matter. But the advent of it, and the strangeness of how it proliferated was only because of its extreme need. The CIA made it popular in this country. Let's not forget that. It was a government official named Alfred "Cappy" Hubbard that popularized it in the US. That's not an accident. Only he could have done that.

— And why was that? Was it because he himself became devoted?

It altered him. The most dedicated people or the biggest acidheads are the acidheads that have been altered by the substance. That's why they're into it: because it changed them. "Cappy" opened a chain of clinics across the US and Canada where he was trying to cure addicts with LSD psychotherapy. But that was just one front. He gave all the acid to Oscar Janiger and to Tim Leary who snuck it to Kennedy. That's where it gets muddy and political. But only a CIA agent could have proliferated it because anybody else would have been killed. That's the tricky part of it. No one really knows that; that it was made popular by the CIA.

— Have you ever regretted that you've been so frank and overt about your interest and your collecting?

Sure. When you're in court and facing a life sentence, you wonder why you didn't stick with your origami or your coin collecting. Regrets, I've had a few, yes... I'd say during that big trip where you get to the bottom of hell and spend an infinity there, there's some regrets there. Even during your psychedelic experience you should be able to recognize your mistakes. It would have been very nice if I could have a blotter collection without ever having problems with the law. That's a regret of mine. But as I look at it, I realize that they came hand in hand. I wish I hadn't eaten all those early ones… I sure didn't have to. You will always measure things against that big trip. You know, the TRIP. Everything will always be measured by the big one you had. And not all those hundreds of little ones.

In early 2006, a few years after my visit to San Francisco, Albert Hofmann celebrated his 100th birthday. There was a big symposium of lysergic minds in Basel, Switzerland — "From Problem Child to Wonder Drug" — with birthday boy Mr Hofmann occasionally present. I couldn't attend, unfortunately, but Mark McCloud was there of course, working hard at bridging the divides between the various environments that have all integrated LSD as a sacrament of sorts. I returned to San Francisco in the autumn of 2006, and decided to talk to McCloud about his experiences in Switzerland.

– The biggest thing that's happened since our previous conversation is of course the Basel show. What are your impressions of that?

One of the participants, a young translator from Basel, called it the "Oscars of Psychedelics." That's what it was in a way. The event itself was totally magical. For me it was a dream come true. Hofmann has quite a blotter collection himself. It was a dream come true to be able to show it all to Hofmann and have him react. I had never expected that. It did great things for the movement. Together, we sent an appeal to all the major governments who have these incredible prison sentences for LSD. That was a major achievement, to have the scientific community and the underground come together in one appeal.

– It's obvious that events like that transcend the concept of "preaching to the already converted."

Sure, but the converted also need to remain excited and alert. The conference was good for them too. I saw a lot of old-timers come back to life. It re-awakened their interest. There were many more people outside picketing. That's the nature of the beast. The conference crossed all social classes. There were English Lords and Ladies together with Seattle street kids. The conference was so enormous that anyone who took active part in it knows how much they missed and how little of it they saw.

— Has there been any noticeable effect from the stuff that was sent out? Did you get any replies from any governments?

I don't know about that, but there sure is some great acid around! To me, that's important. The acid today is better than it has been in the last 20 years. The DEA claimed they'd shut everything down, or 90% of it. At the time of the conference they were still bragging about the Pickard bust.[9] Although the scientific community was well represented, the underground was also very well represented. I saw beautiful blotter works there, made especially for the occasion. The whole event not only re-initiated an interest for LSD but sped up the process through which many of these governments are deciding whether or not to implement psychedelic studies again. Since the conference, many governments have responded positively. Gaia Media, who organized the conference, has a newsletter, and in the last one they reported about very positive things.

— When you say the scientific community, is that then the clinical, medical or the psychological?

All of them. Anyone who's overground and legal. The underground are those that are in the illegal LSD trade, and that's huge. The coming together of both those worlds is not always an easy thing to do. The scientific community is mostly interested in regulating the substances while the underground communities are not so interested in regulation.

— It must have been a great event for everybody who was been involved in some way...

Many of the people I talked to had come to beg forgiveness for being the problem children of LSD.[10] Some of them being chemists; others being dealers that had been busted. There were truly all kinds of people there. There were people there just to kiss him for the wonderful product. There were people there who'd been involved all of their lives. There were people there from his childhood who'd never tried it and have no interest in trying it. It was a beautiful rich cornucopia. Albert was totally unfamiliar with the renaissance of the underground. That's what

---

9 The arrest of chemist and psychedelic advocate Leonard Pickard (b. 1945) in 2000. Pickard was released from prison in 2020.
10 Reference to Albert Hofmann's book *LSD – My Problem Child*, first published in 1979 in German.

startled him and made him declare that his problem child had now become a wonder drug. He saw the incredible input that had been given by people who had not regulated the substance. They had used it anyway.

— Do you think that the scientific community in the mean time have been beating around the bush by coming up with alternate methods, when everybody knows that LSD proper is so to the point?

I'm not the right person to ask that question. My respect for Grof and the scientific community may be tempered a little by my involvement with the underground. Their interests are so different than the underground's. Grof's dealing with terminal cancer patients... The underground is more like "four million people tripped last weekend and no-one got hurt..." Two different ways of looking at it. It's been a big problem with psychedelics: the battle between those who think it should be dispensed and controlled and those who think it should be available to anyone who wants it. That struggle goes on at every convention. And even at every rave, if the DEA are there to bust people.

— What's the story on psychedelic prime movers nowadays? Are they championing LSD or are they more into designer drugs?

In many ways, LSD is still a growing phenomenon. It shows in the arts even more so. The stigma has been integrated also. The allusions to LSD can be made without reference. The band can be full on LSD-related without having to put it in the title. That's the advantage now. If you're in the know, you don't need all that re-assertion.

— Can you see an increasing interest in the activities of your "Blotter Barn"?

I see an ever increasing interest in it. To me, the real value of a site like "blotterbarn.com" is not so much the economic benefit but the historical benefit. I'm hoping to get another 50 designs up this year. There's a huge fake blotter scene going on now too. Not fake, but "vanity blotters." As that scene gets larger and larger I notice that the vintage blotter interest increases too. Many people start by collecting vanity blotter. Then they learn and want some vintage. I have Lucky Jeans coming over tomorrow. They're a big jeans company. I'm trying to pitch them blotterbarn images. They have a big T-shirt line. My job is always the same: how to sneak it into the museum and affect the culture? There's going to be a show at the Whitney called "The Summer of Love" next year. It's starting at the Tate. They're going to put three blotters from the 1970s in there. That's a first. I think that's a major blow. I keep reminding everyone that there wouldn't be any psychedelic art if there weren't any psychedelics. I usually stay on the path of least resistance. If it's not happening, I'm not going to push it.

— Have you been an inspiration to other collectors, you think?

I hear that but I really don't think so. It's more than an inspiration. They wouldn't have any without me. I wouldn't call it an inspiration. It's more like a hate-love-relationship.

— Do you still come across blotter that you haven't seen before?

Sure. Two years ago an old-timer showed up with a huge portfolio for me. It had lots of stuff I'd never seen before. It still comes in. I try to keep up with the new stuff too. If I can't get it I at least try to get an image of it. There's a lot of great new stuff coming out.

— Have you ever thought of turning the collection into a reference web site?

We're working on a book. I like people coming in who are serious about it. I've had people here who've been just looking for hours. I like that. To me it's not so important to be a museum, as long as it's culturally indoctrinated. I don't expect LSD to be legalized but I don't want it to be discriminated. It's very simple: my job is to minimize suffering in prisons. The best way to do that is to grab the subject that's controversial and shed some light on it and see that it's not that big of a monster. A book is great, a museum is great... But my job is to see that it continues to happen. It's not the T-shirts or the books that really entice me though. What entices me is a little guy in England making his own blotter, soaking it, eating it and being enlightened. To me, that's real art. The art you can ingest and paint in your mind. Spiritual food as art. The most effective art pieces as I was growing up was the movies. When I saw "Spartacus" I knew the power of art. I came from a very anti-art family. They were all industrialists. When I saw the effect of art and realized it could actually change your fucking mind, I went for it. That's my fascination with blotter. I've seen many amulets that did not work, but to find the amulet that works — that's truly a miracle. Nothing short of a miracle. People don't give that part of it, that attribute of acid, enough credit. If you can re-initiate the miracle or keep that miracle as the currency, then that's the propagation of the miracle. The rest just follows. It may not be your book but it'll be a book. It may not be your movie but it'll be a movie. I shed light on it and charge a nickel for it. That gives it more value and attention than it had. That's all. I love my job. I looked a long time to find the thing that irritates society enough to give my attention to. My art was always that way, and my blotter art is always that way. I don't even like to make the blotter too pretty.

Ralph Metzner, 2004

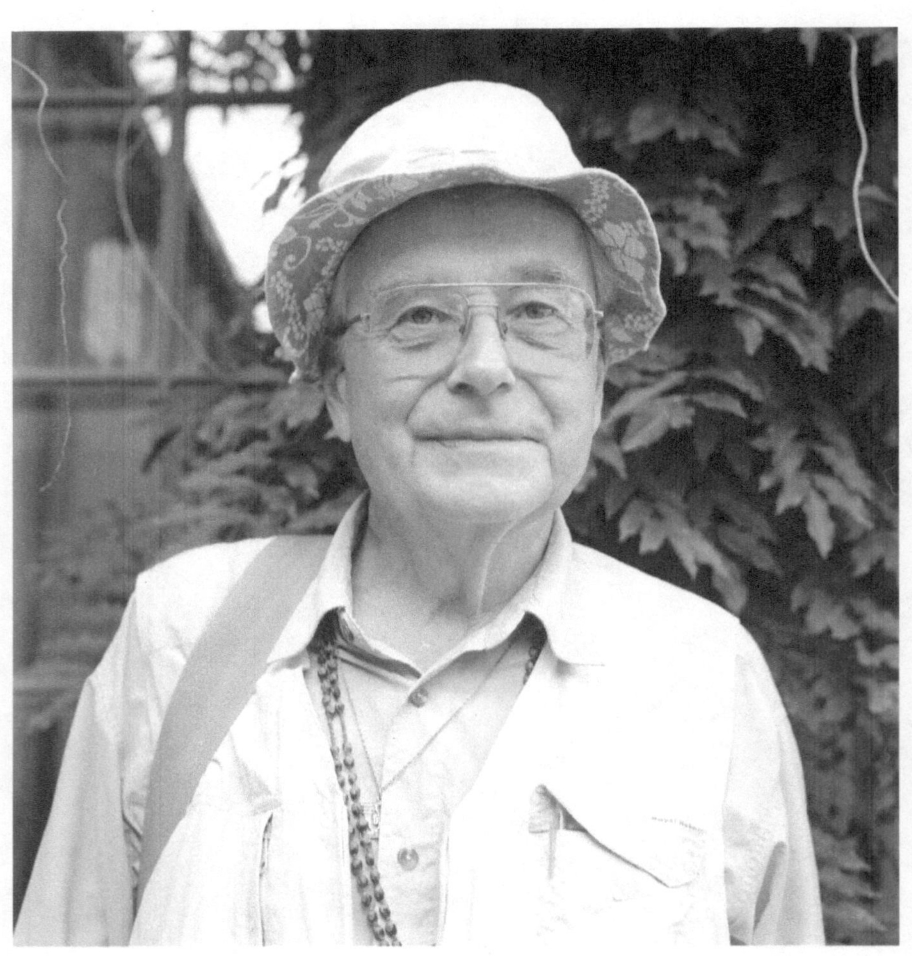

Ralph Metzner

"When you have a vision, you shouldn't neglect it."

When American psychologist and author Ralph Metzner passed away in 2019, it was hardly noticed in mainstream media. His old friend Baba Ram Dass (né Richard Alpert) received slightly more attention when he traveled onwards, also in 2019, but then he was always a slightly more flamboyant character. Yet Metzner had been as much part of that pioneering and paradigm-shifting trio at Harvard in the early 1960s as Dass and their prankster partner, Timothy Leary.

Where Leary enjoyed his Western stardom, fame and infamy, and Dass publicly retracted into his Eastern spiritual trip, Ralph Metzner kept on working diligently in the center to find alternative routes to human enlightenment; routes not necessarily connected to either illicit drugs or established religious practices. Not that he was against any of them per se, but he wanted to achieve a "non-partisan" and available breakthrough so that the wisdoms could be integrated by more people, and from different walks of life.

Studies of ethnobotany, shamanism, ecological awareness, meditation and yoga, and collaborations with scientists like Stanislav Grof turned Ralph Metzner into a savant and sage, a gentle giant who persistently pushed on to nurture the nature of the lysergic big bangs of the 1960s. Emerging from the clinical experiments and ensuing benevolent chaos of the 1960s, he too drifted out into the world to literally spread the word that the spiritual dimension is the "core" dimension, and that it's not an "add-on" in the psychedelic experience; it can be a reconnection to what's already there but can never really become a replacement.[1] Metzner was neither a proselytizer of wild experimentation, nor a salesman of accessible and attractive paths of trippy bling. His integration of concepts both complex and simple, both eternal and present, both revelatory and already known, helped turn himself into a smiling wizard that it was impossible not to love and appreciate. He didn't shove anything down anyone's throat, basically.

---

1 Ralph Metzner in conversation with Stanislav Grof: https://vimeo.com/392870297

He may have freely and gladly talked about the positive effects of LSD, and arranged workshops in "holotropic" breathing à la Grof's interpretations, and organized boundary-crossing seminars all over the world, but he was still always himself in the center; always willing to share whatever he had found in his long life of exploration.

In the summer of 2004, Metzner came to Sweden, and we spent a lovely afternoon chatting away at the Historical Museum in Stockholm.

— When you talk about personal illuminations, regardless of how they're achieved, my experience is that once people have reached a state of illumination, most of them seem to want to retract to a normal state of mind and life in general. What was it that spurred you on or inspired you to move ahead and just keep going in this eternal quest?

My interest in transformations of consciousness started when I was at Harvard, with Leary and Alpert. It has just continued from that time. At first I thought it could be useful as an adjunct to something, like psychotherapy. But it quickly expanded beyond that. Leary felt it, and I did too. The area of art and religion attracted us. It went a bit beyond psychotherapy as we saw it. We also saw challenges in how we should understand it. How should one understand a psychedelic experience? We didn't really get anywhere with Freud. At that time at Harvard there was only psychoanalysis and behaviorism. Neither had anything to say about altered states of consciousness at all. Jung had a bit more but he was more interested in Eastern mysticism. The question was "An expanded state of consciousness, and then what? What do we do with it?" I felt like tuning in to the shamanic tradition. The concept of "set and setting" became important. The intention was to find out what could be done; a very experimental attitude. I could see tools for a spiritual path that could be used or misused. Or perhaps only recreationally. I'm not opposed to that but it is a different thing. As long as one doesn't hurt anybody else. My interest is the knowledge and understanding that can be gained from expanded states of consciousness. States of consciousness can be contracted and pathological as well. But the expanded ones are more interesting for me. How do you build them and turn them into a lasting condition? Say, if someone is depressed, they don't want to be un-depressed for a little while. How can you hang on to a state of mind that's lasting and get to bottom of personal problems, for instance. How to integrate such states? I became interested in various Buddhist traditions and wrote a book called *The*

Unfolding Self where I used ten-twelve key classical metaphors that were used in spiritual traditions over and over. A process of transformation. From a dark state to an enlightened state. The idea of death and rebirth. Taking a shamanic journey. Using myths, according to Jung and Campbell and people like that. Basic themes that exist everywhere. Life like a journey of self discovery, of aspiration, and the altered states like a journey too. The shamans don't talk about altered states of consciousness, they say, "I'm going on a journey. The beat of the drum is my horse or my bird." Quite often, they go for a purpose, say, of healing. The intention of shamanic travel is usually healing and envisioning. Not making predictions, that's a common misunderstanding, but rather divination. I call it shamanic divination or alchemical divination. Alchemy and yoga I see as the Western and Eastern descendants of shamanism. Symbolic systems of transformation, technologies of transformation. Psychoactive plants and drugs, drumming, fasting. The basic idea is healing on all levels: physical and emotional. Healing negative experiences from childhood. Envisioning or divination is looking ahead into the future, and that's where I see that psychology can expand. Psychotherapy doesn't really think that one can predict, but every day people predict all the time. But envisioning isn't prediction; it's more like looking into probabilities and seeking guidance. It's not just curiosity. Almost all the indigenous people have an active interest in the future. The difference from shamanism is that you go into a normal state of consciousness and use tools like the runes or the I-Ching or tarot cards. But the core process is a question and answer process: "How can I heal this painful thing? How will this or that turn out?" Back in the old days people would go see a Völva and ask for advice or vision, for answers. Those people had high standing and were active professionals. They would go into an altered state with their questions, which would then serve as a key for where to look. "Will this battle turn out OK?" If the Völva wouldn't say Yes, then the people backed off. It was accepted as a normal practice. It's just our general world view now that says we can't possibly anticipate things like that. But we do it all the time. In English there are two words that are interesting in this regard. One is "Forethought" and one is "Foresight." But they're hardly used anymore. If you look in a dictionary for "divination" it says "prediction of the future for supernatural reasons." Wait a minute! It's not supernatural, and it's not about predicting either. It's about guidance. Should I do this or should I not do this? When the native American Indians would go on a vision quest, it was all about their life. Big questions. What am I going to do with my life? They prayed, fasted and perhaps were granted a vision. Or, like in the

Black Elk Quest, where they had visions for their entire people. When you have a vision, you should not neglect it. You should express it, tell it and make it real. If you don't it can make you sick. Or even worse if you go against it.

— Isn't that essentially what happened after the 1960s? People thought it was a wonderful thing, but they let it slide for the most part.

I don't really see it that way. I don't think the 1960s faded away at all. We recently had a gathering in Sonoma in California where we asked the question "Whatever happened to the 60s?" People were a bit amazed because we found out that that actual spirit was very much alive. What I think happened was that the states of consciousness that people got into triggered a cascading wave that changed the culture and the society. I'm not even sure all those people took psychedelic drugs but the general quality of the change of society was comparable to an expanded state of consciousness. Six or seven movements started in the 60s. One was the environmental movement. Another one was the civil rights movement. People could understand that the environment was in danger and they could see Southern policemen beat up black people. The Vietnam war was another important factor. People started asking questions in a new way, I think. Many of the hippies became organic farmers and turned their psychedelic experience into an environmentalism. When you expand consciousness you become aware of things you weren't aware of before. Also, when the women's liberation movement started, they called their meetings "consciousness raising." The sexual revolution was important too. The pill was invented and made contraception much easier. In all of those movements people were saying, "Let's not take for granted all of what we've been taught." Like the movie "The Stepford Wives." A person who has taken LSD can never look at the world in the same way again. The old way of looking at the world is no longer working. Leary said, "Turn on, tune in and drop out" but he was very much an Irish trickster. He didn't mind making people confused. He himself didn't drop out, and it wasn't his intention that everyone should. But he wanted people to think about it.

— Why do you think that all of these things coincided at the same time?

It's interesting, but I don't really know. I've been looking at cultural collective transformations and historical trends and I've certainly speculated about it. The hard work is for the people now who inherited the enlightenment, to try and integrate it. To make everything real. That's true of any kind of visionary process. If a child gets a vision, they want to hang on to it. But later they will need specific training and schooling to get there, to make it happen and real. It was a series of cultural changes. I'm a devoted student of Gurdjieff and interested in stages of development. I can see the end of the second world war as especially interesting, with the making and exploding of the first atom bomb and the discovery LSD basically happening at the same time. It's almost as if someone was saying, "Wait a minute, we have to give them something to change their minds..."

— The minute fragmentation of the atom compared to a very big holistic worldview?

Einstein said that the atom bomb has changed everything except our way of thinking about the world. I used to say that LSD may not change the world but it definitely changes the way we think about the world. Anyway, something happened back then. The whole story of that is so fascinating in terms of synchronicity. Hofmann had already synthesized LSD some five years before. And then he says that he "accidentally" absorbed it in 1943. Wait a minute... Here's a Swiss chemist... A guy like that shouldn't accidentally absorb anything! An amazing thing, that chemicals can affect your consciousness in that way. He didn't really know about that then. He had no idea. He's a chemist, not a psychologist. He had his magical bicycle ride and started understanding. He realized the trip had taken him to the same place he'd been at as a child, to his nature-mystical experience as a child. He felt in touch with everything and realized there must be something in the substance that activated this. That was a major starting point. Then, in the 1950s, Gordon Wasson researched the cultures of indigenous people and the mushroom cults. He wrote an article about it in *Life Magazine*, which had something like five million readers. Ancient visionary mushrooms, with pictures of this mushroom man handing this Wall Street banker some mushrooms... In *Life Magazine*! Suddenly people became interested in these old cults and their practices with entheogens. In the 1960s, our Harvard project was a bunch of people talking to psychologists, psychiatrists, doctors and ministers about how we should handle LSD. At the same time, people like Ken Kesey were more artistic and hedonistic, and they were giving psychedelics to thousands of people at the same time, at concerts and gatherings. That shocked us. We were trying to keep everything clinical and controlled in a way, and these people were just going crazy.

– Do you feel that that impaired your work, with Ken Kesey's "Merry Pranksters" getting more attention than your scientific work?

No, not really. It was a phenomenon. What could we do? It just happened and we were all amazed. Later on, the professionals on the field blamed Leary that the government wouldn't allow LSD to be used clinically in research. But first of all, we weren't the people who were giving out LSD at these mass events. And secondly, I think Leary became a scapegoat for everyone. The government didn't want this kind of research anyway, so Leary's actions and comments were just perfect for them. But it wasn't Leary in himself that got the experiments banned. In retrospect I don't think we failed with our experiments. On the contrary, I think we succeeded within what was possible. Our misson was never to make LSD legal; it was to make it used. We got people thinking about it and they're still thinking about it. And people are still taking it too. And taking it seriously. They're being healed and they're getting visions and they're getting a deeper understanding. Research is still going on, whether it's the government or not. Whatever people want to do, they will continue to do. As soon as a substance is discovered, people will try and figure out what to do with it, whether it's legal or not. It's interesting to note that the war on drugs and the war on terrorism uses the same rhetoric. It very seldom has to do with drugs or terrorism, but rather with instilling fear. The war on drugs isn't working for people who are using drugs. They're obviously not afraid of drugs, plus of course they don't believe the government either. It's not addressed to them. The people who use drugs don't care. It's rather addressed to the people who don't know about drugs and who vote. Big middle-class people who are afraid and suddenly want to make everything triple-illegal. The war on terrorism is the same thing. It's the government terrorizing the population with fear. So that they'll vote for more police and more control.

– Don't you see changes in a good way happening, too? In the UK, both ecstasy and marijuana were downgraded recently.

Sure, many European countries are moving in a much more sensible direction. They seem to accept that people want to take substances like that and instead focus on harm reduction and information. In America, more effort is put into draconian measures. A lot of good things are happening in the world, but people don't hear about them. The media are all part of the empire; they're just part of the official lies. But even in America good things are happening. One thing is that more people give birth at home and more people choose to die at home. They're taking both those facts of life back to themselves. It's not an illness to give birth. It doesn't deserve to be medically treated. People are also questioning the prolonging of vegetative life. What is the point? I think more and more people will try and take responsibility for their own health. People will say, "I don't care what you say. It's my life and I do what I want with it."

— A lot of the problems that we have today are stemming from an anthropocentric point of view. If we turn that around and adopt an holistic world view, couldn't one say that essentially the human being in herself is the problem? If we play the Devil's Advocate, we could also say, "Why should we bother? Why shouldn't we be allowed to kill each other and become extinct — the earth will be happier for it?"

I think it's a false dichotomy. Earth First were radical and said, "No compromise in the defense of Mother Earth." The politically active people have to make compromises all the time, even in order to have access to politicians and legislators. In a way, it's a valid position not to want to make any compromises. It's a matter of making the humans equal to the rest of nature; not putting the humans down. I think a world view transition is going on and it's being worked out in different areas. It has to do with systems of interconnectedness, but it's not a reversal of hierarchies for its own sake, like "Earth first and humans second." Everything is inter-related and inter-connected in complex ways. You have to look at how the effects work out. You have to think systemically. I'm a big follower of Thomas Berry and his equal eco-systems. There's a danger in protecting certain species but not others. There has to be an eco-system that balances everything out and creates a really tangible harmony. And all we really have to do is look at traditional tribes and traditional ways of life, how they took care of things and organized themselves. Everything is interconnected in invisible ways. But you can know about it and you can understand it.

— That's another great advantage of psychedelic use: you get aware of the notion that everything is inter-connected.

Diversity on a biological level is protection against degradation. Biological diversity is the same as cultural diversity: a key to sustaining vital pieces of knowledge. Ecosystems must have diversity. On a higher level too, the universe is extremely, unbelievably diverse. Also theologically, it's important. For us, it's been "One god, lawgiver, rule-maker." But we have a whole variety of deities of many different kinds and I think people are beginning to honor that more. Who are we to say that someone else's god is no good or doesn't exist? On an individual level, it like psychic multiplicity: each individual is a multiplicity of parts that are interconnected. It's also the same in a family, with different parts that are related and communicate and work together. It really is very hard to be an individual without relations. Everyone is made up of different aspects. One person can be a father, a son, a brother, an employee or an employer. To not have any relations is not really an option. It's more or less impossible.

– Here's another Devil's Advocate topic... With illumination comes insight and all the things that we've just discussed. However, those involved or inside are still quite few compared to those in theistic structures with aggressive monotheistic views. How could one turn that right and how could one defend oneself against possible oppression? Being free is not only having the rights to do things but also to actually do them; to use the rights.

Some people argue that it's even the other way around. It's the same with the death penalty in America in a way. How is it that almost every other civilized country has abolished it? It's like Michael Moore says in his movie: the Canadians have just as many guns as the Americans but they don't use them to solve their problems. They just have them. They don't need them to settle their differences. Perhaps it's the same thing with drugs too. There's a ruling elite that has its own agenda: to preserve their own wealth and to enlarge it. They don't give a shit about anything else basically. This small elite has basically hi-jacked the world in a way, but mainly the American government and their allies. Just like the Roman Empire in many ways. It's like Rome at the time of Julius Caesar. Or not; he was actually a reformer in many ways. The politicians got him in the end and blamed his egotism. "He's so ambitious... Let's kill him!" Another analogy is to Hitler's Germany. It's the same kind of power tripping in America. Abolish parliaments or reduce their real power, increase police and military power, find scapegoats. But one can only really act where one is. We're like cells in the body of earth, and the knee can't save the whole person. But the organism in itself can always look after itself. We're a small part of it, that's all. But I do think change is going on, and people are becoming more aware of things. The Vietnam war went on for a long time before any newspapers even wanted to tell the nasty details. What's happened in America during these past years is like a coup d'état, organized by "neo-cons." There are books about it and investigative journalism too, and I think that's very healthy.

— Usually people in power try to get away with more and more once they've started...

That's part of it, unfortunately. They're also using incredible rhetoric, saying, "Maybe some day you'll get some weapons so we'd better strike first now... We reserve the right to hit you first! We're not interested in self defense, we're just protecting our self interests..." In history, that's usually called fascism. One analogy I often use is called the cosmic game of catastrophe, and I think we're in the middle of it. The earth has a trump card of course. Playing the trump card would be like "The Day after Tomorrow," with enormous natural disasters that would force all the military forces to help humans and to deal with it. Flooding, floods of refugees and many other things. And thereby not having any energy left to make war. Those kinds of huge sacrifices in human lives have happened before. You never know when the Earth is going to play that trump card. And another wild card is the Internet. All kinds of campaigning and information spreading that can be used for a lot of good things. And of course it can be used in the other direction too. It can be used to spread lies, defamatory information, etc.

— The mere availability doesn't really guarantee anything at all.

Exactly.

— It's the same thing with Gnostic thought and the possibilities of illumination. You can basically get what you want. But that in itself doesn't really guarantee anything.

No, but still the knowledge and information exchange is there. The inter-connected networks are important; that's what it's all about. Spreading knowledge and making information available throughout the system on many different levels. It's a complex transition we're in right now. I think the more unpredictability we can put into the system, the better. We need all the perspectives, because so many perspectives we have nowadays are really non-functional. They're really obstructive. So why stick with those? Why not consider other possibilities? Even the Pentagon has its own unit that studies sudden climate change. They call it "Low Probability but High Impact." The government doesn't have a clue. That means the people still have to do something. One should always consider all possibilities and probabilities. The same with the attitude towards psychedelics. I'm not saying everyone should take them; that's just highly unlikely. All I can say is that this is what other people have found. They're human beings and they're not stupid. They found things within themselves that led to positive changes in their lives. Here's the information; you deal with the choices. The government basically says it's OK to drink alcohol and smoke tobacco, but they put a ban on psychedelics. Come on! People should be able to make up their own minds regarding that. They're individual as well as relational beings and have to be able to make choices. I don't go along with the statement that this is the information age though. It's just as much about disinformation. A lot of the information that pours over me is information I don't need to have. Knowledge is good, but we need wisdom too. What are you going to do with all the information? What's the intention? Are we working towards supporting life and towards healing and towards empowering people? It shouldn't be beyond us as a species and a civilisation to accomplish that. All the knowledge and calculations are already there and I think it's high time to deal with it.

– With this at hand, would you say that you're a Dystopian or a Utopian?

I don't think I'm either, or perhaps a little bit of both. There are so many levels to everything. I'm not saying that to be diplomatic, but what we need is an open-minded system. Things are far too bad and it's far too late to be passive. I support anything that supports consciousness. I go with the Buddha. We have to deal with the evil that's in the illusion. We have to strive to become more conscious of that and what we really can achieve. A starving child in Sudan may not need empathy as much as food. It's better to give food than teach him to meditate. But right now I'm sitting here trying to do what I can in this situation. There's no point in taking on the responsibility which you really can't be responsible for by yourself. I was born in Germany as a German national and I went through a period where I felt personally responsible for the Holocaust; personally responsible for the murder of millions. Until I was able to expand my consciousness and realize that I couldn't go on feeling like that anymore. It doesn't help anyone. That doesn't mean I don't care. It's just a mistaken thinking. It doesn't mean I don't have compassion. Nothing human is strange to me. If I were born a Palestinian I might become a suicide bomber... What do I know? It's very much about how you grow up. Consciousness and life are two values that matter to me, and that I work for, and what I teach.

— Speaking of that kind of Buddhist approach, you integrated the Buddhist Bardo concept early on at Harvard. How was that looked upon by the Buddhist community?

As far as I know, everything was OK. There's a great book out now, called *Zig Zag Zen*,[2] that talks about that merging of psychedelics and Buddhism. Charles Tart, a psychologist, sent out a series of questions to Buddhist practitioners and teachers. Those who had psychedelic experience were happy about their experiences as spiritual beginnings. It gave them experiences of the possibilities of expanding consciousness that you're aiming for when you're doing meditation. The psychedelic experience tells you what's possible. It might even be a great motivation to experience that in order to be able to meditate for months or even years. An inspiration even.

— But isn't that decimating the value of the psychedelic experience in a way? If you look at it through order structures and you have to go through years of work and initiations and training... Can one experience really replace that? That criticism was there already in the 1960s; the question of whether a chemical illumination can be spiritually valid...

I don't think that was the message though. I think one should look at it as a preview: a vision. In the end, it can differ a lot from various kinds of spiritual experiences. In Zen they're striving for a kind of ultimate simplicity. According to them there's a danger in spiritual structures too, that the ego might get in the way; that you look at developments as spiritual achievements. Tibetan Buddhism is more shamanic and very much a cultivation of the visionary experiences. I think psychedelics are tools and it's great if you can integrate them into your spiritual path. If you take them only for recreational purposes it can be OK but it's not going to make any contributions to your spiritual path. The impact of my first trip had long term consequences. It's harder for me to resonate with

2 Allan Hunt Badiner & Alex Grey (eds), *Zig Zag Zen: Buddhism and Psychedelics*, Chronicle Books, San Francisco, 2002.

people who take LSD now, because of the drug association. Back then, it was very much "set and setting," and an emotional and psychological experiment into the unknown. People nowadays usually see it as three letters and a trip that unfortunately becomes associated with some kind of stigmatized underworld. But people have always wanted to exchange states of consciousness and drugs have always been one way of doing that.

Peter Beard, 2005

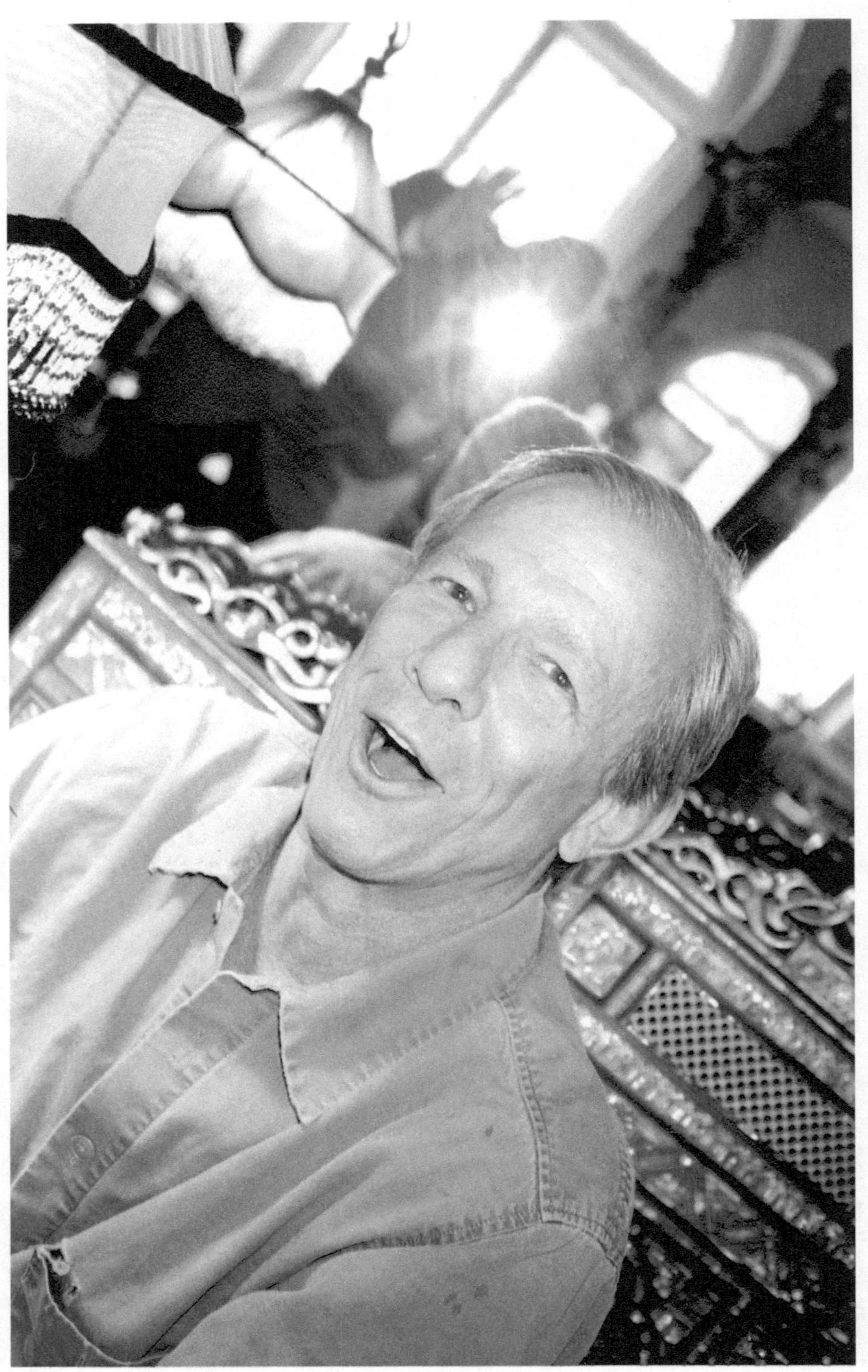

Peter Beard

"You've got to carve out a niche!"

I have been thoroughly blessed to meet a great number of fascinating artists. One of the most remarkable, and certainly most inspiring for me personally, was American photographer/diarist Peter Beard (1938-2020). His multidimensional artworks, which include photography, collage, writing and even sculpture, are psychedelic juggernauts displaying not only life experience but also constant potential. One single Peter Beard image is so filled with depth, mystery, and essence that you find yourself tossed between what you're actually looking at and what it could possibly "mean." But what it usually always means is simply that the image projected itself from the mind of the artist himself. So that's where you have to begin if you want to find out more about the process.

After having studied art with Joseph Albers at Yale, Peter Beard traveled out into the world in the 1960s. Inspired by Karen "Isak Dinesen" Blixen's *Out Of Africa*, he went to Kenya already in 1955. And also to Denmark in 1961, where he met the then dying Blixen. He bought land next to her former estate just outside Nairobi. "Hog Ranch," Beard's own sanctuary of houses and tents there, was a place to which he regularly returned and which distinctly influenced his art.

The African years (that turned into decades) meant for Beard a photographic documentation of a critical and depressing phase in African history. Conservationism and the construction of compensatory habitats for elephants and many other animals led to a plethora of unwanted effects. Many species were almost made extinct, not so much by local shortsighted butchering but by Western misdirected altruism and insane compensations.

Beard's two powerful books *The End of the Game* (1965, mainly about elephants) and *Eyelids of the Morning* (1973, about crocodiles) contributed to an increased awareness about this highly complex situation.

At the same time, Beard hung out with international high society and artists in New York and other hotspots around the world. Salvador Dali, Francis Bacon and Andy Warhol were three central and influential figures in this stage of Beard's life (1960s-1970s). He married "Society Girl of the Year" Minnie Cushing, and later on supermodel Cheryl Tiegs, before settling down with Nejma Beard (née Khanum) in 1986. Interesting, wild, beautiful, successful, wealthy and free people have constantly passed by in his life and Beard preserved them all in photographs, collages and memories.

For decades, Beard hopped between Kenya and his place in Montauk outside New York. But it's mostly in Manhattan he acted when it came to displaying his art and himself. From the 1960s wild partying, over the 1970s wild partying, over the 1980s… And so on. But this is predominantly a media image that he was stuck with and which perhaps also haunted Beard during all these years. The handsome, affluent artist with the entire world at his feet, and with all its demigods and goddesses as playmates. An (epi)center at Studio 54 who charmed and inspired generations of esthetes and sans souci arrogants.

But one should never forget that Peter Beard already from the very beginning took his art seriously, unaffected by the media image mentioned above. In the form of diaries (or, rather, ever swelling three-dimensional collage-collections), photographs and texts, he documented his life and thereby indirectly many others' in a way that has created a new kind of esthetic: naked, non-edited, chaotic, irregular, violent, bloody, passionate and, lest we forget, painfully beautiful. All that a human life can handle, corroded by time, dented by experience and constantly redefined, in that new experiences are added to the old and represented again and again, forever.

The people who have questioned Beard's value as a serious artist are often stuck in their own class hate/envy or, at least, in their critique of supposed social privileges and benefits. Beard looked at this casually. He was pleased with his life and was in no way ashamed of it. And why should he have been?

He just continued to create his enormous collage- and photo-based images, enhanced by quotes from his favorite books (in his own beautiful handwriting). If you'd ever want to illustrate the manic will of an artist to assemble loose fragments and create a new kind of external order — and at the same time document life as it passes right before the artist's eyes/camera — a Peter Beard image would be the perfect choice.

When you entered his Manhattan home you were swept away and into his mind frame, and you couldn't really escape. And you certainly didn't want to. The entire apartment was like a studio or a large, three dimensional sketch pad that spread out on the floors and walls. Sheets, photos, images from other sources, glue, scissors, ink, books… Beard enthusiastically pulled out images to accentuate whatever he was talking about right then. Then, suddenly, on to something completely different. It could be a cut out image from a fashion magazine or an original drawing by Francis Bacon casually placed in a pile of other papers. The outer very much reflected the inner, just like the "inner scanning" medical photographs he was so fascinated by. Peter Beard could on the surface appear to be somewhat incoherent, but once you'd had a peek inside his creative chaos it was very easy to understand his greatness. It was not a simple, causal process but rather like an extremely colorful and multi-versal pulse emanating rays of awe, wonder and delight.

If Peter Beard liked you, he was incredibly generous with his time and willingness to show you the many magical things he housed. He made me feel like we had been friends for a long time, and made sure to inscribe a copy of his great anthology of African memories, *Zara's Tales – Perilous Escapades in Equatorial Africa*, with his trademark ink nib and fingerprints: "To Carl, in mad haste!" And "Special delivery to the most patient and extra enthusiastic Carl, en route to Sweden (lucky)!" Not only it is a wonderful book; it is now one of my most treasured items, period.

In early 2020, Beard walked out into nature on Long Island and was lost for weeks. When he was eventually found, he was dead. Apparently he had been suffering from dementia during his last years. I had last seen him mingling happily at the opening of a retrospective exhibition in East Hampton in 2016, and it was great to catch up briefly with his wife Nejma. But it was during a NYC visit in 2005 that I had the good fortune to visit and interview the great artist-magician himself.

— I'm up all night and try to avoid the daytime, Beard stated as we sat down to talk.

Newly arisen but definitely awake he pointed at some of his own images and at some African objects in his living room. He'd said many times before that the objects can tell stories much better than he himself.

— I'm a night person. I'm not into the day. It sounds pretty selfish, but that's the way I am. I just did an inner scanning, looking for polyps and things inside my body. It's kind of fun with inner scanning. It just shows you everything. I've got lots of plates and pins inside and broken ribs and I'm missing some bones too. Then they can put the muscles over that and the skin over that. It really is amazing. From the inside out, it's unbelievable. It's definitely the most interesting kind of photography there is. It makes regular photography a drag; which it is, really.

Despite the fact that Beard belonged to a clique of the world's most respected photographers for a long time, he was often critical when it comes to medium itself. Photography is a tool that can document, but no more than that. In his own case, the integration of the photographic image itself into a larger context of painting, collage, mixed media and, not least, his own diaries became his trademark. Only very, very seldom was a photo a mere photo.

— I'm not really into photography. It's just so easy. I believe in common sense. If you take pictures, you parasite on subject matter. That's it. If you pick better subject matter than the other guy, you'll get better pictures. I'll tell you one thing about photography though… It's life thickening. You feel you are punctuating it all the time. Then you have a time capsule. I like the time capsule aspect. Life just becomes so short, so you might as well thicken it up. I liked to photograph my class mates, as we went through the horrible schools. Then of course you get some funny pictures by accident. And then I simply started to be interested in better subject matter. I'm still just interested in better subject matter.

Picasso was a really artistic photographer. He did double exposures with himself against his abstract paintings already around 1910-11. Lartigue was a very artistic photographer early on. When he became an adult, it all became so boring. Then he started doing horrible paintings too. I photographed him on his 90th birthday and he took some funny pictures of me too.

I like Brassaï, Diane Arbus, Matthew Brady… The photography I like is like Weegee's… Murder, suicide, accidents… "L'hazard est le plus grand artiste…" Astronauts taking pictures, weather photography, lunar photography, inner scans… Everything is better than what I do! Photography is supposed to be magic. But there's not much magic in the photography I see around. It's all cleverness and technology, lenses, assistants, equipment dangling over their necks… But no visual acumen whatsoever. All you get is technology photos.

The girls are taking all the good photos now: Ellen von Unwerth, Deborah Turbeville, Bettina Rheims, Sally Mann… Paolo Reversi is very good. Guy Bourdin was good. Helmut Newton was good. But now it's all cleverness, all manipulation. Irving Penn's a good friend of mine but I'm not very excited by him.

Avedon was the greatest manipulator in the world, so clever. He was actually the opposite of Diane Arbus. He hated his subjects and he put his hate of himself onto his subjects. He made Ezra Pound wince by asking him about anti-semitism. Avedon was an evil man. He was the best fashion photographer though, because he had a great early period when he was working to get into the business. He had enthusiasm then. He wasn't pleasing the magazines with studio work.

You have to push for better subject matter, and that's what Arbus did. She was a good friend of mine. We used to trade bondage pictures for animals. Unfortunately, everything I had from her burned. She was great.

The fire Beard refers to happened in 1977. His old mill on Long Island was destroyed and with it a number of Bacons, Warhols, African objects and books. Also many of his own works and diaries.

— The caretaker went to the movies. The fire was started by the only piece of American equipment in the whole building, which was a 1928 mill. I got the call at 8.30 that the thing was burning down. The caretaker took those pictures (of the burning mill), by the way. I was just so busy with the deadline for the book I was working on... All my African books were on the second floor and there was a grand piano there too. I opened up the roof, which was fantastic. I found a piece of wood up there saying that "If anyone finds this, call my family. They built this building." I did call the grandson who was still alive and living in Miami. Carl Fischer who was from Montauk actually built Miami.

We were close to the deadline of the book.[1] I was even doing the retouching right there and then. Everything was so last minute and we were just throwing together this hunting chapter. I didn't get out until 3.30 in the morning. It was raining, it was July 28th... I was staying on my tax man's sofa in New York. I had to walk back because I couldn't get a cab in the rain. I thought about the mill then. I was lying down and started to feel the self pity and little tears started to fall... I had a realization then. I've only had two, one on Ecstasy and one at that moment. "Well, you can do two things... Worry and regret it or just forget it!" I just took the forget-position. It just seemed terribly logical. Everyone thought I was pathological and didn't care... But what can you do? All I can say to someone whose house has burned down is "Forget it!" There's nothing you can do. The firemen flooded the cellar with water, because the caretaker had told them that all my diaries were there. I did get a lot of burned pages. I had a show once in Japan of the burnt pages. There were a lot of good ones left.

In this attitude lay an important key to Beard's creativity. Life is no more than a palette and a canvas, if you will. Life is all about filling the canvas with color. You use what you've got, regardless if it's super models on a leisurely safari in Africa

---

1 Peter Beard, *The End of the Game*, originally published in 1965, but which was at this time being prepared for a new edition.

or scorched old diaries from a burnt out mill. Beard photographed objects and other photographs and then used these as images for new projects and collages. Which were in turn re-photographed. It never ended, like in an eternal creative loop where everything not only can be recycled but actually also is.

In Africa, Beard sometimes called his images and creations "living sculptures," something that in equal parts referred to the animals and nature itself and to his own visual formulations of them.

— There are so many animals that are sculptural. Originally, it was just the title of a show, with loads of elephants in there. But I did "Living Sculpture" with Salvador Dali too, years ago. We put shaving cream on Verushka over the FDR Drive at Riverview Terrace. Dali was so eccentric and I actually did a whole movie with him. The movie stretched over a ten year period. Every time something insane happened in New York, we picked him up at the St. Regis. We had a lot of fun together.

Peter Beard pulled out old photos he'd written on in his beautiful handwriting. Predominantly photos of elephants from Africa; either breathtaking aerial shots or snapshots very close up — dangerously so (Beard was actually thrashed by an angry elephant in 1996, which actually killed him for a moment. A massive blood transfusion brought him back to life a short time after being declared clinically dead.).

— Look at this, that's 3000 elephants sweeping an entire area... We actually had to shoot a lot of them... That's how I know that the separation of the sexes is the first effect of exceeding caring capacity... Overpopulation! We are having a huge separation of the sexes right now, an avalanche... Lots of limiting factors like mad cow disease and mad cowboy disease, sars, heart disease, etc... Every elephant we sampled had heart disease. It's mentioned in the epilogue of *The End of the Game*.

Beard helped out in Kenya's national parks to document the elephant population and later also the crocodiles in the Lake Rudolf region. This not only meant invaluable opportunities to take pictures of a rapidly changing environment, but also laid the foundation for Beard's laconic misanthropy.

— That area was bigger than New Jersey and Israel... It was eaten clean by elephants. Of course, nobody noticed. They were too busy buying the elephants a drink!

I wondered if Beard thought that attitude of over-nurturing and over-caring is something that is being applied on humans too.

– Well, you can really contemplate that. We are experts, not only at the libido for the ugly, but at wrecking whatever we touch... Now we wreck things through sentimentalism. Now that everything is almost out, we're sentimentalizing it like hopelessly religious people. It's nauseating. It's like photography. I think most photography is extremely nauseating, because they think it's art. As far as I'm concerned, it's subject matter. It's a capture.

My experience is that you don't change anybody's mind. The galloping rock goes further, and we make the same mistakes generation after generation. Because of desperation we're becoming more compassionate. The slaughter is becoming more noticed, and more televised. That's the good part... People are so scared of death. One hundred beds turned by one nurse. Gaga vegetables lying in their own excrement. We worship it. We have no interest in the quality of life because we're obviously ruining it.

To be pro-life is to be emotionally and politically correct according to these people. Every sentimental program on "wildlife channels" is actually ruining the future of the wildlife, because it's just irrational bunny-hugging.

I actually like the horror of it. It's like Joseph Conrad's *Heart of Darkness*, my favorite book. When I was doing that piece over there I was listening to that book twice. Listening to it as an audio book is like music. Every sentence is magic. He was such a writer. It's also very comic. "The Horror" is not necessarily bad news.

I suggested that perhaps the USA of today is a better general metaphor of decay than the elephant population crisis in Africa ever was. Beard nodded in agreement.

– There's nothing healthy here, I'm telling you! Horrible looking people. Diversity, we've got that! I'm thinking of H.L. Mencken's "Libido for the Ugly"... It's home is America! We can do it!

Beard brought out a copy of a Mencken anthology and enthusiastically quoted the brilliant German-American journalist:

"Here is something that the psychologists have so far neglected: the love of ugliness for its own sake, the lust to make the world intolerable. Its habitat is the United States. Out of the melting pot emerges a race which hates beauty as it hates truth..."

Peter Beard never denied deny that Africa meant a lot of positive things for him, for decades. If he wasn't on safari, he'd be working on his diaries. If he didn't help out in research projects in the wildlife reserves and national parks, he was philosophizing about the meaning or possibly meaninglessness of development and progress.

A steady stream of friends visited him in his "jungle camp" outside of Nairobi (Andy Warhol once described Beard as the "Tarzan of our times") and brought with them their own myth-making stories about him to Europe or the States. The inspiration from Africa never seemed to end. I wondered if the African experiences had perhaps been the central inspiration of his life?

— I don't know how to answer that actually. I would love to find some inspiration in Sweden. I'm actually a total Scandophile. I longed to go to Scandinavia already during my first trips to Africa, in the late 50s and early 60s. Karen Blixen was inspirational in that sense also.

Karen Blixen, Andy Warhol and Salvador Dali in all their glory... But the Irish-English painter Francis Bacon was probably the overall most important artistic inspiration for Peter Beard, who even modeled for Bacon a number of times. I asked Beard what he thought of John Maybury's 1998 Bacon biopic, "Love is the Devil."

— It looked so faggy and so camp that I just didn't get into it. But the guy who played Bacon actually looked just like him. But I did see the BBC movie. They sent that to me, because I'm in it. It's embarrassing. They just love to emphasize the homosexuality, the S/M. That really had nothing to do with Bacon. On a personal level, sure, it had something to with him. But Bacon was major, like an oasis. An oasis of common sense. He liked photography very much too.

My art teacher at Yale was Joseph Albers, and his definition of art was "the ratio of input to result." All the lines in this Bacon drawing are very Zen, very economical. Bacon was very Zen. He himself hated his drawings usually and wouldn't call them Zen at all. But he was such a great guy.

Beard lived with incredible experiences and a history that make new generations look to him for inspiration, in the same way as with his own relationship to Bacon. But in terms of general recognition, Beard often pointed out that he was genuinely tired of all the media projections and simplifications.

— It's usually just all of these clichés. They say things like "Jet Set Socialite." "Portrait of a legend"... What is that? It was great to live in Africa and I got a lot of good subject matter. Of course I was very happy. It was great to be on safari. The common sense of it was that it was like the American West... It's finished. We might as well watch the last chapter. Photography can record that. I've got all the pictures that won't be able to be taken again. And I'm finding some good quotes to put on them. The other pictures I take give information about the main picture.
I majored in old master drawings and I try to do artistic borders. Photography is decorative, but I'm not saying that's necessarily good. Decoration is not necessarily art. If you're Matisse, OK... Well, you try and get something that works. I use blood a lot and they think it's sensational. Blood is thicker than water and better than ink. Better than paint. I've got a lot of blood in my shows.

Looking at Beard's art or at his books it's easy to get the impression that a lot in his creativity was totally intuitive and spontaneous. To an extent, that's correct, according to Beard. But I wondered if he ever reconstructed things from dreams, daydreams, visions and ideas too?

— Sure... Then I just build them up and do them. Like this one... it's Danielle Luna lying on the diaries. I do set things up. Those diaries burned a few weeks afterwards, and she died soon after that too. She was kind of drugged out and she died from an overdose. She actually ruined my house and filled it with seaweed. But I didn't care at all because I was planning this picture.

Peter Beard's visual style was unique. There are exceptions to the rule of course, but usually we see a central photograph with a group of smaller images creating a visual frame around it. Handwritten texts, glued in objects, other people's drawings or images and smeared out blood and/or ink as elaborate and violent frames. Forceful Africa meets the sophisticated Western esthetic mind. Quite often, psychedelic and mind expanding effects occur. I wondered if he came across artists who try to emulate or plagiarize his style?

— All the time. But I don't care. I went to art school. I never use the word though. I'm an escapist. If you go to art school, it takes you a long time to recover. They're teaching you all the clichés that make them failed art teachers. Art teachers are failed artists. They're giving you homework in art. And they all do the same thing. It all looks like Jasper Johns or somebody else. Even Jasper Johns looks like an art school victim to me. You can barely survive art school. It's so full of clichés. I was so bored that I got into doing my diaries instead. I'm not trying to be superior but it was just so boring to be there.

I liked my teacher Joseph Albers though. But the rest were all just homework people. They never teach you how to develop your own nervous system or any of your own individual things. I know they don't know the definition of art. Albers had "the ratio of input to end result," which was quite good. I've read a lot about "expressions," but the one I like the best is from the art historian Bernard Berenson, who did the great collections for all the rich people. His definition was "whatever is life-enhancing." They definitely don't know that one in art school! They just fuck you up big time.

My diaries were and are all about getting out into life and getting away from art school. They're meant to be unartistic. People think they're artistic because they're expressionistic, but they're basically just raging against the homework... I'm just collecting things that are fun. I'm an escapist. I'm just looking for subject matter and life enhancement.

Duchamp's interviews and Bacon's interviews tell you everything you need to know about art. The common sense of it, enlarging the bouquet, finding a niche, all the common sense obvious things... All the things they'll never give you in art school. All they give you is their tragic lack of individuality. It's important... You've got to carve out a niche!

Bill Landis, 2005

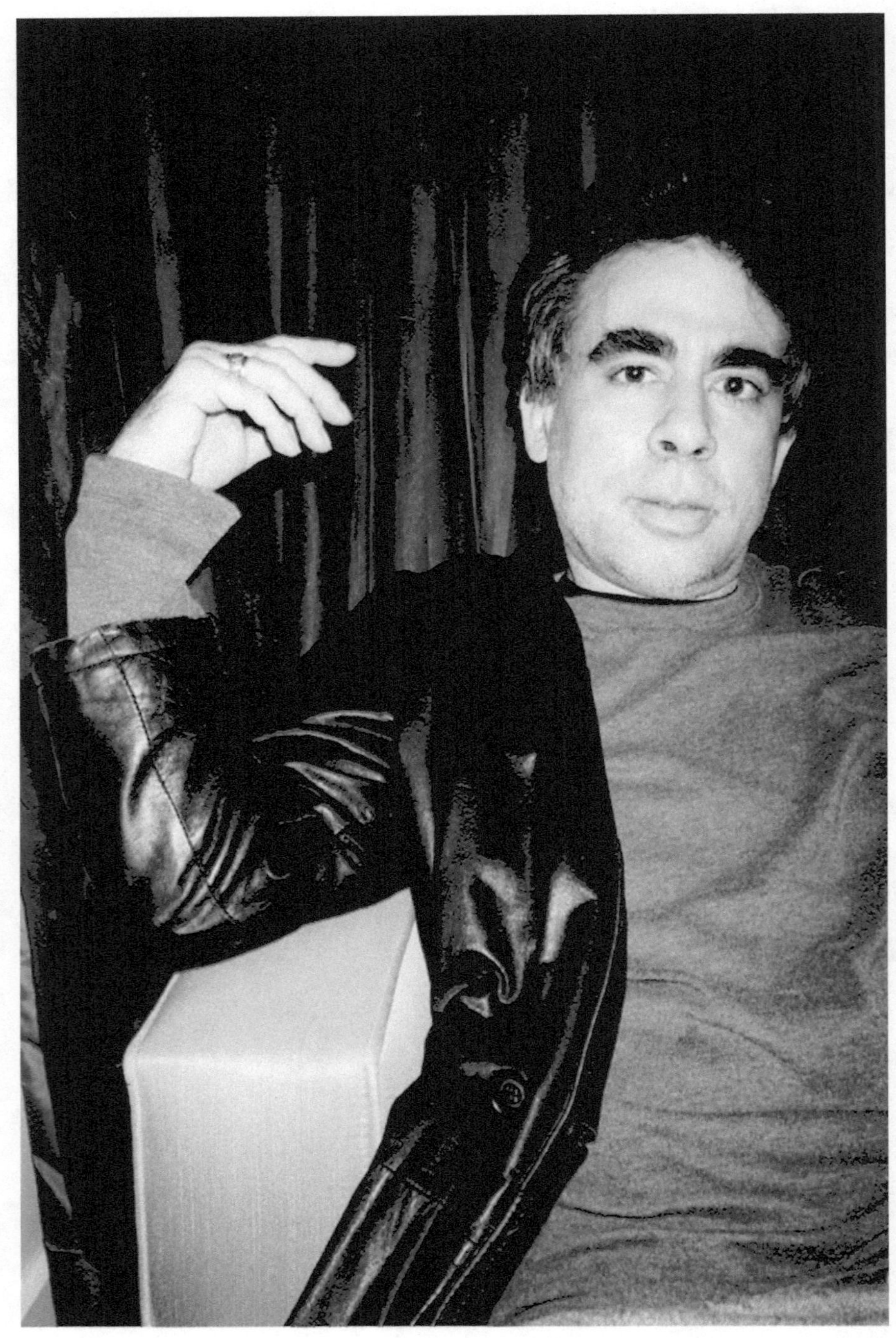

Bill Landis

"Every movie is a work of art."

> "Shaped by an overwhelming sexual history, and dotted with a pro-liferation of blatantly sex-related businesses, the Deuce remained the most intense venue one could ever hope to see a movie in. The Deuce grindhouses were showcases for the wildest and most extreme films in cinematic history, and ticket buyers were of all sorts: depressives hiding from jobs, sexual obsessives, inner-city people seeking cheap diversions, teenagers skipping school, adventurous couples on dates, couples-chasers peeking on them, people getting high, homeless people sleeping, pickpockets. This disenfranchised audience had nowhere else to go, and the grindhouses were where they all wound up."[1] (Bill Landis)

Growing up as I did in a very safe and highbrow environment, I naturally delved into unsafe lowbrow culture with a passion (vengeance?), basically as soon as I could spell i-n-e-r-t-i-a. One important part of that soul-searching process was exploring extreme expressions in cinematic form. Experimental films, avantgarde gems, surrealists, splatter pioneers and gore-hounds galore stirred up an intellectual but also existentially valuable knock-out cocktail that was truly dizzying – as desired.

As this was long before internet saturation, us gore- and sleaze-hounds had to work hard to secure our movie kicks (quite often just privately copied fuzzy-imaged VHS tapes) and magazines by real postal networking and trying to figure out who did what out there. A time-consuming but utterly delightful experience!

On the grand source scale, there was Michael Weldon's *Psychotronic Encyclopedia of Film* (1983) and RE/Search's *Incredibly Strange Films* (1986). But beyond those rather slick books were fanzines like Jack Stevenson's *Pandemonium*, and

---

1 Bill Landis (with Michelle Clifford), "Introduction," in *Sleazoid Express: A Mind-Twisting Tour Through the Grindhouse Cinema of Times Square*, Fireside, New York 2002, p 3.

even more primitive sheet-style fanzines like Rick Sullivan's *Gore Gazette* and, of course, *Sleazoid Express*. The latter differed a lot, in that it not only chronicled the 42nd Street culture, with its bizarre films and "trans-hygienic" theaters, but it did so from the inside, so to speak. Main writer Bill Landis didn't just write about sleaze culture and organize underground film screenings. He was part of it, as they now say, "24/7." Landis starred in many a skin-flick under the name "Bobby Spector" — no relation to music producer Phil Spector, who packed a different kind of gun, entirely. This unique insider perspective, and the superb dead-pan writing style of his lowlife observations, made Landis a strange shapeshifter in the New York underworld.

Post-Sleazoid, Landis wrote for *The Village Voice*, various mens' magazines, Al Goldstein's *Screw*, assembled a *Sleazoid Express* book and also penned the unofficial Kenneth Anger biography, *Anger* (Harper Collins, 1995), which angered Anger to the point of cursing both Landis and Michelle Clifford, Landis' partner in life and writing.

Curse or no curse, Bill Landis died in 2008, aged 49. Not that many people seemed to care or even take notice. When I got the news, I remembered a rainy but interesting spring New York evening in 2005, during which an enthusiastic Landis entertained me and my friend Peter Bisley in a mid-Manhattan hotel room. Landis was then totally willing to enthusiastically talk about his life and career in an underworld that simply doesn't exist anymore. The following interview was conducted by me and Peter Bisley.

— How did you get involved with what eventually became the foundations for *Sleazoid Express*?

I first saw 42nd Street when I came back to the US from England. I was about six years old. That was the "Midnight Cowboy" era. Everything seemed neon and black and white. It was just an amazing, sexually driven place. Occasionally I'd go to Broadway shows with my parents, but my eyes would be looking at other things. "The Devil in Miss Jones," and things like that. I went to college early. I was bored at school and started going to 42nd Street all the time. Sometimes it was nine movies a week; every kind of genre. Pornography, Kung-Fu, Horror, anything that wouldn't play in a mainstream theatre. One day I saw "Let me die a woman" at the Anchor, and I figured that it wasn't going to be reviewed by anybody. It was not going to be recognized by anyone. It must be recorded, so it'd better be me, I thought. I printed a whole bunch of them and typed it all up on a manual typewriter at the

George Washington Hotel. I gave it out at every place. How could you argue with something that was free?

Soon it was bi-weekly. I tied in with the hipster crowd at Club 57 and started a film series with it. I designed my own ads for the series. Kenneth Anger was a big fan of it. I got into trouble with censorship early too. There was something called the "Sex, Sin and Sadism" festival that I had. I made a nice flyer on heavy red stock with a picture of a girl who hung in a cage. A lot of people wouldn't hang that up. That was an early resistance. We had showings at the Mudd Club and the Danceteria. In that minimalist way, it was hard to put out something with a lot of thought in just one piece of paper. A lot of movies were coming out then, so I got the bright idea to expand and have a feature story in the middle. It grew. And when I started working on Times Square, I wanted to document all of that too. Suddenly it got all the attention. *Rolling Stone* wrote about it. I later expanded that article for *Screw Magazine*. I also wrote some things for mens' magazines. Later it became more of a kind of personal diary.

I always wanted to document what I experienced honestly. Between the lifestyle of living in vice constantly... It takes a toll on you, working in vice. I started as a projectionist, a manager, a ticket-taker, everything... Then I graduated into doing other stuff, "participationally." Michelle wrote to me after seeing the *Rolling Stone* piece and we decided to hook up. In a way I wanted to leave. People saw my image on cable TV. Movies are made and then released and re-released years later. I revalued myself. I was a young star for many years and did a diversity of things, like the Eric Stanton wrestling tapes, which were heavy sadism. I was also working for Damiano, which was a lot of fun.[2] I did all kinds of things. By the time I'd been in this for four years and living under an assumed name – living it, breathing it, working at the theaters – I got tired...

There are people who stay in it for life, like Jamie Gillis, and then there are the four-year-people like me. I left the city eventually, went to Florida for a while, came back, and then worked on the *Anger* book. With time, things change. I felt vulnerable at the time and was trying to integrate more into straight society. Michelle came along and I wanted to get away from all these people. We wanted to write and start collaborating. It took some time, but eventually she put out the fanzine *Metasex* and we put out *Sleazoid Express* again. She encouraged me to have no shame in writing about all the things I wanted. Michelle and I collaborated more and more to the point where we finished each other's thoughts. Then we did the *Sleazoid Express* book. That's my story in a very small nutshell.

---

2 Gerard Damiano (1928-2008): American director of pornographic films.

— You said you felt vulnerable when being active in vice. Did you feel that writing about it and publishing those writings had any kind of cathartic effect?

When I did the "Body For Rent" story in *Sleazoid Express*... It was about someone who realizes that the fantasy is not the real thing. I can't think of any other piece that so clearly showed the motivation behind it. And then what the experience actually was, realistically.

— That was published later on in *The Village Voice*...

That became more integrated in *Metasex* too. Drugs played a big part in everybody's life, too. It became like a perpetual motion: doing the movies to get drugs. You can't be in the movies without self-medication. I think the people who do it without the self-medication are either tushed in the head or are doing it as some kind of hobby.

— Do you think all the sunshine stories from the era, from people like Annie Sprinkle, are self-deluded? Is she trying to delude us?

At first I had a lot of suspicion about Annie and that kind of feminist rhetoric that she was trying to promote. We did a story for *Hustler* on live shows. We talked to Annie about it. She wasn't the greatest dancer, so she did something else. I don't know if she's deluding herself or what's going on up there with her. She's been a hooker all of her life. Some people accept that as a way of life. It took me until middle age to lose any kind of guilt trip that I had. I wasn't feeling guilty about it when I was young. Later on it became some kind of strange guilt trip. I was doing S&M-things with girls at an early age, and it cut into what I was doing later as an adult. Eric Stanton had his own room for sessions. Stanton's wife really knew how to hurt. She really knew the pressure points. You really needed some kind of medicine when she was through with you. It was very primitive, like in the Bettie Page era with Irving Klaw and his camera. It was well paid and ended up in a Taschen book, so I'm not ashamed about that.

— Did you get *Sleazoid Express* fan mail more or less immediately?

Of course. There were people who liked it and people who thought it was all about negativity. Jonas Mekas was really mad that I'd given it out during a screening of "Chelsea Girls." He was really offended by that. I got some nerds writing me asking where to get this or that material. I used to write for *Fangoria* but they attacked me when I wrote about the Toby Ross movies. We xeroxed that letter from *Fangoria* and sent it to the subscribers. But of course, I didn't advocate the movies I wrote about. I described them. Like "Farewell, Uncle Tom"... It's a vile fucking movie, but it's remarkable.

— In terms of chronology, when did Michael Weldon's *Psychotronic* guide show up?

He started after we'd put out three issues. He thanked me in the first issue and we were friendly for a while. He hated typing. I learned to type in seventh grade. It was one of the most valuable things I was taught at school. I also experimented with speed reading, like skimming pages really quickly. I was really grateful to learn that. In High School I was on the High School newspaper. That was a lot of fun and I even had my own column.

The magazine started out dealing with offbeat movies. But later on the Forrest J Ackerman-crowd were really offended by the new direction and material...[3] It was so completely different. It was addressing a lot of issues in a very straightforward manner. The more sexually oriented I got, the more they would attack it. The more I'd attack the sacred cows of horror movies, the more pissed off they'd get. I got banned from Spring Street Books and from Forbidden Planet. This was because I had an image from "Barbed Wire Girls" on the cover. That was my first real ban. Fan mail was fun though. Michelle sent me a fan letter and I answered it. Anyway, when I and Michelle had gotten together we started talking about writing together. We talked about Ken Anger a lot. He hadn't been written about and he was a celebrity. We focused on that book and didn't put out the magazine for a while. As we were finishing that, she wanted to do a more sexually oriented magazine. That eventually became *Metasex*. Michelle suggested I write down stuff about all the movies I'd seen. Otherwise they'd be forgotten. They will never be shown again.

— The *Anger* book and the *Sleazoid* book were published by major publishers. How did that come about?

With the Ken Anger book, I had a proper agent and a really good editor. I originally wrote a very rough treatment of it, which included some rough stuff. Then I had to write about him as a proper artist too, so that we could actually sell the book. I had

---

3 Forrest J Ackerman (1916-2008), editor of the legendary and influential magazine *Famous Monsters of Filmland* (1958-1983).

a 40-page interview plus pictures too. I made some money from that book during the recession, but it did take four years to write. There was also a lot of pressure involved. We had a two day legal reading, so that he couldn't sue us.

— How much of an edition of *Sleazoid Express* was distributed by you to stores and how much of it was subscribers' copies?

It varied. Michelle told me to re-issue the old ones and to make them sensational and throw all my fetishes into it and all those nice stills from "Sadomania." She told me to go for what I really, really like. To make it kinkier than anything these other guys would ever have done. I had a lot of rare stills that I had accumulated over the years. This was the first time people got a chance to see that kind of material and read about these movies in detail. With age, the old issues sold more and more. Material by the pornographer Lasse Braun was in there too...

— How did you come across that? Some of it is beyond belief...

Michelle knows him and worked for him on something. She got him to write that story on sadomasochism for *Metasex*. Some people wanted us to have some kind of disclaimer on the covers, but I don't believe in that kind of bullshit. Some stores and companies have made huge amounts of money from the ads in our magazines but have still given us a hard time. Something Weird is the most legitimate of all these outfits.

With both *Sleazoid* and *Metasex*, we wanted to kink everything up. We had some competition, some imitators. We were trying to go into the unspeakable. The fourth *Sleazoid* had the sadism picture from "Performance" on the cover. There was a bit of Karin Schubert history. I believe that art and exploitation is the same thing. There's no distinction between them for me. For me, an Ingmar Bergman movie is the same as an exploitation movie that's sexually oriented. Every movie is a work of art. The distinctions have to be destroyed.

— Were there any notable or famous people among your subscribers?

Larry McMurtry, who gave me the quote on the back of the *Sleazoid* book. A guy from *Los Angeles Times*, and many other journalists. Roger Ebert, the movie journalist, was a subscriber.

— It's never been disputed that *Sleazoid Express* was the magazine that defined that whole era. It's simply the best document. All the others were lightweight in comparison.

A lot of those people wasted time in trying to attack me. *Gore Gazette* attacked me and called me different names. The guy couldn't even write. One time, together with my ex-partner, we went to his house and creepy-crawled him and threw Sleazoids at his door. When I printed the Toby Ross pictures, he made remarks like *"Sleazoid Express* is merging with *Boy Magazine."* Anything that's sexually ambiguous makes these nerds very nervous. One even wrote me saying to remove him from my mailing list because I'd said that "Forrest J Ackerman is an old queen." Some of the nerds contacted me after a while about things like that. I guess many of them hoped I would come to a bad end. Sure, I've had rough times, but I'm still alive.

— Did it ever bug you that a lot of other people capitalized on that whole thing?

There are very few that I get along with. But I usually don't send out review copies to certain people anymore, because I know they will just rip off the ideas. Bill Lustig took me to lunch once.[4] He was upset about the bad review of "Maniac" but wanted me to write some liner notes for another movie. He said, "Think of the publicity..." But I wanted to hear about payment. I thought he was cheap, but then I heard he was actually working out of a trailer. He spends money on buying old prints. I get along a lot better with European people. We're about documentarian work. That's why I like to work with Michelle. It's great to have a woman's voice talking about that kind of stuff. Some people have said they think both magazines should merge together. But I don't really see how that could work out. One is just sexually oriented, and one is movie oriented. *Metasex* is developing into more of weird stories about weird people. I think sadomasochism is an important part of the life force of this age. I don't think people should feel guilty about it. When I was 17-18, I don't think people knew about it as much as they do now. People seem less inhibited about it now.

— Do you think it would be better if some things were actually forgotten, or do you think that everything should be dragged up and remembered?

---

4 William Lustig (b 1955), an American director of exploitation films.

Part of the fun many years ago was the actual struggle to find the material. It was like an adventure of sorts. It was great having actual rare prints too, and showing them at parties and things like that. Now, everything is just so available.

– Would you like to write about something that's not related to this kind of scene?

I've also written extensively about the drug subculture. We've also written about different urban areas. The first cover story I did for *The Village Voice* was about the weird block where I lived on 14th and 3rd. That was the area where Taxi Driver was shot. I lived there for a while.

Ralph Gibson, 2005

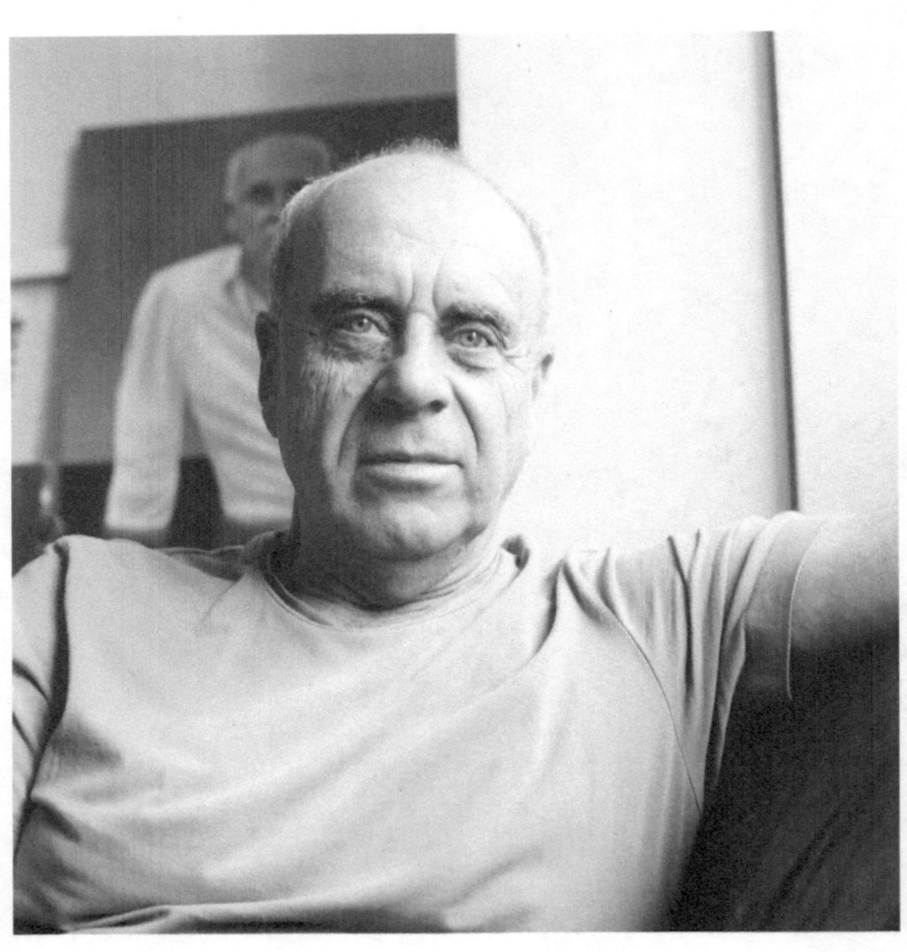

Ralph Gibson

"Melody is to music what reality is to photography."

Saturation. Detail. Drama. That about sums it up. American photographer Ralph Gibson (born 1939) has consistently taken, treated and given back images that draw you in; tempted by and lost to the mystery of creative compositions and daring displays. Since the early 1960s, Gibson's roving eyes and cameras have been the hyperactive filters of a huge amount of images that are not only influential because of their iconic status; they have also become like entities in themselves, seductive on the surface and revealing as you sink deeper into whatever story you may find. Basically, Ralph Gibson is in many ways a magical photographer.

The consistency and determination of his vision has led to many exhibitions, books, awards and overall successes. This might at first seem strange, as his most potent images are basically abstractions of recognizable items, structures and human forms. There is paradoxically a distancing in the close-up esthetics of his images. But the very force that these abstractions wield (not only on their own but also together) will drag you relentlessly into the web of attraction. The high contrast, grainy black and white images, as well as the saturated color ones, are all messages of sorts from a highly refined esthetic mind. Very few of his images – and we're talking about 60 years of ardent clicking here – lack that signature: the immediate dream-like punch.

There is something about that cross-over aspect that I really love, and always have. Where the esthetic sense of the photographer truly amplifies the image itself, and adds to the subject or object in question – regardless if there's a mutual awareness of it or not. It's a forceful vision, and one that sticks.

I met Ralph Gibson in his Manhattan studio in 2005. There was a great number of guitars there, photographic prints, equipment, books... All signaling a curious and creative mind that has also managed to build a successful career of his passionate endeavors. Gibson himself was calm, controlled, courteous, relaxed; very much reinforcing the impression of an ardent seeker who has actually also found something substantial along the way.

— What are you working on right now?

I'm deep inside a project on Brazil. I just returned from my second trip this year and the deadline is coming soon, this summer. I showed a dummy for the publisher that was 80 pages and he said he wanted to do it but it had to be 160 pages. That's a reversal of the usual enigma. I've been enjoying this a lot.

— Your style is distinctly poetic. How did that come about in the early days? Was it an intuitive development?

My early work reflects my inner needs at the time. I had worked as a photojournalist but I found that the documentary mode wasn't bringing me the satisfaction I was yearning for. I evolved my look in response to personal needs. That's the only way you can get actual content into a photograph. You can decide to get a different look, which is a formal issue. You can say that you need contrast here or all grey there, that I'm going to only use a wide lens, etc. Some people mistake that formal consideration for their look. What I want to do is create the impression I've had when I was looking at something. When I seriously look at something it creates a set of inner emotions which I attempt to evoke in the subsequent photographs. You can argue that my pictures are what it feels like looking at those things; not the things in themselves.

— The first picture that comes to my mind is from the Japanese garden; those well ordered pebbles...

I find a lot of satisfaction in a point blank look at essentially nothing. I find the idea of a subject matter like the president or the pope... None of those things or people would make me reach for my Leica. It's the humble subject matter that counts. I could take a picture of empty space before my nose.

— Does that come from or stem from a specifically spiritual outlook or a philosophy?

Yes. I'm studying yoga and yoga thought. I'm also deeply immersed in a kind of metaphysical pursuit. I've studied Gurdjieff and other prominent masters and I realized that I had to deconstruct or unlearn a lot of things before I could actually see what I was looking at. That's just one sentence but it requires several years of total concentration.

— Simplicity is hard sometimes... Do you ever get images in your head that you try to find or arrange, or is it all intuitive...?

There's a phenomenon that occurs in my pursuit, which is that there will be a picture that I've been wanting to take for many years but it will function primarily as an emotional hunch. It'll be like a whiff of a feeling that I have. Then I can instantly recognize it when I see it in the so called world of reality. My colleague Duane Michals is very good at pre-visualizing things like that. If I could pre-visualize and then go straight towards it, I would love to do it because I'd eliminate a lot of search. I still feel that the essential nature of photography has to do with its peculiar abstract relationship to reality. I find myself functioning in harmony with and parallel to that vector.

— Would it be correct then to say that you're more of a flaneur or a stroller than a constructor?

I'm definitely a flaneur. I know it when I see it. In my 1975 book *Quadrants* I didn't know what the next picture would be but I knew where to look for it. This goes back to the point of departure theory of Dorothea Lange, which continues to inform my efforts. I'm working in Brazil and I'm looking for the roots of its culture. That tends to help me look in a vast country the size of America with 200 million inhabitants. It tends to slightly narrow the search.

— You've mentioned how different places have helped define yourself and your work. Has New York been the best one for you?

New York has essentially defined my intelligence. I travel continually along with others in this age where it's possible. It's hard to decide where to live but I've been here in New York for 35 years. After all my travels, I still consider New York to be the center of my culture and civilization. It's changing, and Berlin is very exciting; primarily for young artists, I think. But I have an infrastructure in this city that continues to amaze me and enthuse me. You need to live where you stay inspired. I solved that a long time ago. I came to New York with $200 in my pocket anticipating a two week stay. I never looked back. I was like a guy coming out of the closet. Finally I'm complete; I'm me. This is just the way I am. At one time I contemplated living in Paris. But I don't want to live there, or in Rome or in Rio. I like going there.

— Well, you once wrote that going to France is like going to a beautiful woman...

Yes. I'm going at the end of the month to lead a workshop on nudes, so that'll be fun.

— Watching you from the outside and watching you work, it certainly looks like a blessed life. You've stuck to your integrity and you haven't done ad campaigns you haven't wanted to do. And apparently that's worked out quite well. Have you ever had doubts along the way?

No, never. One of the things that happened to me was that when I was in the Navy I had the epiphany that I was going to be a photographer. One of the things that a vocation includes is that no matter how bleak my circumstances — three cameras in the pawn shop, two flat tires and an eviction notice — I still knew I was going to make it as a photographer. It's just true. And for this reason I can apply this sentiment to the endeavors of a Palestinian terrorist. I know what blind faith is. I understand those people from the point of view of my own Jihad as an artist. For that reason they're not quite the mystery to me that they are to other people. When I see a young photographer walk through the door I can tell from across the room if they are so inclined. It doesn't guarantee anything; it just happens to be the way you're born. I always knew the purpose of my life. This requires me to stay pure and true to the work, to engage in the work above a level of mediocrity. That then becomes one's moral code. During this period when a lot of people are discussing many religions for many reasons, one of the things that occurs to me is that deeply religious people need to have a moral code provided for them. I do believe the artist provides his or her own moral code.

— Do you think that sense of purity comes from having seen your father involved in a very constructed world of make believe in Hollywood?[1]

Sure. I was always fascinated by the extreme importance that was attached to the formulation of an image. I would be on the set and I'd watch the precision and diligence with which they created images.

— Another logical progression in this work of purity must have been setting up

---

1 Ralph Gibson's father worked as an assistant director to Alfred Hitchcock in Hollywood, and the young Gibson often visited sets.

your own publishing company? Was that a conscious decision in the sense that there weren't any other options, or did you want to have your own press?

In fact, with *The Somnambulist* I had an offer from a very prominent publisher.[2] I created a sequence over a three year period. No other editor would have been capable of arriving at the same conclusions. I did it because I could. I had learned lithography in the Navy. I had demystified the process. You have to remember that in those days you were constantly made aware of how much an image lost in a magazine or a book. That had to do with the nature of the medium at the time. When I arrived on the scene with the possibility of doing a book I said to myself that this printing process will amplify my image a lot so I thought it necessary to work with this, with the medium in itself in a way. I discovered I could over-ink, which was how I got my bigger black shapes. I didn't see the lithographic process as an opportunity to lose something but rather gain something. It continues to be that way for me. Technology has evolved right along with my perception of photography. I can do two or three books a year now. I work over there in the computer and I can send a PDF-file to my publisher in Italy. It's very satisfying to make books now.

— The sequence you mention, where you're putting together a beginning, a middle and an end, does that help when you're actually shooting the stuff too?

I'm a musician and I'm deep into music theory right now, harmony, etc. I find that in free improvisation, you can introduce, perform and exit a theme any place you want, as long as you adhere to very minor signpost guidelines and rules. Not rules, but indications. To keep it sort of within the range of what you're doing with the rest of the piece. I've been back from Brazil for a week and a half and I've been doing nothing but darkroom and layout work; printing, scanning, printing, scanning. I like to introduce little sub-themes in the sequencing, like four-page sub-themes. In *The Somnambulist*, I discovered that if I had the sequence of 48 pictures correctly and really perfectly drawn as a sequence, I could open the book every two, four, six pages and the subsequent pairings would continue to resonate in an effective manner. That's one way of sequencing. I could also use that for one segment of the book and then go back to another way of sequencing. As long as there's structure. The real pitfall, the real shortcomings of many peoples' sequencing in books is that they attribute content that really isn't there. The theory of the visual overtone: the visual overtone has to actually resonate. It cannot be projected. It has

---

2 Ralph Gibson's first book on his own Lustrum Press: *The Somnambulist*, 1970.

to be something that emanates from the page towards the eyes.

— Do you think that's a sign of the times: a constant bombardment of images that loses itself and just keeps on going?

I think it has to do with the ease with which graphic design ideas can be applied in computers. In the old days I had to make a copy negative from the original print, and then I'd have to make work prints to size…

— Speaking of contemporary technology, you also have a great website now. Is that something that actively interests you?

I have my site. It's like having a cell phone: everyone has one. It's not really a sign of being hi-tech. It's so simple to do. I have an appointment this afternoon with a guy who's going to put in some Flash and motion stuff. And I also want to incorporate some of my compositions. I get many compliments for the way it is, so clearly it's functioning. There are hipper sites around but mine is at least functioning. I don't want to lose any of that functionality.

— In terms of photographic inspirations, have there been any constant ones?

Yes. Painting. The history of two dimensional art. Music. And my coterie of artist friends, with whom I exchange my most personal thoughts and vice versa. A dictionary would define esthetics as the philosophy of beauty. I find that as I accrue information and experience, as I make more images and add them to the previous, I find that my esthetic evolves. It explains the difference between the pictures I was doing in 1960 and the ones I'm doing in 2005. They will always be interdependent… You can't have later work without earlier work. On a purely esthetic issue one continues to evolve and pursue additional personal concerns.

— Have you noticed that photographs can have a very memetic quality? If someone documents something, it can help your memory in the sense of "I remember being there." But it can also evoke or re-evoke emotions. Does that occur in your case?

I have a folder called "False Emotions" in my life and I file different emotions in that folder, and I'd immediately file that in that folder…

– That could be an interesting book...

I will be doing a book called *False Emotions*.

– What about contemporary photography? Do you try to keep up with what's going on?

I know that there's a lot of interesting, good work being done. Who's going to deny that Gursky is a master when he dies? I'm friends with Cindy Sherman and see her all the time. But you're basically only interested in your own work. There are 25 guitars in this studio. I'm constantly refining my hands, my technique on the instrument. I'm applying these things on my use of the Leica. I'm constantly refining my camera handling. When it comes to photography I tend to look at and admire those photographers who have excelled or advanced their camera handling techniques to the extent that they can have access to the image which they couldn't otherwise have had access to without this virtuosity. I see pictures I admire all the time. Roger Ballen came on the scene a few years ago. That's point blank photography. What do you think Diane Arbus would have done with Roger Ballen? She might have knocked off even sooner. The medium in itself has defied definition since the first frame.

– Have you noticed an increase in photography collecting? Prices are going up and auctions are more frequent.

I fully understand that. It's all based on the fact that there is a creative aspect of collecting. Part of the success of the photography market is based on the fact that people can come in and photographs are still accessible, price-wise, even now. One of the most creative things about collecting is that you can get young talent and then see him or her evolve through the process. You can do that as a collector.

– Have you noticed your own work going for higher and higher prices?

Not necessarily in my case. I have an awful lot of work out there. I'm prolific. My auction prices are stable. I've had some books go very high.

– You once had the "Sex & Drugs" rock'n'roll band... Do you still play with other people?

I do, but it's not rock'n'roll anymore. It's pretty much avant garde improvisations, atonal, textural... I improvise and I make tracks on the computer... I find it quite tough engineering sound in a computer though. It's amazing how narrow my vocabulary is when it comes to actually engineering it all. You have choices of these endless curves and you can do so many things with a signal.

— Do you see music as having therapeutic qualities? In the sense that it's not your main chosen way of expression?

Photography is my love and music is my passion. I have a book coming out on Steidl, about my esthetics.[3] I realize that melody is to music what reality is to photography. As an artist, I'm interested in both those points.

— What about other artistic disciplines? Writing? Painting?

I write a bit. I've never been tempted to paint. I've always remained very firmly under the impression that what I should do... If I ever want to achieve what I want to achieve, I have to really concentrate on that. I don't do many things that are not related to the idea of enhancing my abilities. Music helps my photography. Language is also help. Tennis helps me too. But I don't do things that aren't a part of the bigger picture.

— In terms of preparing for major book projects, do you usually factually prepare or do you want to come and be taken aback on a spontaneous level?

What happens is this: It's not a multiple choice. While I'm working on a project, it starts indicating other possible paths to follow. I have another book project called "The wounded nurse and other nudes." I do two or three workshops a year on the nude. I realized that I can put together a body of work on the figure. That's how that evolved. The "False emotions" project is based on a deeper examination of how photographs are looked at. In the creative process, you never go directly to the solution. You try various things before you get to that solution. The things you're not looking for specifically quite often open up doors. I keep that in mind and I study my work intensely. Book-making is the very best discipline. That's how I work basically.

---

3 This became *Refractions – Thoughts on Aesthetics and Photography*, Steidl/MEP, Göttingen, 2006.

— A technical question: the very contrasty images... Was that something you had seen before or was it something you stumbled across yourself?

I got that basically from movies. Film Noir, from when I was on the set in the early days as a kid. I move in and out of it in my current work. I tend to be a bit contrasty in my printing but not as much as I used to.

— Even your color stuff is really saturated...

That seems to be the result of Photoshop. When it came out I said that I wouldn't start saturating. But your eyes change with time.

— When you first came into contact with digital imaging, was it like you didn't want to get into it at first?

Yes. I don't use digital cameras, that's for sure. But computer use is really great for color photography. You can get your palette exactly where you want it. You can beautify your colors. It's great for setting inking levels.

— Here's a nerdy question concerning your favoring of the Leica M-series: Have you ever worked in medium format or with other brands?

I know how to. My very first camera in the Navy, when I was 19, was a Rolleiflex, which I then cropped to make it look like 35. I went to Leica in 1961 and I've been there ever since. That got rid of all that ambivalence; that kind of identity crisis that some photographers have... You know, the endless bags of cameras. I can go around the world lightly. I like to choose the best camera, the best lens, the best film and then just forget about the rest.

— What's a perfect day like for Ralph Gibson?

It's like today. I do yoga every morning and some push-ups. Then I can tell how I'm feeling physically. I then adjust that as much as I can. I get over here at around nine. I usually print in the mornings or have a harmony lesson. I have lunch with friends. Today, I have a lot going on. Spring is an intense season for me. I love packing my bags and going through which cameras I should take... The quantity of films have increased over the years. Now I shoot both in black and white and color. There are a lot of different ways of working. What I try to do is evolve ways of working that make me want to work. I write in my journals about my creative process and I attempt to enhance it.

Maja Elliott, 2006

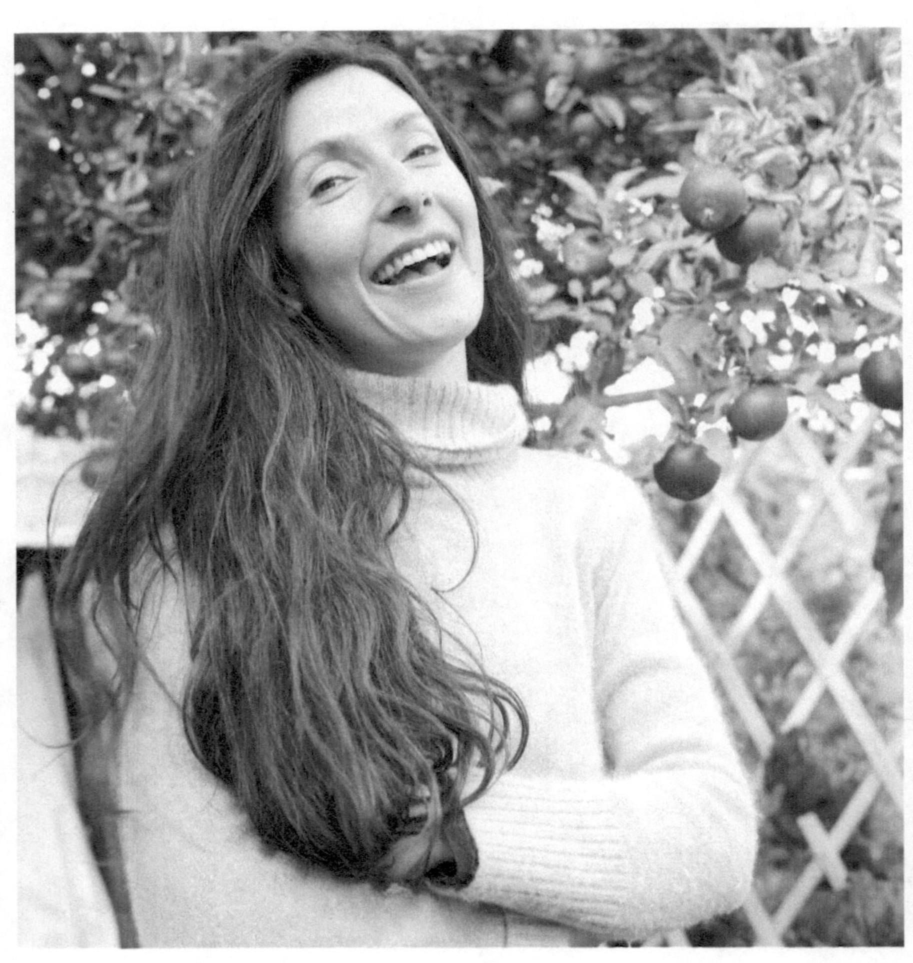

Maja Elliott

"Music is a language that can be taught intuitively."

I first met Maja Elliott in London in 2003. We were performing at the same music festival: Maja with Current 93, and I with Cotton Ferox (together with Thomas Tibert). It was a pretty relaxed event, and we had the chance to talk and exchange ideas. I immediately liked her playing, too. This particular festival presented a kind of low key Current 93, with a David Tibet simply presenting his romantic poetry over Elliott's subtly dramatic piano music. I realized then that Maja Elliott is a "drifter." She lulls you into sonorous safety, and then pushes you onwards when things have become too comfortable, and then back again. It is true in live performances, with or without others, and it's true in her own recorded music (such as the absolutely brilliant mini-album "1000 water craters on the sea").

This of course requires real musical skill, and that she truly has: being classically trained in piano, song and composition, and having gone off on jazzy tangents of her own, Elliott's keyboard treatment is seductive and perplexing at the same time. And, yes, unpredictable; undefinable. Her own recordings also take you for ride in other ways than merely through the keys. Sometimes they are pure ambient or sound collages, snugly cloaked in emotional reverb, and evoking mysteriously sensual scenes. Quite often also including her own voice — at times completely audible and understandable, at times merely as another mood-maker in the mix. And sometimes her keyboards erupt into full forte mode and basically run amok in sprinkling harmonies that completely knock you out in their fierce beauty.

Her position as a poetic satellite to the later incarnations of the music/culture scene depicted in David Keenan's book *England's Hidden Reverse* makes perfect sense. Traces of the playful yet poetic attitude of Steven Stapleton and his "Nurse With Wound" project float up to the surface at times, only to sink again and reveal her very own greatness.

Maja Elliott paints too, and the "scapes" are somewhat similar to her music: abstractions in muted colors, drawing you in to see if there's anything approachable or tangible there — something to hold on to. It's an attractive and magnetic pull, that then sets you drifting in new directions.

And, yes, she's part Swedish, too! When she was visiting family in Gothenburg in 2006, I decided to meet her again, and to talk about how she looks at her art.

— Recollections of your very first musical memory?

Just from what I was told afterwards. I first moved to London when I was 18, and I listened to some Indian classical music. I had this amazing feeling of déja-vu. I talked to my mother and she told me that I'd heard a lot of Indian music when I was a baby. I was born in Abu Dhabi. At that time, they had a whole lot of Indian people there working in construction. It was just desert at the time. There were big Indian markets, with sarees and carpets. I had the feeling that I'd heard that music before and I felt very much at home with it. Then I found out... So that must have been my first musical memory. I just rediscovered it later.

— That's a good start.

I tend to love music from the East. I like Arabic music too. I think Indian music has more depth but I love the Arabic scales too. That's what I loved about being in Romania too. They have this fascinating Latin and Middle Eastern mix. When you see the gypsies dance, you realize it's very similar to Persian dance. The gypsies have a form of hip street music which is a mix of Turkish influences and disco beats. It's quite fun! It's got that Oriental, Eastern tinge to it. Very danceable.

— You started playing at an early age. Was it your parents' choice or did they encourage you in your own interest?

I just started myself. We had a piano that my father had bought for 20 pounds. He didn't play, and my mother didn't play at all. I was never pushed. Later on I had some lessons at school but that made me almost want to give up. My mother took me to a piano competition and I ended up studying with a man who was composing music: a mix of jazz, contemporary and classical. It was really good training for me. I learnt about my left hand, my rhythm. Boogie basses, Bossanova rhythms, Blues... I studied classical music with his wife. But always in an open way. I was never forced to do scales. It just came naturally. Then I got more and more into the classical, but I was always writing little songs myself. I was never pushed to play pieces I didn't like. I got a good technique by playing big romantic pieces though. I know from then that music is a language that can be taught intuitively. You have to teach students by teaching them to open up. They'll learn much more quickly then. You don't really have to separate technique from expression.

— You were hooked on music from very early on. Were you also involved with other creative outlets? Did you ever feel tempted to leave music and pursue other creative things?

All through my childhood, it was piano. I just loved it. When I studied with the composer and his wife, they never pushed anything. Painting came later.

— The music that you're composing yourself, how would you describe it?

It's changed over the years. But the music is always quite dreamy. I love music that takes you into a different space. Music that expresses an emotional state. Music which lifts you up. I tend to like composers like Debussy and Arvo Pärt; music that puts you in a spiritual state.

— To what extent does improvisation and composition differ for you when it comes to achieving this spiritual state?

It works in different ways. I usually start with some motif I find when playing around. Sometimes a melody or a particular chord. Before I start I'm usually directed by what I want to express. I try to get into that feeling. What is it that I want to express? It's emotional first and then I find a structure for that once I'm really in touch with that expression.

— Are you predominantly a "major" or a "minor?"

I love uplifting music and I think my music is happy but tinged with melancholy. I've always had that touch of melancholy. When I was about nine years old I didn't know what melancholy meant. A teacher in school explained what it meant and she said that it's rather like a color and that I had that and that it's not a bad thing to have it. Even at nine, I think I had a touch of that color! I tend to love minor music. For instance, that's what I love about Swedish folk music. The Swedish fiddle. I've played the cello and am learning the violin now. The Irish music is much more in major.

— Now that you're approaching a digital world, do you still find that the keyboard maintains its stronghold for you?

It doesn't really hold the strongest fascination but it's been my most used tool up until now. It has sometimes felt like a limitation these last few years. I've wanted to explore more of sound in itself. Soundscape music. Sound sculptures. I've always loved ambient music. When I was at college I enjoyed playing contemporary music. But at that time, what I could relate to was more modern Jazz, in terms of composition. I was studying the contemporary classical music, and it's very cerebral. It's changed a bit now, with Arvo Pärt and Michael Nyman. You can use conventional harmonies. It doesn't need to be all abstract. I didn't relate so much to the totally abstract. I was writing modern jazz for a few years. When I moved to Ireland I started to arrange music for string quartets. I wrote an orchestral piece and everything I did contained influences of all the things I like. Quite a few repetitive things, like, say, Steve Reich. But also quite romantic, rhythmic things. I really like Bulgarian folk music which has these very fast dancing rhythms. But I do like music that makes you think as well. Compositionally I was more into contemporary jazz. In Ireland I got these commissions and explored that. Recently I've been doing a collaboration with an English drone composer called Paul Bradley, whom I met when I did a concert with Scribble 7, with Steve Stapleton and Andrew Liles. That was very inspiring. I finally decided to set up my own studio because I want to go more into using the beauty of sounds and breaking out of the conventional forms. I've always been a piano player, and as much as I love the different forms — Chopin, Liszt, modern jazz... — I now find that all these forms can be limiting. I'd like to be able to explore more. I'd like to explore in my own way.

— What is it that you'd like to express with your music?

I tend to like art that expresses love. I've always felt that this is just a way to express love, joy, beauty. I think of art as something that can really touch and give people something. I like art that touches people. There's so much suffering out there. Art can remind people that there is actually some joy too. That tends to exist in the artists I like.

— Is music and art a sort of food or nourishment then; something that we all need?

I think so, yes. Music can touch people in such a powerful way. I like painting that is uplifting. I love colors. There's a lot of optimism in my music, but also pain and sorrow. I think we need to get through all that. I've been more exposed to darker kinds of music through playing with Current 93. It's been good for me. When I grew up I was playing a lot of classical music and I didn't hear so much from the darker side. I think it's good to express that too. There has to be a balance. I think it's good to let all the pain out. At the end of the day, there's hope. I feel very strongly that musicians can give people some hope.

— Do you have any examples of bands that are able to combine the darkness and the hope?

Arvo Pärt is probably a master when it comes to that. It doesn't always sound particularly hopeful but there's always an amazing outpouring of human sorrow and spirituality. I think that because it's so exquisite and beautiful, it is hopeful in itself. I also like Steve Reich. There's a kind of hypnotic positive state there. I like Steve Stapleton. I think what he does is amazing. He's actually one of the best musicians I've ever met. He doesn't actually play an instrument, but still… It's great for me to have met people like that. Even though I play an instrument, I've always appreciated so much more someone who doesn't perhaps have a technique but puts so much feeling into what's being played. It has to do with sound and the intent and the emotional intensity behind it. That means so much more than mere technique. For me it's quite a challenge to leave the piano and try to learn other instruments so that I can use different sounds in my studio. I'm interested in the sounds of the violin for instance. On the latest CD single I did, there's cello on it, but not played in a conventional way. I did a long piece that was then time-stretched and then we erased the original signal and just kept the echo. It was incredibly ghost-like and moving. I learnt some good things from Steve Stapleton in the studio. The violin can really sound like a lot of things when treated in an unconventional way.

— How did the collaboration with Current 93 come about?

I met Steve Stapleton through Aranos. For a long time Steve was just a mysterious figure I heard stories about and who released his own records and was on the underground scene. Out of the blue he contacted me to play on an album that his friend was doing. I'd never heard of Current 93 or David Tibet. That was for the album "Soft Black Stars." He came over to our house. I didn't know quite what was expected. Michael Cashmore was there. We had a piano in the house and Michael played some themes. I asked him why he didn't play it on the album, but he didn't feel confident enough or something. He wanted me to elaborate. The themes were quite clearly defined and very beautiful. Like simple, early medieval music. So I learnt those and the particular patterns that had to fit to David's texts. I kind of fleshed out the chords and made them richer, and added some bass lines. A lot of the themes that accompany David's words are repeated, but the secret is that they always change. It's never quite the same. The theme is the same but each repetition is different. It's mostly piano but we added some viola. They said to me, "Imagine that you come across an old piano in an attic and that you haven't played for years." They wanted me to sound like the music had been rediscovered, like forgotten melodies. I played a little bit hesitatingly, so that was fun.

— That was recorded in 1998, quite a while ago. How has it been to be a part of Current 93 since then?

Nothing much happened after that. I left Ireland and decided to go to Hungary and learn the Cymbalom. I've always loved Eastern European music, and piano is not an ethnic instrument. The Cymbalom has a very fascinating sound. I love gypsy music. Particularly Romanian music. I went off to Hungary, from Italy actually, where I'd been into experimental circus and acrobatics. It was quite mad. I made friends with some kind of gypsy mafia and I had to run away from them. I ended up not learning so much cymbalom but I did touch my dream, so to speak. I was renting it from a gypsy. While I was in Budapest I got a call from David to come and play in London, out of the blue. That was at the Bloomsbury Theatre, which was unforgettable. I didn't know about Antony then.[1] He came over and played support with his group. It was great. Michael Cashmore was there too, and others. After that we've played once a year or so. I moved to Hungary and there was going to be a concert in New York. It was cancelled because of 9/11 and that was quite catastrophic because I was living on peanuts in Budapest. I'd even been singing on the streets to make a living. It was fine and fun but I relied on having that concert with Current 93 in New York. Then I had to start selling my extra clothes in an underground market! But I started teaching English instead. I wasn't destitute anymore, but 9/11 had big consequences for me too. But since then, we've played once or twice a year.

— How much creative input do you have in suggesting variations or themes?

---

1 Antony Hegarty of Antony and the Johnsons.

David usually has an idea of what he's after. He may have a theme that he presents to us and then we play along with it. He then tells us if he likes it or not.

— What do you prefer? Big concert halls with people or to play alone in a setting like this? What's most rewarding?

I think any genuine exchange is the most rewarding experience. It could be here in the cottage or in a concert hall with Current 93. It's usually such a warm experience; it's like playing in and for a family. We all know each other so well by now. David is so in touch with the people who listen to his music. It's a very devoted crowd. We always have a lot of response. There are people who never miss a concert. Anything that's a genuine exchange is a rewarding experience. The worst is when you play in a place and people aren't listening. That's what a lot of musicians are forced to do, like when they're playing in cafés. Drowned out by too much talking.

— Do you also teach piano playing?

I have taught in the past but I'm not doing it at the moment. I like teaching. I need to see what they really want. If you're really in touch with that key, you can really open them up and they'll get more out of it. It's very creative. But at one time I was doing a bit too much teaching. I didn't have any energy left. You only have so much energy. I'd rather express my own colors.

— I was going to ask "Why Sweden?" but that has already been answered by the fact that your mother lives here.

She moved back and I came for a visit. I thought it was a lovely town, and with friendly people. I'd been living in Ireland for nine years and I fancied a change. There's a lovely Nordic tradition in contemporary jazz and contemporary music in general. It's very atmospheric and quite transcendental. I really love that aspect of music.

— Do you have any favorite Swedish artists or composers?

I don't know so much about the contemporary scene. I've met some contemporary jazz musicians. The Nordic sound I like is kind of inspired by Keith Jarrett and Jan Garbarek. Now I think I've moved on but at the time it was quite a breakthrough.

Jazz hadn't been so transcendental before. I love that space. There's a lot of space and contemplation in the Nordic tradition. I like a contemporary jazz group called Atomic. I'm still discovering what's around.

— How do you think your traveling lifestyle has affected your music?

I can see traces. It's quite subtle sometimes. I'm inspired by Bulgarian rhythms. In some of my compositions I'm using rhythms inspired by them. It's not really recognizable. The Irish influence is easier to hear in some of the pieces. They were consciously written in an Irish style. I love the Irish singing tradition. I speak Gaelic as well. Clannad was a big breakthrough at the time. Enya is a bit too commercial. I love folk music, folk voices.

— Have you noticed similarities between Irish and Swedish folk music?

There are different traditions in Ireland. I was in one section, Connemara, to practice my Irish. They have a harder style of singing which is more reminiscent of Arabic singing. Harder and very, very moving. In Sweden there's a mix. I love the open-chested quite strident singing. There are different folk traditions in every country of course. My own voice is usually softer, more whispering. I think Swedish folk singers have a very natural delivery. They have an edge but it's usually quite soft.

— If you compare your musical compositions with your paintings, what kind of similarities can you see?

They're very similar. They're dreamy, spacey... Inner landscapes. You can often see elements that are very watery. There's a lot of water in my paintings. I was born just by the sea and could swim before I could walk. When we moved from Arabia to England when I was three, we went straight into the water. My brother and I came back screaming because it was so cold. We had colds for months. My relationship with water is also present in my music and my paintings. Inner emotional scapes.

— Do you wish to communicate with others through your art or is it just the actual expression that's important to you?

I think it's important to write music that really touches people. If you start with that aim though, it gets people-pleasing. It's dangerous. Unless you're moved yourself, you rarely move anybody else. You have to be very honest to yourself.

— Does that happen, that you don't like something you've created?

It's very easy to go off into clichés. Because I play the piano, it's always a temptation. I think it'll be good for me to build my own studio and experiment more, to resist that temptation. I'm very interested in working with natural sounds. The digital set-up has created such a whole world of new instruments and new scapes. Rather like a macro-lens in photography. You can never really appreciate the inside of a flower because you can't see it. The same with music recording now. Some sounds are so soft. Real sounds add life.

— Has Stapleton been an inspiration in that sense, too?

Very much. He would dissuade me from using synths. Having said that though, there are so many means... The main thing is always the authenticity. You can use very good preset sounds. But a piano has that whole range. When I play with Current 93, I really use the piano like a full orchestra. Electric pianos are very useful in their particular space.

— Can you see yourself headed in a distinct, specific direction?

I feel a bit limited at the moment, having to rely on others' studios. I'm very attracted to rich sounds that have resonance. I love bells. I like music which generally is meditative. I'm heading more towards that. As a person I'm changing. The stuff I'm doing now I couldn't really play in the local wine bar. The more pianistic ones I guess I can play out. I want to focus on writing and performing my own music. I've learnt a lot from all the stuff I've done with others. Going my own way is a bit of a leap into the dark. I've been performing my own music alongside some Current 93 gigs, and that was lovely. The pieces I performed were distinctly pianistic, but now I want to go into realms where I use a voice loop, perhaps some violin loops. I want to create different live textures. It's moving away from being just the piano. I've been encouraged by David Tibet to sing more. I like to sing other people's poems. I'm not really a lyricist but I admire people who are craftsmen with words. But David said that no one can write my own words but me and I feel that's a valid point. Music I like, Debussy for instance, can be quite "notey." In my own songs, I'm keeping everything quite sparse.

— Except for the music in itself, are there other things in life that inspire and influence you?

Very much. I tend not to be able to express music unless I'm really living. I'm inspired by nature, by travel. The traveling has perhaps influenced me more on a deep emotional level than the particular forms of those countries. I love the depth that you get from Georgian music, from Eastern, Arabic music. Those cultures are so rich. Traveling certainly deepens me. I also swim almost every day. I just love water.

Michael Bowen, 2006

Michael Bowen

"Life is very groovy."

Michael Bowen (1937-2009) was one of those cosmic protagonists who seem to always be at the right place at the right time. Someone constantly charming the gods to bestow blessings upon blessings, and installing foundations for a good life wherever he may end up. Out of his affluent Beverly Hills life as a child in the 1940s, Bowen drifted into the vibrant 1950s art scene around Wallace Berman and the Ferus Gallery in Los Angeles. Among other things, Bowen worked as Ed Kienholz' assistant. While helping Kienholz assemble his great pieces, Bowen was also developing his own style of painting.

Immersed in esoteric thoughts and in his own naïvistic but forceful paintings, Bowen hung out with beatniks in San Francisco and, a decade later, was a proto-hippie who helped manifest the "Human Be-In" in Golden Gate Park in 1967 (and many other historical events). Together with Allen Cohen, he published the legendary underground paper the *San Francisco Oracle*, which was instrumental in spreading the radical hippie gospel. Remember the famous press photos of hippies stuffing soldiers' guns with flowers at a peace rally by the Pentagon in Washington? The thousands of flowers were bought by Bowen, to spin the "flower power" concept he had helped coin in San Francisco onwards.

From there and on, Bowen lived a nomadic life in America, Asia and Europe. Strangely enough (or not), towards the end of his life he wound up in a suburb of Stockholm with his family and a small entourage. He painted away and gladly talked about his art and his life experience. At the time I dropped by to see him, he was suffering from severe back pains. Morphine seemed to help out a bit, but this also affected his focus a great deal. He would often drift away into another "zone" and then come back and carry on where he left off. Or perhaps this was just the self-styled magician checking out some parallel universe while at the same chatting away about art and life?

No matter what, Michael Bowen died in Stockholm in 2009. I'm very happy to have met a man who was instrumental in many great counter-cultural events and

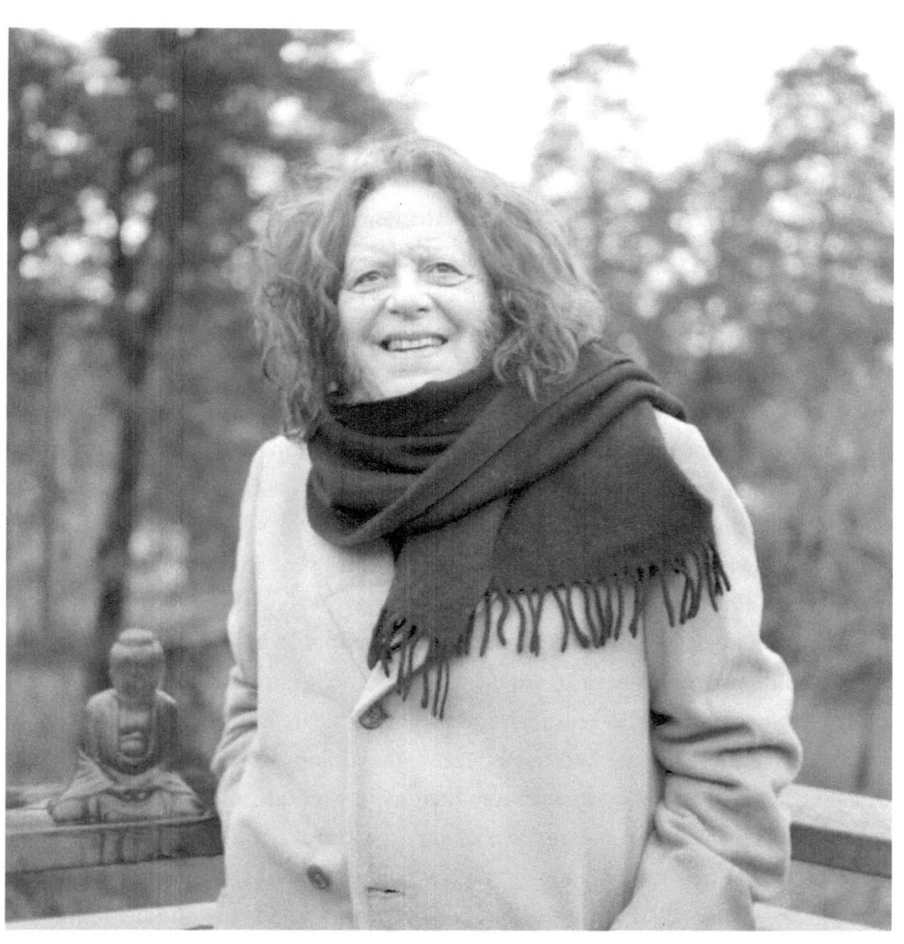

happenings in those explosive decades of contemporary American history. What follows here is a transcript of our talk on November 17th, 2006.

— What attracted you to painting specifically in the beginning?

I was interested in drawing and painting since the age of six. I was never interested in anything else at all. My father was both a doctor and a dentist. He kept his office in Beverly Hills and a house there as well. He was also known as what they called in those days a "Sportsman." Meaning he owned a few great old prizefighters, had a pleasure boat that he and his Hollywood friends would go on to fish, drink, and party with each other. He also loved airplanes and had two of them that held about eight people each. I guess I was an original "Beverly Hills kid." Your question "What attracted you to painting specifically in the beginning?" is a complicated yet simple question for me. Everything attracted me. Now as then I want to know everything I can about everything I see. As for painting or assembling things from my experiences, I have never done anything else. The truth is that I have never done anything else in my life except create art. But I don't mind this funny question, because it reminds me that I am talking to you now rather than working on the big painting on the easel behind me. And I like to talk with you. It is like a little vacation. Usually I become so absorbed in my work that I don't really care much about anything else. I could spend 24 hours out of the day just painting in the studio or anywhere. And this kind of studio action is not like work at all, yet I suppose it seems like very hard work to the few people who see me paint. Only when my body tells me it is tired do I understand that making art is actually definitely hard work. I make these images because I have to. If I did not I would go nuts. All these images crammed in my brain with nowhere to go would be torture. Very exquisite torture, which I would not care for. The very few times I could not work for a day were awful. If I painted only for money, I would be one of the thousands of commercial artists. There is a huge difference between a fine artist and a commercial artist. My interest has always been in the fine arts. van Gogh and Gauguin believed that somewhere in the world there was purity in people untouched by civilization. I do not believe that. I think that there is purity in everyone, everywhere. And that this purity can be found by the people themselves. I paint pictures because I am driven to paint. I like to record what is around me. Sometimes I become interested in my own work long after I made the picture. My observation at the time I made the work has become deeper than my awareness of it at the time I made it. When I see the picture later, it might even turn out to be prophetic. There is a poster over there in the corner of the studio from a show in Italy in 1998. It's a painting called "Eurabia." It was created because when I came to Florence I liked very much to have Cappuccinos and sit and watch the people in the Piazza de la Republica. While I was having coffee, drawing and thinking, I would watch the people in the Piazza. I felt like an art spy while I recorded what I was watching. It didn't really dawn on me what it was that I was actually seeing until later in the studio. Then one night I picked up a magazine from America with a piece by the journalist Oriana Fallaci. She had moved to America because she claimed Europe was being cleverly re-invaded by Muslims. I looked at the painting and there it all was. In the picture are the black people from Africa running from the cops because they were selling cheap sunglasses on the street. They looked like beautiful gazelles running in herds from the cops on horseback trying to catch them in the crowd. The handsome Carabinieri could never catch them. The Africans disappeared like genies into their hidden bottles. There were many people in Western clothing but you could tell clearly that it was a Muslim family. There were many of these people in the crowds I was watching. When I saw Oriana Fallaci's statement, I realized what I had painted. In this way the painting was titled. After the fact; not before it. That seems to be the way I work. I usually do not think before I make a picture.

— You started out early with your vocation.

Yes. I always went to private male only schools; almost all Military Academies. If I was caught drawing I was punished; usually beaten. I kept right on drawing anyway. So much for the paper tiger of authority. They have no power unless they have your mind and/or your body under their control. Even then, they can always be conquered. I feel I am a living example of that great lie they spread about themselves.

— Were you eager to show your stuff to others early on or was it more like a cathartic process for you personally?

I wanted to show my art if it was an easy and simple process. I have never been interested in scrambling after a career. For me, that is a low thing. If it comes to you and you help it out, that is OK. We have to make a living somehow. At the same time, I am not a studio painter. I like to travel around the world. If I would like to get enough to get a ticket to go somewhere to live there long enough to paint something then I project for it. I put it in my mind as a thing already done. Then I do not wonder about it – I just let it cook. Eventually the law of probability produces the ticket and anything else you need. All great yogis know this and they pass it on. I am a lucky person from that point of view. But then I have had great teachers. If I may say so, I am not someone who sits in a studio trying to find out what the next fashion's going to be. I have never done such a thing. However I don't want to make an attack on the art world. It is attackable enough. Besides it is boring and not worth it. The bottom line of commercial galleries is money of course. I have had people who have shown my work and have discovered that some types of my work will sell faster. They would come to me and say, "Look, why don't you paint this some more?" The first time I ever heard that, I was so shocked I got drunk. And drinking is something I really don't personally care for. I had a show in San Francisco and there were many people there. This was after the Beat period. The Beat galleries did not care at all about this bottom line money horror and that is why they are famous today and the others forgotten. I could not believe anyone would ask me to do such a thing. To paint another painting like the one that had sold. I might do that if I wanted to, but not for money reasons. I told the dealer that I just could not do it. He asked me if I was unable to copy my own work. That shocked me even more. In addition, it really pissed me off. He asked me the same question again. I just got up and walked out. I picked up all my work at his gallery that day and never spoke to him again.

– Do you think you were affected then by the attitude or integrity of Kienholz?

No. Those people were very interested in making money. Not Wally Berman or people like that. Ed Kienholz and others, yes. I don't want to give a lot of names. But it was great that Ed did that. There would be no powerful form of assemblage art if it had not been for him. There is no question about it. He may have been an automobile salesman who stumbled into a bunch of Bohemians in LA... At least that's the way it all began for him. But what matters is that he discovered a way to express what he saw. And what he saw America needed to hear and see. I lived with Ed when I was 16 and 17. We paid $7 a month for our place. An old ceramic studio behind Dutch Darrin's Auto Studio on Santa Monica Boulevard, a block from Barney's Beanery where we all hung out. The mental hospital piece that's in Stockholm's Moderna Muséet... I helped him make that, in the sense of screwing and glueing things together.

As far as money, me and LA is concerned, I had just run away forever from Beverly Hills: the place half the world wants to live in or at least smell or hear about.

Ed's friends, great artists that they were, mostly came from backwater America. I couldn't really blame them for wanting a piece of the pie. American pie. But I already had my fill of it. What these guys did between themselves was perfectly understandable. The fact that they sat down and figured out among themselves that, "We're artists, we're broke, we're going to make it financially and we're not going to depend on some lying art dealers for our future. We are going to work out a process by which we help each other quietly. And we're going to advance that way, very quickly like a Blitzkrieg through the art world." And that was exactly what they did. And that is exactly why I left Los Angeles! I was just a kid and I was watching this bunch of people doing the most fantastic things I had ever seen in my entire life. And they were sitting there plotting how to take these incredible things into a whole other world: the world of money and crooks I had just escaped from. There is nothing wrong with that. It is a business thing that they had to do or they would just die on the vine like grapes in a blistering sun. However, to me, there was no romance in it. 500 miles north, there was a city of romance. I knew about it because I had gone there with my mother and her lover when we weren't visiting Las Vegas, where he was building The Flamingo Hotel and Casino.[1] We used to drive to San Francisco, and that is when I first discovered that the projection of a kind of fairyland was real. I was only eight years old then and I was drawing then in San Francisco. I did some of my first drawings in the bar of the Drake Hotel. The Drake was the "in" place to stay with the Sportsmen crowd when they came to San Francisco. The Drake Hotel is still there; still shiny and fabulous. Those were the days when an eight year old boy could wait all day if he needed to, drawing pictures on the table in the plush leather seats of the Drake Tavern.

— What about the interest in esoteric matters? Where did that come from?

My grandmother was an early member of the Theosophical Society. The Society set up their headquarters organization in Madras, India, and then in other places over time. One was a very beautiful property in Ojai, California, just south of Santa Barbara. They put together beautiful properties and their whole interest was in the esoteric meaning behind metaphysical thought and modern art. I was fully involved with that. There was no religion in any part of my family. We are not genetically or racially religious. My family was not even atheist. However, my grandmother was extraordinarily interested in the question of how this miracle happened. How did we get into this situation? The situation is very simple. We are alive in bodies. If

---

1 Bowen's mother's lover was the iconic underworld entrepreneur Benjamin "Bugsy" Siegel.

that is not a miracle, I do not know what is. It was difficult to attain, because I was not with my grandmother every day. It was hard to get to be with her. I was with her as much as I possibly could from the time I was a baby. I saw things from the point of view of the Gita, the Mahabharata and other literature as a child. Later on in life, I discovered the same things I had discovered already as a baby. It all started to make sense. Sometimes when people write about my work, they call me a "mystic artist." I am not really a mystic anything. I have come to believe that there is something called magic. That is when things happen and everything just is. You can take it apart, have all kinds of ideas about it, and even mystify it. Maybe they should describe me as a mystified artist?

— When were your esoteric interests consciously included in your art?

Usually in times of crisis. Always in times of crisis. There is always crisis. You think everything is going along just smoothly and then some weird crisis comes along. It comes from the left field. During times of crisis, you become more metaphysically oriented or aware. It is like people walking in a daze. They are hit over the head but cannot remember it. It is like amnesia. We do not remember what happened before we took our first gulp of air. Someone took us out of the inside of the body of somebody else. We were mixed together in that alchemical container: the womb. So then, you can get out safely with a little help. You get some air; air that exists around this tiny planet. The planet is like dust. If you look in a telescope, you really see spots of dust called planets and galaxies. On this particular spot of dust that we are living on there is this tiny layer of stuff that we have to gulp right away. The miracle has given me a voice box that has the right bones so I can push my face around so that it pushes the air out again and so that I can make a word. It travels across the space-time across to where your ear is, where another piece of machinery is ready to receive information. It really is very slow.

— But it works.

Art works faster but yes, it works. It works for now. However, it does not work in outer space. When we get off this planet and believe me, brother, we are leaving... As the Tibetan lamas have been telling us for a long time, everything is impermanent. Now we have built machines that go around the earth and have great eyes. It can send us back images and we know that stars are born and stars collapse. We now know that everything is as impermanent as those Tibetan lamas have been telling us for 2500 years and other people too before that. However, no one believed it. The scientific accuracy of it all is that we are living in an impermanent reality. In death, there is oblivion, nothing else. All over. That means that this situation right now cannot be happening. Because what formed it? One can just go on forever like that... Our consciousness is permanent. It is unborn. It has always been there. That thought process ends up in my paintings. You can start that thought process from the simple fact that you have to breathe air outside of a womb, which is created for you to be mixed and grow in. Every single one of us goes through this. So... Here we are. And that's it.

— I agree! While we're on the subject of impermanence... For you as an artist, what has been your main development over the decades? Is it mainly stylistic or having to do with content?

That is a big question for an artist. It's basically saying, "Can you draw better now than when you were nine years old?" It's also saying, "Do you have anything to tell anybody that's more intelligent than when you were 12 years old?" The answer to both questions is no. Nevertheless, there is also a yes, because what happens is that I have become able to get across much better now what I knew was true when I was 14. As far as being able to draw something or build something, the same is true. The more you practice it, the more proficient you become, the more subtle you become and more aware of other people's consciousness. You get better at getting a point across. In my life there are points that stand out. Some are so strange that I hesitate to talk about them. Others are so simple that they sound strange in their simplicity. Here is an example. My life as a child in Beverly Hills was miserable from the point of view of being a child. However, from the point of view of having things like Cadillacs crowd your driveway and people make your clothes by hand and black people who are there to clean your shoes and your house, weed the flower beds... That was the world to me in those days before the new worlds were discovered with their infinite possibilities. The memory, at least when it doesn't wake me screaming as a nightmare, I sometimes call "Long ago in Beverly Hills." Anyway. One warm, hot day I was feeling very alone. More alone than usual. I walked up in the Hollywood Hills and I decided to give myself to the universe. It sounds very childish and simple.

— I think it sounds very mature!

I almost feel embarrassed when I try to relate it now. I went up there. I took off all my clothes. If someone found you naked in those days, you would end up in the madhouse. I lay in the sun and spread my legs and arms out like the da Vinci-drawing. And I gave up. There is not much you can say about that. That was all there was to it. After a while, I got up, got my clothes on and wandered back down to Sunset Boulevard. Then I went back to the house with the black people who were just waiting to do nice things for me. I did not know anything else back then. But it was not long before I discovered jazz and I discovered real black people. I discovered that they actually lived somewhere except on a bus. All I knew was that they got on a bus in the morning and came into Beverly Hills and my house; then later they all walked back to the bus stop and went somewhere. This went on day after day. I escaped with the black people one day on the bus. I had never been on a bus. Somehow, I got to Laurel Canyon and the artists. I was happy about that. I'm still happy about it. Things have changed. However, in an impermanent world, this is to be expected. People are still causing suffering for each other. Unfortunately, they have not realized yet that this is not a good thing to do. Again, we have the Tibetan lamas or the Christian saints or whoever... Saying there is suffering and we all experience that. Why? Let us try to not keep that up. Then you think about peace and what is peaceful and then you read about people hurting each other and causing horrible suffering. This is foolish and unnecessary, and I hope my paintings reflect that. One cannot expect truth to be understood by very many people. Nevertheless, you can project for this to happen. Some of the people who caused suffering for other people are called heroes. This is insane and I try to show this in my art I hope. Other monsters are called saints. It is unfortunate. The least suffering possible is the best thing.

– How much of your work would you say is talismanic?

Every bit of it. But I'm not sitting here making talismans. People keep telling me that they see something new all the time. The most common thing I hear from people that have my work is that it changes all the time. People see things and they ask me about things that are talismanic. Many people have for some reason found something in my work that they happen to have experienced. They feel they have a bond with the picture. They feel that something is living in the picture. Moreover, these people are not crazy. They ask me what it means. If it is of any help in understanding my work you can know that I am very familiar with tarot cards. My mentor John Starr Cooke taught me about the real esoteric aspects of tarot, beginning in 1960.[2] I can see that in my work. When one uses a tarot deck, one is trying to get some kind of answer from the cards. That is not why I paint pictures. Nevertheless, it is the same thing in a way. When people come to me with questions that are really for the tarot that puts me in a kind of spot. I definitely do not want to be anybody's guru. The only thing I want to be against is suffering.

– The tarot is a very systematized and esthetic tool. Art and paintings affect through esthetics. Do you think the human mind needs to be opened up by, for instance, art in order to be able to perceive something higher and/or deeper?

Definitely. When there's a war usually the first thing that happens is that the art is protected so that it doesn't get blown up or broken or stolen. Why does anyone protect the art that's on cave walls? Because it's valuable to us. It's the key to the unconscious and, beyond that, to the "connective" unconscious. Jung was a very smart dude with his collective unconscious, and he was close to coming up with the connective unconscious. As a race and through machinery we're developing a connective unconscious. Computers and the Internet are parts of that. It's a precursor to the connective consciousness, where you have accurate communication. It's much faster to go from brain to brain. Ingo Swann is an interesting guy in that respect. Uri Geller is another guy I know from correspondence. To a degree, we communicate. He does not fully know yet what is happening to him. It is all coming about and it has to do with evolution. We are evolving because the life-force wants to survive. Lamas and other people have known the truth for a long time. In fact, in the 60s a bunch of hippies knew the truth. They told the truth but they were weird so nobody wanted to believe them. 30 years later, it is a different story. I illustrated a magazine 30 years ago telling exactly what is going to happen to the planet if we don't stop screwing it up. Now we are at the point where they're all hysterical about climate change. They should have listened to the freaks back then! The people didn't act or look like the average people so they just didn't believe them. The life-force definitely wants to continue on, so it's building escape pods. That's what the space process is all about. The Internet is another thing. Remember Benjamin Franklin and his experiments with conducting electricity. My friend John Lilly experimented with implants in the brain. The scientists back then did not care about how the monkeys suffered during the experiments they conducted. Lilly developed a painless way of inserting implants in their brains. It is all part of a gigantic life-force attempt to maintain itself and to live. Life is a very wonderful

---

2 John Starr Cooke (1920-1976), an American spiritual teacher and magician.

thing. It is very groovy. Suffering or no suffering, it is just very groovy. The way it is moving right now is that there is a lot of fear among people deep in their psyche. People have fear because they did not believe the freaks. They did not listen to the people they should have listened to. Now, they have to catch up. My paintings are about that too. People should carefully pay attention to my paintings. They should examine the stimulation they experience and they should activate their own creative power.

– All of the things you've been involved in – the Beat thing, the flower power thing – these were all movements, leaving things and traces for people to catch later… One couldn't demand at the time that everyone shouldimmediately get it. Everyone wasn't on acid, for example.

You did not have to use the drug. It was more a question of sympathetic feelings. Of feeling for other sufferers. Flowers are among the most beautiful things that this planet produces. Yes, I did call press conferences and we were facing the dilemma of how to tell these hardened reporters about this next thing that is going to be really impossible for them to understand… We were not going to demonstrate against things we hated. We were going to celebrate life. But they were never going to understand that. The only way to do it was by using a different strategy. I had a press conference set in San Francisco, about the "Human Be-In." What to do? One beautiful morning after a fun, playful night I woke up. The sun came through the window and it hit a little flower that someone had put in a little glass. It was absolutely the most exquisite thing I'd ever seen. Then I knew immediately what to do. We got as much money together as we could. We all went out and got as many flowers as we could. The people from my house came back with bushels of flowers. When the press conference came, all these cynical, hardened reporters came up to Haight Street. There were so many beautiful girls there, their arms full of flowers. They were placing them everywhere. Every reporter was handed some flowers. What are you going to do? You see these hippies and you do not know where their heads are at. So you suddenly have these flowers in one hand and your notebook in the other… The whole room smelled so magnificently. It was just an incredible weapon of love. That did it. The reporters wrote about "flower power" and about how dumb these fools were. However, what they did not realize was that they were doing what we wanted them to do. Then there was that other photo with flowers going down the rifle barrels. I had gotten $500 worth of daisies in Washington, DC. There was a terrible war; millions were killed. That was the point of the demonstrations in general: to protest. Soldiers were treated really badly. I observed all that during the war. I hated to see it. Due to a complete accident, I found myself in a position of responsibility in Washington at the demonstration. We had done it in San Francisco with the flowers, so I thought we should do it here too. I thought those rows of soldiers with their guns half-ready would make an awfully nice place to put some flowers in the rifle barrels. It reminded me of that morning in San Francisco when I was sitting in my room and watching that flower. I was living in Mexico after the Human Be-In and didn't expect to come back up to the States. But I did. I managed to get Peggy Hitchcock give me the money to buy the flowers. She sympathized with it and understood it. I dragged them up there. It was just me trying to figure out what to do. We dragged the flowers up through the huge crowd in front of the Pentagon. I was able to hand them out and that was how it happened.

— Hitchcock was quite a benefactor for the early psychedelicists; very much so for Timothy Leary. Did you also hang out at Hitchcock's Millbrook estate?

Leary was a tricky guy. He was a scientist, and at the time, everything was legal. LSD and other synthetic substances were legal all over the world then. I was not up at Millbrook because of that though. I had my studio in New York and I visited some other friends up there. One of them was Peter Fonda, the actor. Leary asked us if we would like to try this substance. Both Peter and I said sure. He gave us small shot glasses of whisky and evidently, he had put some LSD in there. Peter and I are sitting there in this beautiful big room, comfortable. It's around lunch time and I'm hungry. Tim came by and watched us laugh and talk about Beverly Hills and Bel-Air. I mentioned that I was hungry and Leary said he'd be right back. He comes back with a tray with bowls of alphabet soup. By that time, I was not seeing or hearing things as I normally do. There were sounds within sounds within sounds and colors and people were echoing when they were talking. The murals had beautiful hunt scenes because Millbrook was an old mansion and the horses came alive. I was suddenly in 16th century Europe. In addition, we'd just been talking about Beverly Hills. Leary had served us both alphabet soup. You can imagine... The soup was spelling out all kinds of different things... It was quite interesting. To say the least!

— You've moved around a great deal. Is that necessary for you, inspiration-wise? What kind of inspiration are you finding here in Sweden?

Do I need to move around to be able to work? The answer is yes, I do. As the years go by in this body I find I need to move more and more. I also love children. I'm much older than my wife, almost 38 years older than her. We wanted a baby. She saved my life. I had a heart attack from smoking too many stupid cigarettes. She saved my life a year or so after we first met. They fixed me up in the hospital in San Francisco. I was happy that I wasn't living in the jungle then. She told me that she wanted to have a baby. I didn't give it a second thought; I just said "OK, sure." We had our baby in San Francisco. My wife comes from Florence and we wanted to go back to Europe. We gave up our place in San Francisco which was very hard for me to do. But off to Florence we went. Florence is one of the most beautiful places in the world. Moving is very important for me, even if it's within the same city. Moving around the world is my way of life. After you've done it for so long, I guess it becomes your way of life.

Bob Colacello, 2007

Bob Colacello

"We believed in the blurring of those boundaries."

"Like a mother whose worst nightmare is an empty nest, Andy wanted his kids to be popular but unloved, confident but insecure, to be the life of the party but not upstage him. The contradictions compounded until it was very hard to know which Andy wanted more: success or control."[1] (Bob Colacello)

"I loved working when I worked at commercial art and they told you what to do and how to do it and all you had to do was correct it and they'd say yes or no. The hard thing is when you have to dream up the tasteless things to do on your own. When I think about what sort of person I would most like to have on a retainer, I think it would be a boss. A boss who could tell me what to do, because that makes everything easy when you're working."[2] (Andy Warhol, ghostwritten by Bob Colacello)

When *Interview Magazine* editor and excellent writer Bob Colacello's amazing photo book *Out* was published in 2007, I called him in New York to talk about it, and about his times at Andy Warhol's legendary "Factory." Colacello's own Warhol biography, *Holy Terror – Andy Warhol Close Up* (1990), is definitely my favorite retelling of the Factory saga. Not only because Colacello was a first hand witness – at least in the second/final phase of the Factory – but because of his ability to write cultural history in such a great, detailed and entertaining way.

Other Colecello projects have been *Ronnie and Nancy: Their Path to the White House, 1911-1980* (2004), and *It Just Happened – Photographs by Bob Colacello 1976–*

1 Colacello, Bob, *Holy Terror – Andy Warhol Close Up*, Cooper Square Press, New York, 2000, p. 283-284.
2 Andy Warhol, *The Philosophy of Andy Warhol: From A to B and Back Again*, Harvest/HBJ, New York, 1977, p 96.

1982 (2020), plus a long line of portrait articles for *Vanity Fair* (of high profile people like Prince Charles, Ivana Trump, Rudolf Nurejev, Naomi Campbell and Estée Lauder, to mention but a few).

Colacello's outspoken political conservatism has made him a bona fide "radical" within environments that usually perceive themselves as being... radical. Be that as it may or may not, one thing remains indisputable: Bob Colacello is a very gifted writer, and one that has that magical ability to be at the right place at the right time.

Where work at the Factory *Interview Magazine* office was a daily grind (with many surprises), the work with Colecello's own column "Out" became a nightly adventure of excess, fun and many snapshots. In a sense, Colecello diligently collected more material than he could immediately use for his gossip column at the time. In memories, notes, and photographs, he wove his own tapestry of American culture that later on resurfaced as biographies, articles and photo books.

Where someone like Richard Avedon tried his damndest to create iconographic studio portraits of key American movers and shakers more or less wholly on his own terms — and in some ways encouraging revealing weaknesses — Bob Colacello just happily snapped away in unguarded moments of celebration and joy at restaurants, clubs and private parties. It's a different way of writing history, but certainly no less valuable than the structured approaches of American masters like Avedon and Irving Penn. A mosaic of minor moments morph into major myths, if you will.

The kind of casual party photography that Colacello somewhat unknowingly excelled at was also mastered by Andy Warhol himself early on. His documentation frenzy/mania was unparallelled, and absolutely constituted a taste of what was to come later in our own contemporary smartphone camera snaps and selfies. In many ways, Colacello learned on the job, and this was certainly the case with the photography too.

In *Out*, there is a sublimely casual attitude that in a way also predates our own times: if you have a celebrity in front of your camera, you can't go wrong. If a person is glamorous in him/herself, you can't really take a "bad" picture. But it's not just the unguarded moments of apparent inebriation (such as the photo of Bianca Jagger and Mark Shand, with eyelids half shut) that create this immediate poetry: one image that is equally revealing is one of Andy Warhol at a hotel room in Naples, munching on a piece of breakfast bread, and looking exhausted. This is also an unguarded moment that is documented from within the bubble. But also, through the contextualized book form and exhibition, (re)presented as a brick in a building housing an overall memory cluster that keeps feeding the spirit(s) of celebrity.

— Are all the photos in the *Out* book from vintage prints or were they scanned from negatives?

They're from vintage prints.

— Once the project as such had materialized, were you happy about it or reluctant?

It wasn't like I was hiding the images. I left the Factory in 1983 and started writing for Vanity Fair in 1984. In 1990 I published my memoir of working with Andy Warhol: *Holy Terror*. At that point, Mary Boone Gallery organized a little show of these photographs. Maybe 24 of the images. We actually sold half of them; mostly to people who were in the images. Then I just forgot about them. The half I didn't sell Mary had framed beautifully. I put them in storage and that was that. When I was proposed doing this book, which was actually four years ago, I said fine, but I didn't really want it to appear before I published the first volume of the biography of Ronald and Nancy Reagan. I had been working seven years on this biography and I thought that perhaps people would then take me a bit more seriously, because it's about a president and first lady instead of pop cultural figures. Although you could say that Ronald Reagan was our first pop president. Anyway, I wanted to put the photo book off until after Reagan volume one came out. That came out in the fall of 2004, and I got very good reviews. They said it was a very good book from an unexpected corner, from a former *Interview* editor and party reporter... I knew that in the mainstream press they still don't get that you can be interested in both pop culture and be serious. They still don't get the fact that Andy Warhol was serious. My association with him is something that I'll always both cherish and regret at the same time. I have very mixed feelings about it. I think one always has mixed feelings about the past. We decided to look at the book again, after the Reagan book. I thought it was fun. Why not just go with it?

— How has it been received so far?

It's been very well received. They don't really review coffee table books that much. I haven't really seen any reviews yet. But in general, everywhere we've had book signings people seem to just love it. It's selling really well. All the major newspapers in the UK have run photos and interviews. In France too. We've sold serial right too, even to the Greek version of *Marie-Claire*! It's a time that has a glamorous aura about it. There has been a lot done about that time with several picture books. But

I think this is the first one where the pictures were taken by someone who was really in the middle of things. All the pictures are three feet away. I didn't know how to focus the camera if I had to go too far away. I wasn't taking these pictures like a professional photographer. I was just there. I was taking them as a friend. Like the editor of the school newspaper.

— A very good school! Now that you're surfing on this wave of attention, could you consider doing another volume? Is there more stuff among the negatives?

There are at least another 250 vintage prints, probably 3-400. We didn't even look at the contact sheets yet. This is all like a sideline for me. I don't have that much time to give it. But if the book does well and if Steidl want it, I would be open to doing *Bob Colacello's Out 2*, or *Out Again*, or *Bob Colacello's In*.

— When looking at the pictures, people seem to be very open and consenting. There seems to be an allround, funky party mood. Was that a general attitude or was it because it was you taking the pictures?

I think it was because it was me taking the pictures. People didn't suddenly go into a pose or stop doing what they were doing. The attitude that the pictures capture is a kind of carefree, relaxed, open attitude. It was real. It was what the times were about. I think the introduction in the book captures some idea of that hope. First of all, we were all young. There were of course people like Diana Vreeland who were not so young, but they had a young attitude, and who had lived, in the 1950s and 60s, on the forefront of this new openness. The counter-cultural revolution, the sexual revolution and the whole hippie thing, the whole feminist thing, the whole gay thing... All of that was something that had been boiling for a while. In the 1970s all of it boiled over. The pot exploded and we, who were then only in our 20s had the benefit of enjoying the spoils of the battle that the previous generations had fought for us. We had it pretty easy. We were the first generation where you had almost universal affluence, universal college education and universal freedom. Women were liberated by the birth control pill, we were all liberated by penicillin and other drugs that made sexually transmitted diseases easy to cure. AIDS hadn't come along yet. AIDS is what I think really put an end to this era.

— Was it because it was such a mysterious thing at the time or because it hit so hard?

It was very mysterious. It was a disease that gay men in particular seemed to be getting. For years, people were referring to it as "gay cancer." By the mid 1980s, we knew what it was, and it was very frightening. It hit the people who had been most promiscuous first. It took away the feeling that you didn't have to worry. Anything goes… It was really sad because so many creative people died so young. It hit the art-, fashion- and literary worlds the hardest. It hit the places hard where there are these kinds of creative worlds that I describe in my book.

— The ambience at, say, Studio 54 seems to have been quite democratic. The high and the low got together and had a good time. Do you think that *Interview* was a trendsetting force in this sense?

Yes, *Interview* was a trendsetting force. Andy Warhol was a trendsetting force. One has to remember that New York is different from almost all other American cities. It's not dominated by one business. It's not dominated by film, like Los Angeles. It's not a city where old society dominates, like Boston. New York has always been a city of many businesses and there's always new money coming in. New York City is the capital of finance, art, theater, fashion. You also have the publishing industry. There are so many elements that make up New York. It was easier in New York for this kind of mix. I think that both Andy Warhol himself and *Interview Magazine* promoted the idea of mixing high and low, uptown and downtown, gay and straight, black and white. We believed in the blurring of those boundaries or borders or differences.

— Did you ever run into trouble because of the photos or "Out" as a column?

The photos only go so far. No one is really seen taking cocaine or having sex. That wasn't my thing. Where we ran into trouble with *Interview* and also at the Factory with some of the films, like "Women in revolt," which made fun of the feminist movement, was with the Left. The Left and the the gay liberation movement and the feminists felt that we weren't identifying strongly enough with those movements. In San Francisco, the gay bars didn't allow any women to come in. In New York, it was just the opposite. We thought it was great that women wanted to go to gay bars. In the art world, there was a also a sense that artists shouldn't spend so much time with the rich clients. Why was *Interview Magazine* giving so much space to what we called the "Millionettes," the heirs and heiresses, and not to young artists? That was maybe a legitimate criticism. But Andy and *Interview* were all about glamour. We were drawn to beautiful people and glamorous people. In that sense, it was very elitist and probably not so democratic. I'm a royalist at heart personally. My grandmother came from a middle class family in Naples. I don't think anyone's more royalist than middle class people from Naples.

— That's another interesting question. You've approached many elevated social stratospheres through your work. Is there one specific group or class or even nationality that's been less friendly and benevolent to your work than the others?

Not really. It's always been the Left. Putting Nancy Reagan on the cover of *Interview Magazine* in 1981 was a big controversy, almost a scandal within the art world. Someone did a parody of our interview with Nancy Reagan in *The Village Voice*, which had Andy and I interviewing Hitler in his bunker. I was accused of being some kind of agent because I arranged for Andy to do the portrait of the Shah of Iran. But he also made portraits of Golda Meir and Willy Brandt. It wasn't like I was forcing Andy to turn right. Andy was a stalwart liberal democrat. He said to me, "How can you be a Republican? Didn't Franklin Roosevelt help your family during the depression?" I said, "No, he didn't. Italian-Americans don't believe in taking welfare. Not like you Slovakians..." We would joke about it. Even today, the art world and the people at *Vanity Fair* can't understand how I can be a Republican. I'm a Republican because you're not allowed to be a Republican in this particular world. I think it takes more courage to be openly Republican than to be openly gay in New York today. Bush has completely destroyed the Republican party.

— In *Holy Terror*, you describe the incredibly intense lifestyle that you had during this era, with Stolichnaya Vodka and Cocaine as preferred fuel. What do you do to have fun today? Is your quota of excessive fun filled?

I stopped drinking and taking drugs more than 13 years ago. For me, it's just another phase. My idea of having fun now is filing and clipping. I read four newspapers at night and I clip about half of them. The next morning I put them in the files about all the people I might write about. I have my own personal little CIA operation... I have a lot of young friends and I just enjoy life. I don't think you have to be drunk or high to enjoy life. I have very mixed feelings about having spent so much time taking drugs. Cocaine in particular. Marijuana makes you lazy and insecure. Cocaine certainly releases one's sexual inhibitions. After a while that becomes too much of a good thing.

— If you hadn't been given this original opportunity to jump on board at *Interview*, what do you think that you'd be doing today?

I was on my way to becoming a pretty successful film critic. *The Village Voice's* Andrew Sarris had published at least a dozen of my reviews, and the *New York Times* asked if I didn't want to review for them. By then I was already too wrapped up in *Interview*. I think I would have gone in a more political direction. I would perhaps have ended up an ambassador. That's what I started out studying: International Affairs.

— Well, you certainly had a period when you were very active internationally and meeting a lot of diplomats…

I'm more fascinated by heads of state or cabinet ministers than I am by movie stars or rock stars. I'd much rather meet Juan Carlos of Spain or Angela Merkel than Angelina Jolie and Brad Pitt.

— Do you think it has to do with the fact that those you mentioned first wield real, tangible power?

Yes. They have power and they affect our lives. Movie stars have a lot of power too, and the media have a lot of power. But I think it'd be more interesting to have a conversation with people who are actually running governments and know what is going on than with Hollywood stars who think they know what's going on. Popular culture is not what it used to be. It's even a bit too popular for me. It's become so low. Everything has been reduced to the lowest possible common denominator. That's a trend that Warhol predicted and encouraged. I have mixed feelings about my involvement with that. The best interview he ever did was in Sweden in 1968, when he had the exhibition at Moderna Muséet. He said, "In the future everyone will be famous for 15 minutes…" In the end, he also promoted this media take-over of the world, which has led to fame becoming the highest value rather than any kind of accomplishment. It's about becoming famous in any way you can. If you murder someone, you're famous. If you make a porn movie, you're famous. I think we're in the final stages of the Roman Empire. I think Western civilization is committing suicide. It's just a matter of time before the barbarians come crashing through the gates. They believe in something, and we don't.

– That's a valid point. If you really believe in something – religion, philosophy or whatever – it makes you more focused. The culture that we live in today is completely fragmented.

You can blame the liberal media and liberal academics for that, because they have really destroyed our common beliefs in Greco-Roman civilisation. The classics aren't really taught, and if they are taught they're deconstructed to make feminist and gay points. It's ridiculous, absurd and nobody wants to say it. All common sense is gone.

– The era of *Interview Magazine* was of course long and intense. Is it possible for you to answer what the best thing about working there was?

The best thing about working at *Interview* and for Andy was that he allowed me to learn on the job. To make things up as I went along. The incredible variety of people we met and covered. It was a great education. I was lucky I didn't have to social climb. I arrived everywhere with Andy. You flew right to the top with Andy. In Paris you went to the Rothschilds; in Rome you went to the Agnellis. I had an education as a journalist when still very young. There was a time when I was more impressed by movie stars and rock stars. Having lunch and dinner with Mick Jagger or Jack Nicholson, with Deborah Harry, Bette Midler... The experiences were endless. And I edited Truman Capote! Hanging out with old movie stars, like Paulette Goddard. It was all too incredible. Going to Jimmy Carter's White House, and Ronald Reagan's White House, as a VIP guest. All of this before I was 35 years old. I have a lot to be grateful to Andy for. But I also know, as I say to my young friends today, that I can open the door for you but you have to enter the room yourself. I give Andy credit for opening the doors, but I have to give myself credit for being invited back.

– You said that you were learning on the job. Did you have any role models in terms of writing when you realized that you were going to be stuck at this great job?

Diana Vreeland became a role model. I didn't even realize in the 1960s that I'd be clipping pages out of *Vogue*. I wasn't sure who Diana Vreeland was then. She always said to me, "Bob, the job of a magazine editor is not to give people what they want but to give people what they don't know they want, yet." Her philosophy was to constantly surprise the reader. That also became my philosophy. It still is. That's why I thought it was great to put Nancy Reagan on the cover. It was a shock. I think that's what you have to do with a monthly magazine. You can't fall into a formula. Once it becomes a formula and people know exactly what they're going to get every month, it's bound to start going downhill. Even before I met Andy I felt that he was very much, especially in his films, in a line of decadent French, homosexual writers. Writers who I admired in my late high school years, starting with Rimbaud, Verlaine, Baudelaire, Lautréamont, Gide, Cocteau, and certainly Proust and Genet. I said this in my review of the film "Trash" at Columbia University, that it was very much in the line of Genet's "Our lady of the flowers." They quite consciously were playing up the Mary Magdalene-side of Catholicism. It's an idea that we Catholics have: that everyone can be redeemed, no matter how bad the sin. You can still be redeemed, the Church says, through penance and religion. But for someone like Genet it was through literature. For Andy it was through his art and through his films. Andy was redeeming these hustlers and junkies and transvestites through the act of turning them into superstars. Which is another way of saying "Saints." Andy's work was always about creating icons, in the actual religious sense.

— That's very overt in the "Screen Tests."

Yes, they were an almost entirely iconographic form of cinema. Everything I've always done has been a form of portraiture. I consider my profiles for *Vanity Fair* miniature biographies. My goal is to make household names into human beings in a way, for better or worse. Fortunately, *Vanity Fair* gives me the time and money so I can travel and do a lot of research, and for that I'm grateful too.

— Someone should really anthologize all the *Vanity Fair* pieces.

No American publisher has thought of that yet. I guess I'll have to push my agent a bit. Dominick Dunne writes more about American things, and my work is more international. Maybe that makes it a bit more obscure to Americans. I don't know.

— Is it possible for you to pick out one single, most outrageous memory that belongs in the OUT category? What was the most outrageous thing that happened?

Oh, God... The most outrageous thing that ever happened to me, actually happened a couple of years ago. Damien Hirst showed me his foreskin because he wanted to show that it was the longest foreskin.

— Was that the case?

I don't know... I haven't compared that many! In America, we believe in circumcision. But back in those days... It could have been almost any night... Betty Ford and Martha Graham sitting at Halston's house while we all ran in and out of the bathroom back and forth, taking cocaine. They were completely oblivious to what was going on. It all seemed kind of innocent at the time. The 1970s was the innocent age of our decadent era. Or the innocent beginnings of our great decadence. The first time I saw Robert Mapplethorpe's sadomasochistic photographs I was shocked. I thought they were outrageous. Cathy Guinness hung one of them on the wall next to her desk at the *Interview* office. But what I really think is outrageous is people taking Barbra Streisand seriously, politically. Unfortunately, we've almost become un-shockable, and that's what's really sad. Paris Hilton's parents attending CZ Guest's funeral the same week as their daughter's porn tape popped up. That was an outrageous moment of the early 21st century to me. I think I'm too conservative for our time.

— Are you still taking pictures?

No. The other day, I tried to take a picture with a friend's digital camera at a party. I hated it. You're not really taking the image you think you're taking. It's four seconds later. There's a delayed reaction and by that time, people have moved. You get a different picture than the one you wanted. I don't think I really want to take digital pictures. I don't have the patience to walk around with batteries and film. I like the idea of having been a part-time amateur photographer and getting paid for it 20 years later. I love writing, and am so far behind in my Vanity Fair obligations and my second Reagan book. I would like to try writing a novel. I think photography would be too much of a distraction. Writing is my main mission.

— Would you say that the book is filled with predominantly happy memories?

Definitely. But there's an underlying sadness when I go through it because so many people are gone. Not only people who died at an old age. There are also many people who died way before they should have, including two of my closest friends ever in life: Thomas Ammann, who died more than ten years ago at age 44, and Claudia Cohen, to whom I dedicated the book. She died only two months before the book was published.

Different People

— Thomas Ammann bought you the Minox camera you used to take these pictures.

That's right. But that's life. As you get older you realize that happiness is fleeting, but sadness is too. You just keep going.

Dian Hanson, 2007

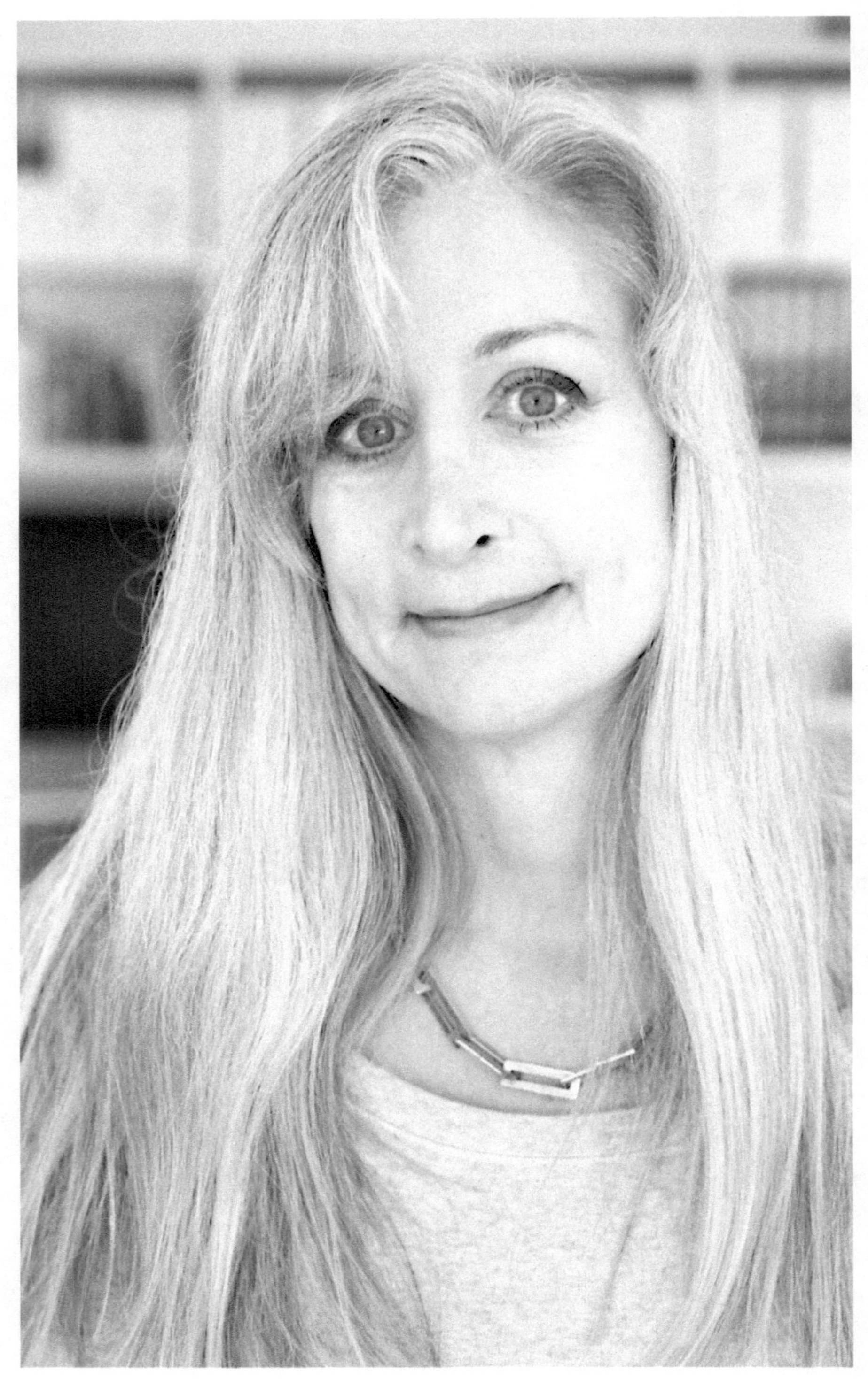

Dian Hanson

"The breast is timeless."

I can't properly recall the details on how I first got in touch with Dian Hanson, Taschen's mighty editrix of Sexy Books. She was always there in the perimeter or grey area between art and sex; often inviting cool and "arty" photographers to shoot stuff for "her" 1990s magazines and projects like *Juggs* and *Leg Show*. Intelligent publisher Benedikt Taschen eventually wooed her over to his amazing empire of crossover culture, and a formidable array of erotic art books started spurting out over an unsuspecting planet. When Dian Hanson puts her mind to something, it will become a very good thing; and that seems true for most things Taschen, too.

Dian Hanson has consistently put together fantastic books that have not only shone the light on a particular photographer or artsist; they have also helped bridge the gap between the "high" and the "low," by contextualizing whatever it is in a distinctly human and cultural setting. Whether it's dust-ridden and kitschy men's magazines, anthologies of big butts, breasts or penises, or classy reissues of Swedish pioneering *Private* porn magazines, or monographs about porn stars like Vanessa del Rio, etc, etc, it's all done in supremely good and contextualizing taste. Taschen in general, and Hanson in particular, ultimately help to de-stigmatize sexual cultures otherwise left to dwindle in the sordid and ill-lit sections of history's own adult store. In many ways, she is a splendid history writer simply by her sharp focus and skillful editing.

In the early 2000s, I was asked if I could write something about the history of Scandinavian porn magazines for her massive six volume series *The History of Men's Magazines*. Which of course I did ("The Swedish Sin" in Volume 4 and "Sweden's Berth of Hardcore" in Volume 6). It was not only fun to research and write, but also great to be published by Taschen.

In 2007, I visited Dian Hanson at the Taschen compound in Los Angeles. This is what we talked about.

— How many of the project ideas come from you?

Probably half. Benedikt always has strong ideas about his books and what he wants. We don't ever do a book that Benedikt Taschen doesn't like. He especially has strong opinions about the sex books. They're not the giant sellers that everyone thinks they are. It's hard to get these kinds of books into stores. We often have to rely on things like amazon.com and other online sources, so often it's hard for people to actually see the books first. They can't actually pick them up. Sex books have always been something that we do because we want to do them. Benedikt likes them. He makes enough money on his other books that he can indulge himself with precisely the kinds of books he wishes.

— So half of it all, ideas-wise, comes from you and the other half from him?

People come to me with proposals or I discover things out in the world or online. I bring ideas to Benedikt. He probably shoots down 90% of what I bring to him. But that's good. I have more than 13 books that I'm working on right now. He will also come to me sometimes, like he did with *The History of Men's Magazines*. That originated from him. He said, "Do this and cover the entire world." The more daunting projects come from Benedikt. When I think up a project, it's something I'll be able to do. Benedikt will think up something that seems completely undoable. Somehow I manage to get it out.

— Which of all the projects so far has been the most successful one?

The Big Book of Breasts. We're just going into our third printing and the book only came out in October. It's been a phenomenal success.

— Does that say anything about the times we live in?

It has nothing to do with the times we live in now, but rather the times we have lived in since the dawn of time. Particularly the times we've lived in since World War 2. When I first started this project, a lot of people were saying that it was too old fashioned and that modern guys aren't into big breasts like they used to be. I knew they were wrong. The breast is timeless. What was set in motion during the Depression and the depravation, and then the following devastation of World War 2... The desire for that maternal warmth and nurturing has not gone away.

— Which project has been the most satisfying for you on a personal level?

I worked so long and so hard on the six volume *History of Men's Magazines*. That's the one I got to know the best. I put the most energy into it. There was more satisfaction perhaps but also more frustration and more angst and more everything. For personal reasons, my favorite project is the book on Vanessa del Rio that we're bringing out in the spring. She's a friend of mine. She was one of the first women I met in the adult industry in 1976. I've run into her off and on through the years. We've become friends and she's a woman unlike any other woman I've ever met. When people say she's the greatest porn star people don't really know what they're talking about. They will find out in this book what Vanessa the woman is really like. She is the male fantasy of a woman. The fantasy that most men recognize as only a fantasy. There are no women like this. But Vanessa del Rio is that woman. She loves sex and will pursue men for sex. She's even paid cab drivers to pull over at a motel and have sex with her. Not because they were so good looking or hunky but just because she was horny. Even when she was young, she'd go with 50-year old cab drivers just because she needed some sex. A woman who made loops back in the 1970s for $40 a film because she loved the sex. She is phenomenal. She still has that personality. She's a very funny woman. A warm and down to earth woman. She's not only a survivor but a thriver. She's been happy all along and has been doing well all along because of her life choices.

— How come you drifted into the world of adult publishing in the first place?

I was interested in pornography from an early age... My first glimpses of my father's copies of *Playboy*. I found his stash of more explicit magazines behind the furnace when I was 10 or 11. I was always fascinated with the human body. I would always draw women's breasts even before I'd seen any bare breasts. I could see that women had these things sticking out. This was in the late 1950s and early 60s when breasts were a big deal. Bras were very pointy. I wondered what was in there. I would draw what I imagined. My father was a house nudist so I knew what that looked like. I was always fascinated by the parts of the body that you were supposed to keep covered. In the 1960s I came into my teens. I was having my own sexual experimentation during the sexual revolution. It perfectly dovetailed with my needs. At the same time I was a very unpopular, bullied child who was miserable in school. I was mistreated by my classmates. I was very tall and thin and weird-looking. My family was weird. We ate health food. The children try to push the bird who isn't like the other birds out of the nest. I was one of those birds. When I discovered sex with older men it was a salvation for me. Here were people who liked me, who were attracted to me, who'd chase after me. My fellows in school despised me. Sex gave me hope in life. It gave me a reason to hang on until I could get out of school. When I turned 18, I started buying pornography. I ended up in Pennsylvania through a series of events. I met someone who was doing publicity for a man who owned some adult bookstores. I was interested and curious. This man wanted to start a magazine. I was more than eager to quit my job and work for the magazine, called *Puritan*. That took us to New York and led to everything else.

— Do you have warm memories from the *Puritan* days?

Not a bit. The guy who started Puritan was my boyfriend and he was very abusive. He was an idiot. He couldn't get the magazine done. He had energy but no editorial skills. And completion anxiety. It took a year to get the first issue out. He spent all the money and it took another year before the second issue came out. It was just ridiculous. I learned nothing then about what real publishing was. My mentor in this business was a man called Peter Wolf. I worked with him on *Partner Magazine* and *Cinema X Magazine* and *Oui*. My years working for him were wonderful years. I learned everything. *Leg Show* was definitely my big magazine. I was allowed to do anything I wanted there and that's why it was such a big success.

— Then you were within the boundaries of adult publishing. Here, you're looking at it. How come you took that step?

I always loved magazines and I wanted to work with them all of my life. However, the man I worked for doing *Leg Show* and *Juggs* died in 1999, suddenly and unexpectedly. Well, he did weigh 300 pounds so everyone knew it was coming. He was an entrepreneur and had left nothing in place to run the company. A brother, a retired construction worker, came from Canada and sort of inherited the company. They threw out the vice president — the one woman who would have known how to run things. It just all began to go to Hell. I stayed on for a year, trying to help them run the company seven days a week, ten hours every day, completely exhausting myself. They also brought in some completely inappropriate people and just tried to milk the company and launder some money. At that point I knew it was time to get out. Benedikt Taschen had been a big fan of *Leg Show* for a number of years. He had been trying to get me come work for him for a number of years. I always knew that Benedikt was going to be the future. It was a hard transition. I was very worried in the beginning that I was going to have to change my style of writing and change my style of relating to things, to make art books as opposed to pornography. I didn't have to change all that much. I just had to change my confidence about what I was doing. I feel very at ease with books now. I find this amazing.

— Is there any competition at all?

Just as with the magazines, I never look at the competition. I will go into stores and see what's being published but I don't think of it as being competition. I think that if one is dissecting other people's work, one gets distracted from one's own vision. I know what's going to do well and Benedikt knows what he likes. We bring these two things together. I feel I have a good understanding of the market and how to tailor a book for the market. I know what men want. We do have books that women like. Certainly *The Big Book of Breasts* is one that women buy. I'm always thinking of the male market when I'm making these books. I never fool myself and think that a book will appeal to everyone. Men and women are different. Their treatment of sexual material is different.

— Do you have an idea about who the typical customer is?

No. I know with each book who's likely to buy it. Unlike what some people think, it's not an entirely different audience from the people who buy the magazines. I hear from my old *Leg Show* fans all the time. And from my *Juggs* fans. They discover where I'm at through buying the books. People who want to get a magazine to masturbate to and people who want to get a book to look at and appreciate are the same person. People have multifaceted lives. They're interested in sex and they're interested in sex. It doesn't mean that they need to treat all sexual material the same way.

— Do you have a dream project?

Oh, I don't want to say it because Benedikt will read this and then make me do it. I have a project that I'm starting on now that I really wanted to do but Benedikt didn't. It's one of the few cases where I really begged and said: "Please, Benedikt, please, please, please..." He kindly acquiesced. I think it can become a really great book. It's about American swingers. A young woman who's a really excellent photographer has been going around for four years to swing parties and photographing these people in action. It's all in the South and the Midwest; it's the Bible Belt of America. Here are these people who are fat and old and middle aged. Everyone's idea of the un-esthetic, ugly American just exuberantly exposing themselves having sex, prancing around in high heels and sexy clothes and guys in thongs with sequins on them. Their happiness with sex is the complete opposite of what the American porn industry puts forth. Here's the fantasy of sex in America, the porn industry, and here's the reality. People who are not full of fear and anxiety about being perfect. They're very, very happy people. I'm really looking forward to interviewing these people and giving the world a picture of this secret world that exists everywhere, in every little town of America.

— From the point of view of you as a very powerful editor, do you ever think about how the book will affect people?

Of course they're affected. Everything around us affects us. I love cookbooks and can look at the pictures and salivate and fantasize about making a dish or eating it. I think sex books are the same thing. People can go through for instance *The Big Book of Breasts* and see women they perhaps saw in a magazine when they were fifteen years old. Some of the women from the 1950s, 60s and 70s who had a powerful effect on them then. They see them again in the book and are transported back to their feeling of wonder and discovery and innocence. That's what I'm hearing from people. I knew this was going to be the effect. I edited *Juggs* for 15 years. At the same time I was doing *Leg Show*. The *Juggs* fans were just as rabidly attached to the subject matter as the *Leg Show* fans. I know there's a power in the breast that doesn't exist in any other part of the body. It not only stimulates us sexually but also our feelings of being loved, nurtured, of being cared for by the mother. When men looked at the print-outs we had from the book, the breasts had the same effect on them all. Their eyes bulged out and it's like going straight into the primitive brain. They don't know whether they're horny or if they want to curl up in the lap and be rocked and comforted. I'm very happy to have an effect like that. I never paid $50-100 for an art book. Who's willing to cough up all this money? It's a person who knows they'll be going back to the book over and over again and get an effect. If they didn't get an effect from the book they wouldn't spend that money. Since I'm a kindly person, I want them to have good feelings. I want them to have that feeling of wonder and warmth and reminiscence.

— Do you think Taschen has helped people overcome inhibitions in terms of getting this kind of material?

They certainly say so. We get lots of messages from people who say that the openness with which Taschen presents sex has helped them to accept themselves. We publish books on foot fetishism, wrestling and areas that are sources of shame for people. We're just about to publish a book with a man called Ed Fox, the successor to Elmer Batters. A very talented young man who loves feet in the same cavernous way that Batters loved feet. He presents them beautifully. I discovered him at *Leg Show*. I know that somebody who photographs the subject matter so well and with such obvious love for the subject himself makes people feel better about it. We do a service with these kinds of books. *Leg Show* did a similar kind of service for people who felt utterly and completely ashamed of their sexuality.

— The main difference being that now people don't have to go into an adult store or an adult section of a newsstand. They can go to a regular bookstore instead.

And put their shame right on the coffee table for others to enjoy. Taschen has been the champion of the heterosexual male. Taschen dares to print books that appeal to the heterosexual male, which very few other art book companies do. It's extremely popular and easy to make books for a gay audience because they're a marginalized community. It's a good thing to make books for a marginalized community, but the heterosexual male has always been reviled. His sexual interests are considered to be loathsome and crass. Why didn't anyone ever make a book like *The Big Book of Breasts* before? There have been many books on breasts, but no-one took what the heterosexual guy really likes and made a book about it. It's because it was considered politically incorrect. Now that the book is out, women love it too. It shows the natural bodies of women as they existed before they had to watch everything they ate and have gym-flat stomachs and breasts that stood straight out. At the same time women have said to me that men don't like these kinds of bodies in the book. They claimed men like Pamela Anderson-kinds of women.

— I'm not so sure about that...

Please! The reason they make bodies like Pamela Anderson's is because men love breasts. Women are attempting to replicate that.

— Now there's even a subgenre of porn: "natural" breasts. I think the preoccupation with modifying tits is really perverted and decadent. I don't think a lot of guys like these "fake" tits at all. It's a girl thing.

You're absolutely right. It's driven by the women and not driven by the men. I wrote an article about pubic hair for a beautiful French magazine called *Paradis*. Everyone thinks it's men who are making women shave off their pubic hair. It's driven by the women. I've talked to man after man after man and they say they like pubic hair. It makes a woman look like a woman. Men are often nervous when women look like little girls. And women think they have to shave because men like little girls. Where is the huge divide, this crack between male and female understanding? It's in women's problems with their own sexuality. All this obsessive modification is in the same league as anorexia. It's actually desexualizing yourself; making yourself so inhuman that you're unapproachable. No odors; no nothing. And it's creating this group of young men who've grown up on it and become effeminate themselves. They're terrified if they find a pubic hair in their mouth. I don't think that guys like that deserve to get laid. You don't ever deserve to get laid if you can't stand that a woman has pubic hair. What are children going to look forward to if they can't look forward to getting pubic hair? Now they look forward to getting pubic hair so that they can remove it.

— Do you think it's correct to say that Taschen is partly responsible for a "mainstreamization" of pornography and sex? If so, is that only a good thing?

There's nothing in this world that brings only good things. It's all Yin and Yang. There's a balance in everything in life. You can drink too much water and kill yourself. I'm sure that there are people who feel very anxious about sex today because they feel that everyone else is having lots of sex so they should have lots of sex too. People feel they must be sexy. They must present themselves as sexy creatures. Otherwise they can't be married. In cities men are surrounded by sexually provocative women that they can't commit to. It's an urban thing though. If you look at small towns, people are living just as they did one hundred years ago. They have a small pool that they can draw from. They go to bed, fall in love, get married. If the marriage doesn't last, they'll do the same thing again. Is it better for human beings to stimulate themselves at will? For some people it is; for some people it isn't. I can look back at how things were when I was growing up and know that the level of sexual repression then was not good. It was damaging and bad. I'm not going to say it's worse now or better now. I think it all just balances out at all times.

— From the point of view of individual liberty it's good. Even though one can feel saturated, all you have to do is close your eyes. That's better than the other way around. Even the porn market seems saturated these days.

I do hear that people in the porn industry say they don't benefit from their annual convention, for instance. The industry is devolving and it makes less money. There's too many people. They're producing tons of product and they can't sell it. There's no place for the product to go. People aren't paying $60 for a piece of pornography like they once did. Remember when videos on VHS first came out? You were paying lots and lots of money for a tape and you'd watch that tape over and over again. Now you watch a DVD maybe once and perhaps not again. It's completely disposable. I talked to my old buddies who left New York and moved out here to the (San Fernando) Valley. These are people in their 60s and 70s who'd love to retire but they can't retire because there's no fallback. They're having to just kill themselves churning out a film a week to keep their heads above water.

— And thereby saturating the market even more.

Even more. It's inflation. In the porn industry, it's like 1930s Europe. There's going to be a crash. We have so many people who want to be porn stars. More of them than can be stars, and there are no stars. The names all run together, the faces all run together. It's all cheap. People need to do more extreme things to make a name for themselves. I would hate to be on that treadmill. I feel for my old buddies.

— In terms of reactions to your books, is there a big difference between Europe and America?

Yes, there are books that sell better in Europe and books that sell better in America. Roy Stuart, who does very well for our company, has the largest readership in Europe. He uses natural-looking women, very little make up, pubic hair, armpit hair. It's a look that many Americans don't like. They're repelled by the naturalness of the women. Readers of *Leg Show* would sometimes write in and say they could almost smell the women and they were almost disgusted. In Europe, a lot of people are turned on by exactly that. *The Big Book of Breasts* has been a complete success in both places. *The History of Men's Magazines* has been a little more successful in the US. *Naked as a Jaybird* was about the faux nudist magazines of the 1960s. That was more popular in Europe. Europe has a long history of nudism. This kind of faux nudism was funny to the Europeans. We always make books that we know will appeal to a world wide audience. We turn down books regularly that are too

American. There's almost never a book I have to turn down because it's too French or too German or too Japanese. Those people understand that they have to think globally. Americans always think they are the world. Vanessa del Rio mentioned to me yesterday that I should do a *Big Book of Fake Tits*. It could be fascinating to the world: the modification extremes that Americans go to to turn themselves into sexy robots.

— What do you do to kick back and relax?

There's no time for that. I go to the gym in the morning three days a week. I've lifted weights for about 25 years. We go to museums, and to the desert. I like both the empty, desolate aspect and the more sophisticated places like Palm Springs. I also like to shop on eBay. The possibilities are endless. When I lived in New York I used to go to auctions. I love that form of gambling.

— You're a very good writer yourself. Do you have the time to express that?

Not really. I'm frustrated in the sense that I don't have something like *Leg Show* where I did all the writing and had to do it as work. I felt very free with it and could do what I wanted. Here I often have to write on subjects that I'm not that interested in or stuff that's needed to help sell the books. I'm not really a person who loves to write. I would never ever sit down and write for a non-professional reason. It's always hard for me to get started. It's the most gratifying part of my job but also the hardest.

— So you haven't nurtured the idea of a book of your own?

It puts a chill up my spine. I wrote a book once called *How To Pick Up A Man*, in 1983. I was working a full time job and I had to write that in a very short period of time at night. It was agony.

Anton Corbijn, 2007

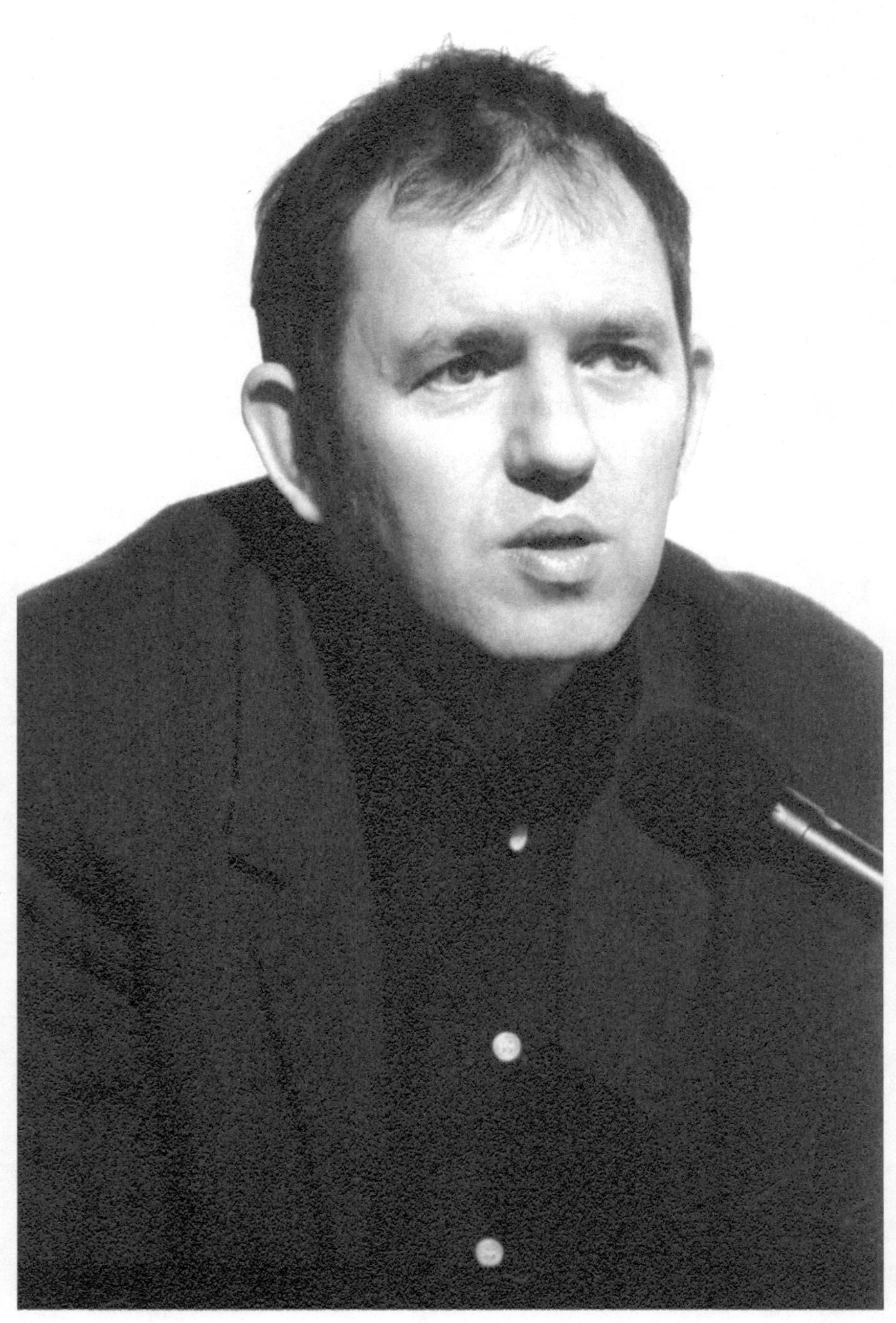

Anton Corbijn

"If I make it with love, it's going to work out."

In 1980, when I was 14 years old, there were many revelations in my life. One was that there was an insane amount of interesting things going on musically in the world. Another, that I was becoming interested in the power of photography, simply via exposure to great images. And then there was the combination. Meaning, looking at amazing and soulful photographic portraits of bands and artists making amazing music, and record covers using these kinds of portraits, and so on. It was an awakening that helped shape my life and helped turn me into a perpetual fanzine journalist and photographer, terminally ridden with the wonderfully satisfying documentarian disease.

There was plenty of great American music at the time, sort of "post punk" and "new wave." But my closest and dearest watering hole – the legendary Pet Sounds Records store in central Stockholm – focused on the British imports. Every week I'd be there, hungry for new vinyl singles and LPs, as much as my tiny purse would allow. Each record savored and adored for a long time: listened to, looked at, touched, smelled...

Then there was that other aspect: the music press. The only way to really keep track of everything that was happening was to read about it. The Swedish music press at the time was, like most Swedish things, epigone with the wind. I needed real international news, and that fast! But I very soon realized that there was another fascinating element in this adventure: the NME ("New Musical Express"), specifically, had such great photos. Although printed on the cheapest form of pulpy paper, you couldn't hide the fact that something very interesting was going on here.

Where their interviews and writing in general was most often ironic in the most snidely ridiculous British ways ("alcoholic logorrhea"), the NME was mainly great for record reviews (as a guide of what had been released that week – yes, it was a weekly!) and for the photographs. It didn't really take me long to realize that all the good pictures were taken by one and the same photographer: a young Dutchman called Anton Corbijn. His photographs made me buy the NME almost every week. Whoever Corbijn photographed interested me. This gradually turned out to be an illusion, however, as he has also taken great photos of many artists who actually don't interest me a bit. But his photographic vision and overall visual acumen is so strong that he can attract people to listen as well as to see. With his dramatic contrast and subtly surreal yet always casual details, Corbijn can weave spells that are at the same time pure and timeless portraiture art. His are images made by an artist, and this was very clear right from the beginning. He quickly became a status- and star-maker: if you had been photographed by Anton Corbijn, you were on the map.

In the late 1970s, Anton Corbijn moved to London in order to be closer to the music he loved. He worked hard, and became part of the very scenes he himself admired and was inspired by. One of the main bands of influence was Joy Division. Some of the most iconic images of the band ever were taken by him: the group in the London subway, looking down a staircase while their singer Ian Curtis looked back into the camera; Ian Curtis, tired in their rehearsal room; etc. After Curtis committed suicide in May 1980, the cover of the the June 14th issue of the NME displayed Corbijn's legendary subway photo. His visual imprint was so associated not only with the moment but also with the very band itself.

And let's not even go into Depeche Mode land (well, maybe at another time). Corbijn has created an entire photographic and filmic world for the Depeche Mode "brand" that is, I suspect, as strong and important as their music is. And let's also not go into U2, or a gazillion other bands he has helped define esthetically.

In 2007, almost thirty years later, Anton Corbijn went "full circle." His debut feature film from that year, "Control," is the story of Ian Curtis's time in Joy Divison, and leading up to his suicide. For me, as an ardent and avid consumer of both Joy Division and Anton Corbijn (as well as the combo), this was surely a match made in high contrast heaven. I was very happy to see that the film was in every way as good and genuine as one could hope for. In absolute joy and excitement, I called Corbijn in London to talk about the process and the memories.

– What has been the most difficult thing for you working on the film?

If you've never made a film before, the most difficult part will be the acting part. Working with the actors. I had never experienced that before. You also tell a story with your photographs and visuals. The visual aspect comes more naturally. Getting the story told through the actors was the hardest bit.

— Haven't you been like a director in all of your music video work, giving people commands...?

Well, they're not actors. You try and get them to do certain things, yes, but it's different. It's very hard for a non-actor to interpret certain things. Music video is such a different discipline. If you have a great song, it's hard to do a bad video. But in a film, all you have are the actors. You can control the setting and the look of the film and possibly with music underneath it you can create a mood. But still you have to get the acting right. Actors are very different people than musicians.

— What has been the most rewarding thing?

Again, I have to say the actors. To see what actors can bring to something is so amazing. It was a daunting prospect to work with them but it worked out and we achieved something. That felt great. I keep thinking that my experience last year was the hardest I've ever had but also the most rewarding one.

— How many people did you have to go through and interview and look at before you found your preferred cast?

Many. With some, it was easier. Samantha Morton was the only person I had in mind for Debbie. For Annik, I was initially looking for a French actress. But I realized that Alexandra Maria Lara had studied French and was educated at a French Lyceum in Berlin, so she spoke fluid French. She became the ideal person to play the role. Sam Riley was an incredible find. He was a total unknown so we were incredibly lucky to find him. Not only does he look a lot like Ian Curtis, he also brought a non-actor quality to the role.

— Do you think it has to do with the fact he has a band and can relate to the lifestyle?

I think it might have helped a little bit. But really it's just persona. Apart from being a very nice guy, he is a film-lover. He also understands intuitively how to play something. He plays it as a person and not as an actor. That helped. You can feel that he becomes the person in the film. Not because he mimics him, apart from onstage of course. But in the rest of the film he breathes the character to a degree where you think it's so real it must be documentary.

— Were there any other sources for the script except Deborah Curtis' book?[1]

Sure... the people. We talked to his mother, his sister, the New Order guys, Debbie, Annik of course, Tony Wilson.[2] We met as many people as possible.

— The book obviously is the framework. The scene where he's writing the letter to Annik surely isn't in there?

Absolutely not. The book might be the basis for things but that's Debbie's story. The story we're telling is Ian's story. We had to go much broader and try to be as objective as possible. Including Annik's role in it all. In the letters, which I've seen for real, you can tell that Ian was very much in love with Annik, and most of the relationship was driven by Ian; not by Annik. That myth of her trying to break up a marriage is really not fair. Annik has always been very quiet about it, in order to have her own life. Therefore, all we had to go on was Debbie's book.

— So that's also one of the reasons you wanted "Control" as a title rather than stick to the book title: "Touching from a distance"?

Sure. "Control" sounds good, and I like it as a word. What you do realize in Debbie's book is that Ian was a control freak. He tried to have his way in the marriage and in the band. There was a part of his life he couldn't control, which was the epileptic part. I thought it would be a nice word to sum all these things up.

— How many of the cinematographic decisions were yours? Did you have a lot of input in Martin Ruhe's work?

Very much. For me, that would be very hard not to do. Martin is a very good person and we've worked together before. We have a good understanding of what we want to achieve. We always go with who comes with the best idea. Some of my strengths are maybe that I can think in certain moves and images. One of his strengths is that he can make very simple things look really good. He also had a good understanding of how many shots we needed to tell the story.

---

1 Deborah Curtis, Touching from a distance, Faber & Faber, 1995.
2 New Order is the band composed of former Joy Division members, Annik Honoré was Ian Curtis' girlfriend, Tony Wilson was the founder/owner of Factory Records.

— In terms of "Control" as a movie, was it important for you to try and not make it too much of a Joy Division movie? To have a more general appeal?

To a degree I didn't want to make it a music film. I'm very happy there's great music in the film. But it's a film about Ian Curtis from age 17 to 23. You follow this boy really, through happiness to depression, and as someone who internalizes a lot. He doesn't really express his problems; it's all internalizing. That's hard for an actor to play. In the end, it's a love story. That's a universal theme. I think the appeal of the film is far beyond Joy Division. We can also see that in the response to the film.

— I've only seen good reviews from the festivals. Have there been any bad reviews at all?

Some people wanted Sam to express himself more. I took a very specific look at it. The way I wanted the film to look and how I wanted the feeling in the film to be. I didn't want to explain everything because I don't know enough to explain it. I think I made it in a quite European tradition, where you leave things open a little bit. In America, everyone wants answers. But it's not that kind of film. I'm very happy with how I made the film and the emotions it expresses. To be honest, most reviews have been ecstatic. We had a great review in *The Guardian* yesterday, which is my main newspaper. Not only did we get five stars, which they only give three or four times a year, but they've already made it film of the year. It's been amazing.

— What about the people within the sphere? Deborah, New Order, Nathalie?[3]

New Order love it. They've been very supportive. They were anxious the first time they saw it. They did a score for the film after they saw it. They've been to Cannes, they came to the London premiere, and Peter Hook and Steve Morris were in Manchester also.[4] "Hookey" is coming to Holland next week. It's been very positive. I just got an e-mail from Tony Wilson's son and he was really happy. Carole Curtis, Ian's sister, has seen it too, and she really loved it. Debbie, I'm not sure. I think she's fine with the film, but I can't read her so well. I think both Annik and Debbie are still having problems with that whole period. Emotion is still raw.

— Did Tony Wilson have a chance to see the film?

---

3 Deborah Curtis was Ian Curtis' wife; Nathalie Curtis is Ian and Deborah Curtis's daughter.
4 Members of New Order.

No, he didn't. I was sorry about that. His illness went much faster than I antici-
pated. I tried to show it in Manchester but he had to go to hospital. He did come
to the set a few times. He met the actor who played him. I'm happy about his son's
reaction, saying he was very proud of the film.

— I know how important Joy Division were for you. But how did you hear about
them initially? Were you still in Strijen in Holland at the time?

No, we moved quite a few times. The last town in Holland I lived in was The Hague.
I had a friend who bought records. He kept playing Joy Division to me. He per-
suaded me to listen to it.

— What was the appeal for you? The sound? The Zeitgeist?

Yes. Totally. That was what it was. I didn't really understand the lyrics because my
English wasn't that good at the time. But the whole vibe appealed. The look of the
sleeve. You felt there was an urgency in how he sounded. There was an importance,
a weight, a gravity to the music. It just seemed to be right. It had all the things I
felt at the time. You're looking for some meaning in your life. And I had already
had enough of Holland in the sense that I felt that my photography wasn't really
appreciated. I felt a little stuck, I think. So I just thought I should go to England, to
where this music is coming from. I didn't even realize they came from Manchester.
I moved to London.

— Once you'd met Ian, what were your impressions then?

They were all much looser as characters than their music was. I didn't speak much
English so I didn't really have conversations. The first time was just ten minutes.
But it was only within days of arriving in England, so it was all very quick. The
picture has gotten an incredible life now. People assume I spent so much time with
them and they all associate Joy Division with this picture.[5]

— It's so iconic. Had you already been in touch with people at the NME before you
moved over to the UK?

---

5 The band are facing a subway staircase going down so we only see their backs, while Ian Curtis
looks back and into the camera.

I had sent some pictures to the NME, and they'd published a few. Costello, Joe Cocker, those ones, I think. I asked if they'd give me some work if I moved to England, and they said sure. But they had totally forgotten about me when I came to England. I went to the NME and they just went, "Who?" I had no jobs in England. I moved there because I wanted to be closer to the music. My friends in Holland thought I'd be back within six months. That's how they said goodbye to me.

— When was the last time you saw Ian?

I saw him late April 1980. They were doing the video for "Love will tear us apart." They had liked my picture so much that they invited me to come to Manchester. They wouldn't pose for me but they wanted me to document it.

— It was shot in their rehearsal room, right?

Yes, that's right. Then I took that picture of Ian that's also quite well known.

— Do you think that anyone could or did foresee what was going to happen? One doesn't get that impression from the book or the film.

No, I don't think so. People were young and you don't really think things like that will happen. I certainly didn't think so, but I didn't know him very well. I had no clue really. The other Joy Divison guys have said in interviews that they started to read the lyrics after his death. They probably could have seen it coming in the lyrics. They never bothered at the time, because that was just the stuff that Ian wrote. In England, people don't really talk about emotions. You can see in the film that Bernard tried to help him.[6]

— With the hypnotism?

Exactly. There was an effort being made, but it wasn't successful.

— One of the first scenes in the movie is the chemistry class, where he's daydreaming and focussing on the word "Oh," like a revelation, while the teacher is talking about chemical imbalances...

---

6 Bernard Sumner, member of Joy Division and New Order.

Yes, you can see that a few times. But basically it's one of those experiences that suggested that a chemical balance was the reason for the epilepsy.

— I was also thinking about the "Atmosphere" video that you directed, with the monks carrying either a plus or a minus on their backs...

That's true. I hadn't thought of that. But plus and minus are indeed an atmosphere in electric terms.

— Do you think that these very iconic images that you took helped propel the myth of Ian Curtis?

I don't know. Maybe the shot I took of him on his own. But in the end, if he hadn't made great work, that wouldn't have happened. It's always down to the work. He left incredible work behind him and yet there's very little known about him. Even in our research for the movie, we never found a filmed interview with him. Nothing exists. It's pretty incredible. That would never happen these days. Everything is documented now.

— Can you see any similarities in character between Ian Curtis and Kurt Cobain, who you also photographed?

I think they were very different. Music sometimes attracts artists who really want to express everything in their music. Art attracts very intense people. I think that's the only similarity. They're very different cases. If you look at it in terms of being well known, Kurt was at the height of his fame. Ian wasn't a household name. He was definitely not on the front pages of newspapers when he died. It was well before they had a hit.

— I remember when you were here in 2002, for the "Mortals" show.[7] You were telling us at the press conference how you usually had 200-250 days of travel per year. I assume that you enjoy that. Was it frustrating while working on the film not being able to live like that?

No, it was a revelation. I really enjoyed it. I'm going to focus on the next movie now.

---

7 A traveling Anton Corbijn retrospective.

— What's that going to be?

It won't be linked to any music. It will be in color and fictional. I won't tell you much more...[8]

— Do you think that on some level you're tired of your very hectic lifestyle?

Well, I wish I could say yes to that. The problem is that making a movie is more tiring than anything else I've ever done. My promotional schedule is worse than any of my photography schedules ever was. I'm flying back and forth, just as normal. Worse than normal. Nowadays you have to talk about the same thing all the time. It is really energy-sucking.

— What would you say is the reason for working so hard? Obviously, you can say yes or no to an assignment.

Sure, but there's always the chance that you can make something beautiful. You go for that then. I have a strong work ethic installed in me anyway. It's the Protestant work ethic I inherited from my parents.

— Now you're working with movies, and then there's the design work, the stage design work, as well as the photography. Isn't it very frustrating to still be labeled a "rock photographer"?

It's totally frustrating. I'm always fighting it. It doesn't really do my work justice. What can you do? People find it so easy to label. Rock photography is about who's in the picture and not what you do with it. I photograph very many different artists, and I'm always very aware of the photography side of things. The initial reason why I didn't want to do the film was that I was afraid people would call it a "rock film." It would miss out on a very important audience. That's what I don't like about labeling. You cater to one audience but another audience is excluded. Unnecessarily so, I think.

— Were you ever hesitant during this long process about if you were going to pull it off? Did you ever have doubts about your own capacity?

---

8 This project eventually became the film "The American," starring George Clooney, 2010.

From the start, I think I was quite determined to see it through. What was hard in the beginning was that there was no money, and all the things I wanted to do were reasons for people not to support the film. I was a first time director and it was in black and white. And the main actor is a total unknown. But all those things are now the reasons why people love the film. I had to make the film with my own money and that was an incredible pressure.

— So you weren't approached by a team of producers?

Well, I was approached by two producers from America. But they had no money, so it was an unusual set up. One guy actually went back to America when we started shooting, and he wasn't a part of the rest of the project. That's why I had to become a producer, because it was my money. I had help from two friends: Herbert Grönemeyer and Martin Gore. They both helped me out. A month after we stopped shooting, we managed to close a deal. Then the movie was safe financially.

— So it was really an adventure too?

Yes, because if accidents happen on the set or someone gets ill or there's a major problem, your money is just gone. It is quite a risk. If you have all the actors and all the locations, it feels right. You don't want to wait six months until you have a deal. If you believe in what you want to do as an artist, to a degree I think it's OK to put your own money into it. Also, I had come to England for Joy Division on an intuitive basis. I had no work, no money, I lived for a long time in a squat. I felt this was similar. England worked out for me. I had the same feeling now. If I make it with love and all these people, it's going to work out. I became quite philosophical about it.

— You're very prolific and also a strong brand name in yourself. Had you ever been approached before with movie offers?

Yes, I've had a lot of scripts over the years. But unlike designing a logo or something that you can do at your desk, with a film you have to clear your desk for a year. You have to be very sure you want to make the film. If you're not skilled as a filmmaker... You can like a script, but will you make a better film than someone who's skilled? The answer is always no. With this film, at least I had an emotional connection to it, to compensate for any film skills I might be lacking.

— Is there something in the film you don't like?

I think I will do a special edition in a year's time. I can make the film longer. I had to take a lot of footage out because it became too long. There are a lot more scenes that I want to put in. I might change something.

— Do reviews and people's criticism matter to you?

I try not to let it affect me. It's hard not to get excited about some things. If someone doesn't see it the way I see it, that's fine. People should have their own enjoyment of the film. Sometimes I think that the problem is that my film has a very European approach. The English or the American would perhaps like it different. It always has to do with cultures. In France it's been out for some weeks and people come back a second time to see it. It seems to be a film that stays with people. That's amazing. What I try to do, also in my photography, is that if you make something about something else, in this case music that touches you emotionally, what you make has to touch you on the same level. It's always very irritating in music videos when you see that the feeling in the video is nowhere near the one you had when you listened to the music. In a film even more so. You have to make it so that it touches you. The story in itself and the music touch you.

— Yes, I can clearly feel that you have a relationship to the subject.

And the music is still so now. When we worked on the film, of course we heard the music very often and I never got tired of it.

— In the live segments, it's so stripped down and raw. The movie conveys very well the energy they had live.

Yes, and the actors play their own instruments. I'm in love with the fact that we had such a great team. Everyone wanted to make a really good film. It was very special.

— I know that you've had such a busy schedule with PR work and it will probably continue for a while. Once everything is over with "Control," what are you going to do? A paradise island for a month?

I'm going to move to The Hague. That's quite a different life, a different energy. I want to be there for a while; a couple of years at least. I'm still thinking of getting a place in Sweden. And I'm going to work on the next movie.

— What do you listen to these days? Are you finding a lot of new interesting music?

I'm not really searching so much at the moment because I'm just so preoccupied with other things. Some things pass my way, like Arcade Fire. Sometimes I listen to new stuff, like the White Stripes and Arctic Monkeys. I love Antony and the Johnsons. I have to say that I get lazy and just put my iPod in Shuffle-mode. When I sit down, I'm sure I'm going to play records again. I just received a box with all the Joy Division re-releases. All the vinyl albums. It reminds me why I fall in love with these things. A vinyl album is something to fall in love with. It's hard to fall in love with a CD.

— And the very first scene in the film is Ian carrying home a new LP.

Yes, that's very close to my heart.

June Newton, 2007

June Newton

"I had to do my own thing."

When I was casually waiting for Kenneth Anger outside the Chateau Marmont Hotel in Los Angeles in January 2006, a silver colored Volvo pulled out from the driveway and turned left down to Sunset Boulevard. This at such speed I had to very swiftly step aside. I only just managed to see who drove the car. It was June Newton a.k.a. Alice Springs, the widow of one of my favorite photographers ever: Helmut Newton (and herself an amazing photographer). It freaked me out not a little, because this was the exact spot where her husband had had a fatal heart attack two years earlier, and crashed his Cadillac. That was a sad day for all Newton fans, including myself, and now I was suddenly standing right there, trying to avoid being run over by his widow in haste. I forgot about it quickly though, because up the hill came Kenneth Anger. We had a table booked at the lush hotel restaurant, and that became a great experience in itself.[1]

The very next year, at about the same time, I was staying at the hotel again. As I knew the Newtons usually always "wintered" for months at the Chateau and that Mrs Newton kept up this tradition, I decided to leave her a note, in the hope that she would see me and grant me an interview. "Dear Mrs Newton, when I was here last year and outside the hotel waiting for Kenneth Anger, you almost ran me over with your car. Could I buy you a drink? Sincerely, Carl Abrahamsson."

It was a long shot, and I knew it. I went about my business and really thought no more of it. Well, until the phone rang in the evening. It was the front desk saying Mrs Newton would meet me at such and such an hour. It apparently pays not only to be straightforward but also to be almost run over.

We met in the lavishly rustic lobby in the evening. The grand lady had brought her "beau" as some kind of filter and protection from a possibly too weird Swede. But as drinks were downed and chit-chat upped – basically a polite interrogation about the interview I wanted to make – Mrs Newton realized that I did indeed

---

1 To read that particular interview, please see Carl Abrahamsson, *Reasonances*, Scarlet Imprint, UK, 2014.

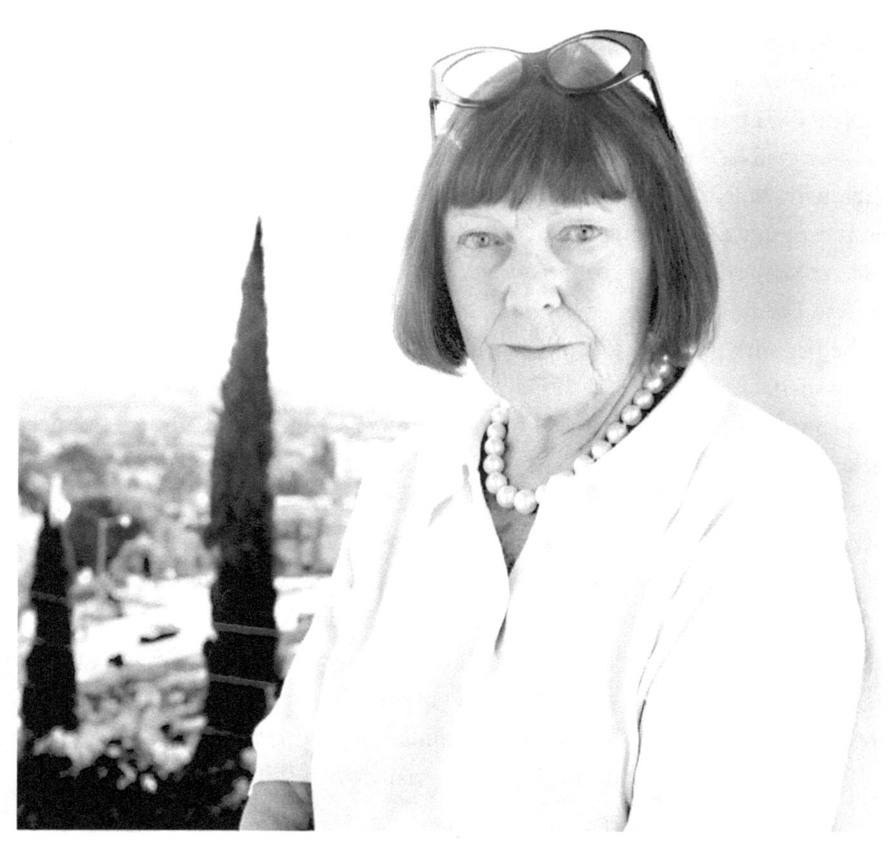

know my Helmut. When I said my favorite photo of him was the one where he's sitting clutching a camera, looking tired, on the edge of a bed on which an elegant model reclined in the nude (as they do), she told me that was one of her favorites, too — as well should be: she was the photographer who snapped it! — and that I was OK.

It became a slightly more than tipsy evening, during which I realized that certain people can do whatever the hell they want to — like smoke indoors in public spaces — simply because of stature and style. Before I retired, and right after we had set up an interview date for next day, June, her beau and a waiter emotionally sang the old Irish evergreen "Danny Boy" for me. It may have been out of tune musically, but it was definitely in tune with my state of drunken bliss.

Next day I punctually knocked on the door of her suite — the same the Newtons always stayed in. Mrs Newton let me in and casually told me she had cancelled a lunch with Anjelica Huston to see me. Did that make me feel special and spoilt? Yes, it certainly did. We talked and talked, I photographed her, and then had a late lunch at Mel's Diner down the street. We also zoomed by the great bookstore Book Soup so I could get a copy of her book Mrs Newton to sign ("For Carl. This could be the beginning of a beautiful friendship...") — another very prized possession on my shelf.

A couple of evenings later, as I was about to have dinner at the hotel, I noticed her again. She waved me over to her table and introduced me to Curtis Harrington, the amazing director of films like "Night Tide" (starring a young Dennis Hopper and legendary LA witch/artist Marjorie Cameron). I was, again, starstruck. Harrington told me he was quite busy at the time but that we could talk later about an interview. Unfortunately that didn't happen. I was also too busy at the time, it seems. And a mere four months later, Harrington died of a stroke. When I visited his columbarium tomb at the Hollywood Forever Cemetery together with my wife, ten years later, I made a vow to never let similar opportunities slip by. One simply needs to strike when the iron is hot — especially when things unfold so synchronistically and serendipitously.

As I write this, in February of 2021, June Newton is still going strong at age 97. A truly remarkable woman and a great photographer. I have many times regretted not staying in touch with her more frequently but quite often think of her as a reigning queen of the lovely free zone of the Chateau Marmont during some literally gilded decades.

— Yesterday you told me about your documentary film "Helmut by June."

I wanted to get Helmut a video camera for Christmas and I took him to a shop. But he just told me he was a still photographer. As if I'd forgotten! I was about to give the video camera back but I thought: "Why don't I buy it for myself?" It became a Christmas present for myself. I decided to shoot him working. I'd seen a few documentaries on him and they were always shot with a big team. I thought it'd be great to take this little camera and just sit in a corner and shoot. That's what I did. I became almost invisible. It was just funny June in the corner with a video camera. It was like peeping through a keyhole. That is the charm of the movie. The big break came when I found the right editor. A young man who came over from London to Paris to see me. As I opened the hotel door he said: "If I'm not back in London by six o'clock my girlfriend is going to leave me." He came in and saw some of the footage. Previously people had told me I really had something great. Well, maybe I had. But this man just said: "You've got hours of this stuff?" When I said yes, he answered that he wasn't my man. He said it was too much for an hour. There were celebrities, naked women, advertising... He wanted me to have a point of view. So I came up with "Helmut at Work." He said he'd go home and think about it. Then he agreed and Canal Plus brought him to Paris, where he edited the film for nine weeks. I came up twice a week from Monte Carlo. That's how we did it. I think he did a brilliant job. He left out a lot of stuff where Helmut didn't really figure.

— How has your book *Mrs Newton* been received?

I haven't heard. I don't know how it's been received.

— Has the book brought with it an increased interest in your work?

Not really. Not at all. Occasionally there are people like you that I talk to and who have the book and like it.

— Did Helmut have a chance to see the book?

No. First, I was working on it for another publisher in London, just before 9/11. Many books went to Europe after 9/11. But these people went bankrupt and I just put the book away. It was a completely different book. One day Benedikt said that he wanted to have a look at it. He looked it over and said he'd do it if it was changed completely. That's how it came about.

— People mainly see you as a photographer. But your work as an editor has been massive too.

We collaborated a lot on the books. All of a sudden we left Australia. In Paris I had absolutely nothing to do. No acting possibilities as I couldn't speak French. One Christmas Helmut bought me a box of paints and I painted for about two years. Very amateurish but still the paint's endearing to the canvas. I gave a lot away. Then I took up photography. But I didn't know what to do with it. I could never be in competition with a giant like that. Helmut said I should do portraits. He thought my portraits were better than the actual fashion stuff I'd done. Little by little I started doing portraits. The moment my book *Alice Springs Portraits* came out on Editions du Regard in 1983, Helmut wanted to do a book of portraits too. That's how his book happened. We had a wonderful collaboration. He trusted me. He threw the contact sheets at me and told me to choose. That became my department. He wanted to take the pictures and that I should do the rest. It was very good. He would check of course, but very rarely he wanted to change what I'd chosen.

— When you live together for a long time, you learn each others' preferences.

Sure.

— Have other people approached you in terms of being an editor for their projects and books?

Not at all. I remember the very first book Helmut did: *White Women*. I got the title on my way home from Hollywood to Paris. I was thinking about a title. He really didn't want to do a book in the first place. He wondered what a book could do. "I'm not into books...", he'd say. But someone came along with some money and said they wanted to publish the book. Helmut looked at what he already had and he also started working a bit for the book. On the way to the airport I just said: "White Women" and he liked the title. Then I thought it was horrible. But that's what he wanted. Then *Sleepless Nights* came out too. I did all the books. He took the pictures and I did the books and exhibitions. And I'm still doing the exhibitions.

— Is there anything big coming up exhibition-wise?

In 2009, the Fine Art Museum of Houston wants a big retrospective. The National

Gallery of Melbourne wants one too. There's a lot of interest in Helmut, and that will increase too, as time goes by. I asked a person in Houston how they want to show him. They answered that they want to show the man who used photography, his lenses and his cameras, to tell us who he was. When he was doing it, America wouldn't touch him. He was a threat to the Midwest, a threat to the family and family values. It was alright if you were a homosexual but to the family values he was a real threat. And the women at the time wouldn't touch him. The women's lib movement wouldn't have him. The women curators said to the men: "If you show him, I'll come see it, but I won't show it." Now, things have changed so much. A lot of American photographers who appear in *Vogue* and elsewhere are so influenced by him. He broke taboos and new ground. He opened up ground for others. That's what I think he did.

— There's so much psychodrama consistently present in his oeuvre. It's such an elaborate vision.

Yes, and he also used newspapers a lot. People didn't realize that. "The Big Nudes" series came from something he saw in *Stern*: some pictures of the Baader-Meinhof gang. Full length pictures. He always put things like that aside and said that he would use it one day. With these pictures he said he'd take the clothes off them. A lot of people who were shocked by the work would look at the pictures of people being hanged by the neck without batting an eyelid. I think a lot of this has come up after his death. I used to say to him: "Helmut, why don't you just stop taking pictures for a while? Let's see where we are. Let's take a look at it because there's so much of it." He just answered, "Don't ever stop me from taking pictures." He just kept on doing it.

— Do you think that would have been a symbol of stopping living for him?

He couldn't have lived without a camera. In the film I tell that when he met me he told me that photography would always come first. When he decided to go to Paris, it didn't even worry him that I couldn't speak French. He bought me canvasses instead and told me to get on with it.

— You were involved on so many levels...

I can't tell you how much. I'd go mad. Most of the exhibitions he did over the years are in crates. Most of the prints are very big. They're all in a warehouse in a free-port somewhere in Europe. It's a nightmare to figure out what's going to happen.

— Couldn't they be stored at the museum?[2]

At the moment I'm trying to put in extra space at the museum. It's a building the Kaiser built in 1909 for his officers. We were offered the whole building. But I said to Helmut that we didn't really need that much. I mean, it's a five story building. He agreed and we took the ground and first floors. Later I tried to get the rest back but then it was too late. There's a big parking space on the side of the building and I'm trying to get a permit to build a big storage area there. When he did the exhibition called "Work" we used an entire railway station in Berlin. We had all the work delivered there and it demanded the entire station. It took both sides of the station. Amazing! It was a disused station though, so no trains passed. I think it was the Hamburger Bahnhof.

— At what point did you come up with the idea to create the "Stiftung" (foundation) and the museum?

Helmut came up with the idea. Paris was interested but nothing came out of it. Helmut told me that he wanted to hire a boat and we'd take all the negatives on it out to sea and just dump everything. I said that they would float and even with bricks on we would just pollute the sea. It would be a horrible thing to do. When we were in Berlin someone asked us if we were interested in seeing an old gas and electricity building, ten minutes outside of Berlin. It was a huge gothic, amazing place. Helmut wondered what we'd do with it and I wondered who would come all the way out there. Then we were shown some other places too, like a Jewish department store that hadn't been used since the war. It was kind of creepy. But we still hadn't found our place. Then someone said there was still one place to see, just minutes away from where we were. Helmut got out of the car, looked at the magnificent building and said: "I'm home!" He was sure right there and then. We financed the whole thing ourselves. We used the same architect who'd done the "Work" exhibition at the Neue Nationalgalerie. He did a beautiful job. He'll also do that extra thing if I get the permit to build it. Helmut never saw it finished though. But he was very happy about the progress. When he died, we still hadn't decided what to put on the ground floor behind the Taschen bookstore and the café. We

2 The Helmut Newton Foundation Museum in Berlin.

didn't really know what to do there. But then I decided to take his entire office from Monte Carlo, including his "Newton-mobile:" a very beautiful Jeep. There are pictures there of him working and also mannequins and effigies wearing his clothes that he's wearing in those pictures. It's like an amusement parlor. I think Helmut would have liked it.

— What about your own work then?

The foundation is still in its infancy. I haven't had the time to even think about my own work yet. I have a lot of legal problems, with all of the fake Newton-prints at auction houses and eBay. People say I should just leave it be but I just can't leave it all. So I can't really take on any assignments from magazines. I do photograph a lot of people and friends that I come across. But I don't really have the time to work as a photographer. Even with offers for exhibitions, there's the matter of setting aside time for it. In the Foundation right now, there's Helmut's portraits of men, James Nachtwey and David LaChapelle. A great combination.

— How many exhibitions do you intend to show each year?

Two per year. I'm probably the only one who knows what Helmut would have liked to have in there. The curator and the people who work there don't really know his tastes. It's not their fault. The people I'm putting in there are people that Helmut admired. The next ones will be Larry Clark and Ralph Gibson and *Helmut Newton's Illustrated.*

— Is it possible for you to pick out one specific photograph of yours that is your absolute favorite?

It could be the portrait of Graham Greene, only for the fact that it was the only picture that Helmut was jealous of. He wished he'd had the opportunity to photograph that. I also like the one I took of the both of us in a mirror.

— Helmut said that his own work was constructed and manipulative whereas your work was more spontaneous and intuitive. Do you think that's a correct observation?

Yes, I think so. I could never be in competition with him, so I had to do my own thing. He was a manipulator and a very complicated person. But a lot was also autobiographical. When he was working in London in 1956 they called him "Shifty Newton." Someone asked an editor how she could have Newton working for her. The material was too strong. Someone pointed out that "there's a horse, a man with a whip and boots..." Helmut slipped these things through the fashion stuff. When Helmut was working for Italian *Vogue* in the 60's, there were memos being sent around, saying, "Be very aware of Newton."

— Now everyone is of course very proud to have been a part of it...

Of course!

— Have you ever felt frustrated or aggravated about the "Mrs. Newton" aspect?

I was very frustrated when I was in Paris and not being able to work. My first pictures had been published in a magazine called *Adam*. Helmut asked what I was going to call myself. He said that I couldn't use his name. We had some friends over for dinner, a director and the actress Jean Seeberg. The director told me to get an Atlas and a pin. I closed my eyes and let the pin drop and it came down right on Alice Springs in Australia! An Australian journalist later asked me what I would have done if the pin had fallen on some place called "Woga." I said that people would simply have to call me "Woga-Woga!"

— Let's talk about the book and project *Us & Them*. The concept as such is a loving manifestation of a creative relationship. Were you or Helmut ever hesitant about the project? It's a very self-revealing thing...

We had an exhibition somewhere in Germany together. Somebody said that it would be interesting to see the pictures that we'd both taken of the same people. Helmut liked the idea. We started looking at the portraits together. Then we drifted into the portraits we'd taken of each other. That would be interesting to show too. And then there were the self portraits. That's how that came about. Just talking and looking at pictures basically.

— The concept is great because it brings together great pictures with the couple who've taken them in a very intimate way. I think the same goes for Mrs. Newton too. There are many intimate, endearing passages. For instance, when you're covering the Venice Film Festival, with all of the mishaps, and Helmut commenting at a distance via telephone. It creates a really vivid picture of how it was back then.

It was not fun! But it's probably fun to read about.

—What's a typical day like when you're here in Los Angeles?

A swim. I can't walk around because the cops will stop you and ask what you're doing. I swim and do a few exercises. Then it's lunchtime and then a short siesta. Then I'll work on the next exhibition until the evening. Then dinner and then it all starts over again. I've been under a lot of stress because of all the legal problems. The faster you deal with these kinds of problems, the faster they come. Here, it's so relaxed I'm almost suffering from the stress of not having any stress. Pre-traumatic stress.

— Is that different from how you live in Monte Carlo?

Well, in Monte Carlo I have staff. One secretary and one assistant. We start at 0930 and go on util 6 o'clock. There's a lot of work to do. I do manage to get in a swim and a walk in the morning. I could never live in Monte Carlo without the work. I couldn't live anywhere without work. I can always pick up the camera and bring a few people if it gets bad.

— What would you say are the foremost reasons for not only having lived together for a long time but also having worked together successfully for a long time?

I went to a few places and sets when I was doing the video work. But no-one ever really saw me there. When Helmut worked he would travel but I was rarely with him. In the early days we couldn't afford it. And in Paris I was going back and forth to London to work. I did live television and dramas for a while. All of a sudden it became too much. I couldn't really go over there just for an audition. I was never on Helmut's jobs and he was never on mine. He wouldn't have welcomed me on his and I wouldn't have been able to take the portraits if Helmut had been present. He could never see me work without interfering. And I would never have dared to interfere in anything he did. He would feel if I were present and not liking what he was doing. Sometimes he would say, "Go away, June…" But basically we didn't work in each others' pockets. We had a lot of independence. When Helmut died, someone said that I'd lost the other half of myself. You don't realize that when you're both alive and together. I lost that half.

— Except for Helmut, who or what has been the biggest influence in life for you?

Helmut wasn't really an influence. I didn't want to emulate him. A lot of people tried to see something there but they couldn't prove it, simply because I wasn't emulating him. When I began with portraits, I liked the purity of August Sander. I wasn't keen on Cecil Beaton and didn't like his work at all. But many years later I realized that it was the period. He photographed his period of time, just like David Bailey photographed the 1960s. No matter what people may say, no-one photographed the 60s like Bailey. And no-one took picture of his time like Beaton. I like Man Ray very much too.

— What about someone like Lartigue? You were friends.

Yes, Lartigue was brilliant. He wanted to be seen as a great artist. His photography was just a pastime. They were wonderful snapshots. Amazing. Looking back, I probably prefer the pictures of Lartigue to someone like Richard Avedon, although I'm a great fan of his work too. But there's nothing left to chance there. There seems not to be, anyway.

— So far in life, what has given you the greatest satisfaction?

The acting days.

— So why didn't you pursue acting more?

I had to choose. Helmut actually thought I should live and work in London. But I would have to take that responsibility. He wanted to be a photographer and he didn't want the burden of someone moaning and saying, "What am I going to do?" That's why I gave up acting. I knew that I'd never get over it.

— Are there still any people that you'd like to photograph but haven't yet?

The person I feel I really missed was Beckett. I used to walk through the Luxembourg gardens and he would take his walk at about the same time. He looked like a tall eagle. A strange kind of animal, with his hair standing straight out. I had a friend who knew him well. I wrote him a little note saying we had that mutual friend and wondered if I could do a portrait and I put it in his letterbox. He wrote me a little card saying: "Dear Mrs Newton, thank you for your suggestion, but I would rather not." Beckett was the one who got away.

— You mentioned yesterday how you were singing at Helmut's funeral in Berlin and how Gerhard Schröder cried... Then there's the Stiftung, and there was the big show at the Neue Nationalgalerie. Different but very strong kinds of homecoming for Helmut. Is there a place where you can feel at home like that?

It used to be Australia but it's so long ago now and so far away. Most of my friends are no longer there. I returned about ten years ago for an exhibition of my portraits during the Arts Festival in Melbourne. It had changed so much for the better. Marvelous food. The roads were better. I couldn't find my way about and it was quite unsettling. There is one place called Kangaroo Grounds that I went to and that hadn't changed since I was a child. It was kept the way it was. Small houses and a lot of land. It's never been suburbanized.

— Have they made you an honorary citizen of Alice Springs?

No, they haven't. They're probably too busy drinking beer in the pubs.

— You mentioned having an assistant in Monte Carlo?

Yes. He used to be Helmut's assistant and when he died I kept him on. Now he's a fantastic archivist. He looks after all the archives and he's very fast.

— In terms of other assistants, did you or Helmut have any assistants who went on to become well known in their own right?

There were three young photographers who used to camp outside his door when we stayed at the Beverly Hills Hotel, before we came here to the Chateau Marmont. They were students at the Pasadena Arts Center. They'd be there often, asking if they could follow him. He said they could come and watch. One was George Holz, there was Just Loomis and another one was Mark Arbeit. All three became very good photographers in their own right. None of the European assistants went on to become photographers. Helmut once had a wonderful assistant called Fifi. He's in the film, the boy with the yellow hair. Helmut thought that he would become a great photographer and I thought so too. But he went into production instead. He's doing very well at that.

— What do you miss most about Helmut?

His company. We enjoyed our own company more than that of others. Always at about five o'clock I feel a void. I realize that this was the time we decided what to do in the evening. We often went to the cinema. We took the car up to the Beverly Center and had a look what was on. Then we'd go just anywhere for a bite afterwards. That's what you can never fill. You can't fill it with writing or reading and you certainly can't do it by watching TV. I miss spending time with him, just walking around, buying books. The things I don't really do on my own.

— What are your hopes for the future right now?

I can't really see the future. I must be very close to the end of my life. Especially the end of my active life, although I'm very well and very fit. It's stacked up against me. I'm trying to get the foundation on the road with the right people. To see that in my lifetime would be great. It's already happening but it's got a long way to go. There's a lot of pressure closing in on me. I can't really see ahead. But the foundation is there. It's there.

Kendell Geers, 2011

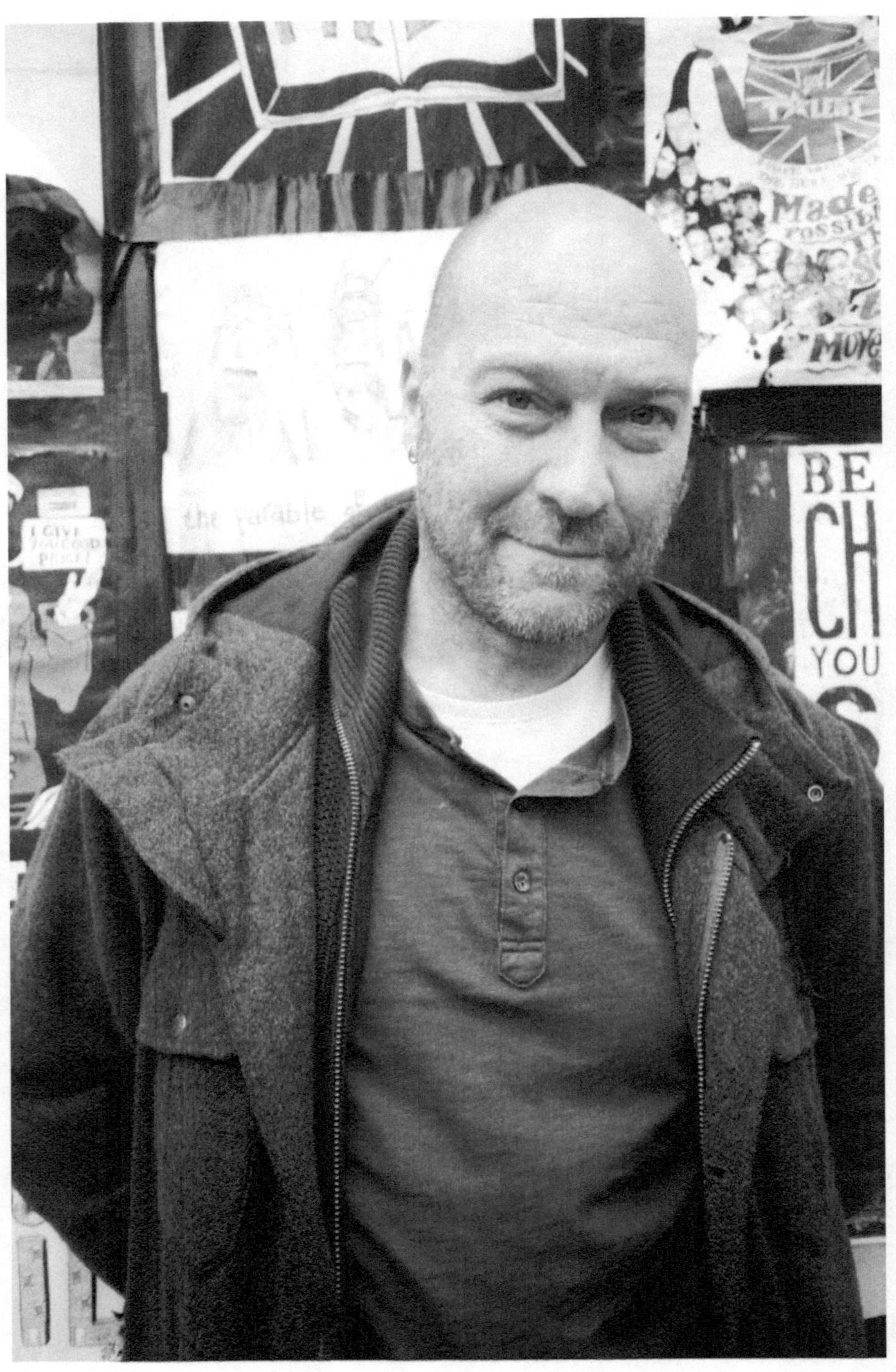

Kendell Geers

"For me the work of art is the materialization of spirit, and the spiritualization of matter."

"Out of sight out of mind, as long as you don't see the children making your jeans in a third world sweat shop, or see the trees being cut down to make space for cattle to graze in order to be processed into your hamburger, or the bees dying from genetically modified crops that will become your croissant, your lifestyle seems justified. As long as the box has a label that reads "BIO" or "ORGANIC" you don't care where the ink it was printed with comes from any more than you care where your garbage is dumped once it's take away from you in a huge iron truck driven by people you don't know, have no desire to meet, much less respect. It's no coincidence that almost half the world's population is either over weight or even obese, whilst the rest are either under nourished or starving to death."[1] (Kendell Geers)

Kendell Geers is one of my favorite artists. This has nothing to do with our friendship, nor with overall thematics, form or content. There is one quality that transcends all of these things, and which is undeniable. It is Kendell Geers's absolute passion. He is a passionate man; an enflamed spirit who emotionally dives into territories most often dominated by the intellect and dry theories. "Passion" is quite a problematic word (to me, at least) because I associate it with cheap and shallow presentations of people who are simply emotional, for good or bad. But in Geers's case, it is, again, undeniable. He really burns for what he's working on. He burns for the ideas and their execution. He burns for a desire to communicate. In this day and age, an inspiring rara avis. But this is perhaps not so strange if you consider that Geers grew up in a South Africa permeated by apartheid and censorship.

---

1 Kendell Geers, *Fin de Partie*, Galleriacontinua, Beijing, 2011, p 5.

Also, one very healthy aspect of his work is the fervent willingness to include what are usually called "spiritual" aspects of human existence to an equal degree as those of the intellect. Whether it's finding morsels of reference in the artworks of others, or in actual personal soul searching activities, Geers is constantly connecting the dots in and of a universe considerably larger than the postmodern art world. Although his works are often satirical and ironic in their intelligent *punnery*, they never cross over to the dark world of cerebral cynicism. They are simply too filled with genuine human ethos and pathos to be too conveniently commodified.

Geers' mind is also hot! It seems to be brewing and spitting out new wordplay every minute. It's a wonderful quality that connotes prankishness in itself, and also ties in with definite streaks in many traditions: art history, literary history, poetry, etc. Whether it's honoring the ghost of Marcel Duchamp or other cerebral surrealists, 21st century meme-sensibilities, "ad-busting" appropriation of manipulation, or simply a neo-Burroughsian cut-up break-down into uncommon denominators, Geers is a contemporary master of word-tumbling, anarchic aphorisms and revealing reconstructionism.

"Believe in what you create and create only what you believe in."

"Use counter-culture to counter the culture of the counter."

"Everything is not for sale."

"Spell mistakes."

"Speak with a sharp tongue in the cheek of expectations."

"Truth exists only within the imagination."

"Inner gods we trust."

"Fuck, it's true!"[2]

Et cetera...

The following conversation took place in London in 2011, after we had both spoken at an art symposium.

— Do you ever find yourself stuck in a creative loop when it comes to the expressions? Do you find yourself stuck in the same thematic things as the decades pass?

Certainly not stuck in the same thing, thematically, but my life as it has played out has definitely not been chronological. It's very weird. I think that looking back over my life it'd certainly be more spiral than a straight line. So I've returned again and again to various themes, but on the spirals. You know, I would be interested in one

---

2 Kendell Geers, "Political-Erotical-Mystical-Manifesto," *Here To Go 2012*, Edda Publishing, Stockholm, 2012.

thing, and then it wouldn't be finished, but five years later I would return to the question and suddenly it would make more sense, and then I leave it alone for another five years. But certainly my overall interest has definitely shifted, and I think shifted beyond ever returning. My early work, in the beginning during the apartheid in South Africa, was certainly political, and it was a time in my life when I certainly believed in politics as a way to change the world. I still believed in democracy, I still believed that politics was an effective modus operandi, or an effective vehicle for working. And that I would work as an artist within the logic of politics. As things have played out post-apartheid and as the world has played out since then, I most certainly don't believe in politics any more at all. Politics is over. The industries have taken over, the captains of industry run the world, the capitalists run the world, the multinationals run the world, and it's a joke and a mockery that they still pretend democracy exists. It's really a joke. I've always had this interest — let's call it the spiritual aspects of art — that is definitely much more downplayed, with politics seeming to be more urgent and necessary at that time. Whereas now it's the opposite; now I'm much more interested in how can I work as an artist in a more alchemical, more talismanic logic; where the things that I make are more than the sum of their parts and more than just physical; in which the work of art is able to function at an almost mythological level, and only working with greater forces. That's becoming more and more important in my process of working; let us say in the way I'm thinking and in the way I conceive my work.

— Did you have high hopes that your specific work in South Africa as a young artist would change other things than merely the kind of immediate dynamic that apartheid dictated?

How I conceived the politics in my work was never a case of me standing up with a banner saying "vote for this party or that party," because I think that would make me a priest; that would make me a propagandist; that would make me a missionary — which I was never interested in. For me politics manifested in my work through that what I would do is construct an ambiguous situation a moral dilemma, you could say, because from the beginning I always was against morality. I make a distinction between morals and ethics. I can be an ethical person but totally amoral. My works of art were morally ambiguous and the viewer was invited into a situation where he would have to figure out what am I doing and what is my relation to what I'm experiencing, seeing, witnessing. This was more like a work of art I conceived as a scene of a crime. The viewer comes along and they see the results of a crime and they have to, for themselves, go through a process of "what happened here?" And in that way they become aware of their own politics. They become aware of their own morals. They become aware of how that would be constructed ideologically, and in that way they become aware of, yep, their politics. So, back then, in a very, very, very isolated country in a very parochial insular self-obsessed climate, I wasn't aware of magic in the way I am today. For me to stir the idea of secret societies and stuff, which was beyond my access or my ability to even imagine, and subsequently having become a member of secret societies and discovered it was a lot of mumbo-jumbo, and then redefining what magic is... I think my work was always designed to be transformative. It was always that need; that I'm not making something to decorate the walls with; I'm not making something which is going to be an out of sight out of mind sticker on the wall that you forget about. There's always this need that the work of art is needs to be a catalyst; it needs to be transformative; it needs to be engaging; it needs to be working with consciousness. In those days it was more an ethical or ideological consciousness whereas now it is much more a consciousness of spirit which is more subtle. The kinds of energies that I'm trying to work with are more subtle, but the desire for transformation remains the same.

— What made you initially interested in making art?

Growing up during apartheid in South Africa we didn't have a choice. Every white man from the age of 16 was forced to go to the military. The only way to not go to the military was to study further. So if you're at school — no problem, you just got a letter from your principal. But once you finished school the only way to not go to the army was to continue studying, or go to jail for six years. Now for me, going to the army was out of the question. I wasn't going to go to the military; there was no way... that was just impossible. So I decided I would study. From a very, very early age, because I have a very authoritarian father, I was anti-authority. Extremely anti-authoritarian. At the time, at school, I had been studying math and science; I had one of the highest marks in the country for mathematics — the more abstract the better for me — and my desire at the time was to become a quantum physicist or something like that. I would go to university and study science and head up towards nuclear engineering. I filled in an application form for the university and they said "you have to put two choices — if you don't put a second choice your first choice is disqualified." I thought this was a very authoritarian fascistic attitude because in my mind there was only one thing I wanted to study. Don't force me to say two! So I went through the list of the things that the university was offering, all the courses, and I thought, "what is the inconceivable opposite of what I could possibly imagine to do as a 'fuck you' to the system?" I found "art." I then had to go to an interview in order for my application to be processed, and I had to bring a portfolio. So for the first time in my life I bought some pencils and drew a banana and I made some still life drawings and I worked up a portfolio for the first time. I went for my interview and for some bizarre reason I got accepted. For the first time in my life I asked the question, "what is art?" I went off to the art class. It was toward the end of the year of the course, and the teacher had absolutely given up. At the back of the class were all the kids, like in the movies: smoking joints and laughing and having a good time, and in the front of the class were two girls and the teacher was desperately trying to teach them. I sat down by the two girls and on that day, by coincidence — if you believe in such things as "coincidence" — the teacher was doing a course on Dada. She just decided to do this — it wasn't a part of the curriculum. It just so happened on this day she did something beyond the curriculum for these two girls. She got it slightly wrong, but she said, "during the first world war there were these people who retreated to Zürich to the Cabaret Voltaire and said that if warfare and all that was going on during the First World War were the results of the rational logical brain, they were going to do the irrational, illogical, opposite." I was deeply touched. "Wow, I can be that!" I was deeply fascinated by the idea of working with something. The thing about science is that I could see my life in front of me; I could see it playing out; I could see the great regularity. I thought that would be kind of boring. Whereas with art, I had no knowledge. I was dealing with something I couldn't even imagine, and decided that, "Okay, I'm going to be an artist." I didn't think I was going to become an artist; I thought I was going to study art. That is how it all began.

— I think most other people become enchanted by other artists or art that they see, but this was more direct in a way.

You know the great surrealist idea of that "chance meeting of an umbrella and sewing machine on a dissecting table?"[3] That is exactly what it was: a chance meeting of me at that moment being accepted into a course which I didn't apply for, going to a class that wasn't supposed to happen, giving me the keys that is the irrational mind and the illogical irrational counterpoints to the over-industrialized, over-technological society. That just becomes more and more central to what it is that

---

3 Originally formulated by Isidore Ducasse a.k.a. Le Comte de Lautréamont (1846-1870).

I'm doing. It is something that started 25-30 years ago; it's crazy.

— When you were there and you sort of found this inspirational environment, what were the actual first expressions? How did you express yourself?

I arrived at art school, and all these kids who were studying art had huge sheets of paper, and great gestures, and expressing themselves with all this confidence. I had the smallest piece of paper and I had to hide it so nobody could see that I, in my opinion, had no talent. I didn't know what I was doing. At that time, I didn't know the difference between Picasso and Leonardo. Maybe the only work of art I might recognize would be the "Last Supper," but that was about it. Because of the huge insecurity complex I went to the library and I taught myself. I saw what the curriculum would be and I saw what they would teach, and then I decided to read the magazines. So literally I went through all the magazines: *Artforum*, *Flash*, *Art in America*, the old magazines, *Studio International*. I read them page by page from the first issue and I just went through it all. I developed a huge knowledge of art from the 1960s until the present. I was also listening to industrial music, and was very influenced by Throbbing Gristle, very influenced by William Burroughs. "Language is a virus," the whole counterculture, and the idea of how language works, and I started to work from the very beginning. Now I know that's a very magical process, but at the time I thought it was simply counterculture. It was hard at the time to find stuff. Some rich person would have a cousin from somewhere in the UK who would send records, or a cassette. In a way, I grew up in a bootleg culture. The kinds of work I was making in the very beginning were very much about that process of bootlegging and working with language; working with the interface between image and text. What you see is not what you get, and how something is described changes the reading of it, and trying to make the experience of art more emotional and more problematic than the cerebral sentence on the wall – the cold intellectual sentence on the wall. What can I do to offset that, to make that sentence on the wall super-emotional?

— Would you say that this is almost like an intuitive approach to dealing with postmodern intellectualism?

Yes. I read all the post-modernists. I did the theory; I was forced to at university. But I was interested in where theory breaks down. So again, my model was back then, and it remains now, the idea of the scene of a crime, where you're driving down the road and you see there's a car crash. You slow down, you stop, and you look. Why? What is it? No matter how much Foucault you read, no matter how much Derrida you read, no matter how much Baudrillard you read, no matter how much you convince yourself it's a "simulacrum," you still slow down and look. Why? You're attracted to it, because we want to see the blood? We want to see the dead body? We want to see but at the same time we are repulsed; we are terrified. We are attracted and repulsed at the same time. We have this "oh my god" experience. We are attracted because it's life affirming. I was always fascinated by that moment where things break down. You have a sense; something is on the tip of your tongue. You know what it is but you don't know what it is called. When language falls apart; when you have these very strong experiences that you know exactly what they are. But you can't talk about it, you can't explain it, you certainly can't write about it and there is no simulacrum and there is no other French theory which can dissect that. That is a process of intuition, instincts, fear... Working with your fear, working with... It's a very tantric process: to actually engage your fear in the production of the work and do things which scare you. All my early work was very much about taking myself to an edge, whether it was with drugs or alcohol or sex or experience. I've put myself in an extreme situation and out of that my fear would give rise to these things that I was making.

— Can you see that you have to enhance the level to keep up?

Unfortunately, we have this thing, this incredible capacity to adapt, and the more you experience, the more it takes to... I always think at this point of my life that we live with this crust; it's almost like there is a crust on my skin that builds up year after year after year that makes you immune. It's like it protects you from the outside world, but in another way it also prevents you from feeling. Then you end up in suburbia; you end up with these fucking middle classes terrified of their own shadow; trying to change the world with a remote control. So you do need to engage more and more in the terrifying. It takes more effort to find things that scare you, it takes more effort to be open and fresh to having experiences. Now I take Ayahuasca because Ayahuasca can certainly take me to areas where I feel fucking terrified, and where I've never been before. Smoking a joint doesn't do it. Ayahuasca is interesting because it isn't about soul searching — it takes you to your fear, without any doubt. It is also an enormously spiritual process.

— You can sort of bring back and keep the inspiration, I guess.

Of course. You need to at a certain age – I guess at our age – use that to turn up the volume of experience in order to stay fully alive.

– Except for those strong experiences of encountering your own fear and letting that be a guide, is there anything on a more general level that keeps you inspired?

Sure! I think it's a very strange moment. You know you're sitting here and you have the "Occupy London" people outside, and I find that very inspiring. Because for the first time in a long time I'm seeing young people trying to reclaim something. For the most part, our lives in Europe and the US have become about creating more and more distance between your body and experience. So we don't go to the book shop any more; we just download a book. You don't go to a CD shop, you just download the album. The Internet has opened up enormous possibilities and also closed down opportunities. So now, you can basically read all the secret rituals of all the secret societies; they are all online now. You can download them. It's like there are no secrets any more, but at the same time it's not the same experience as it should be. Being in a dark room, having that experience of going through a physical process. And the younger generations are content to just read the scripts and not live. We're just living in a world, at least in Europe and the United States, where the privilege has reached the point where there is no desire for change; there is no desire to question the politicians and the banks who are ripping us off every day; there is no desire to make any difference in the world that we're living in. People are happy to say, "well, yeah, this is it and as long as I have my remote control and my iPad and my iPhone I'm happy." I strangely enough find that the classics still work. I read William Blake, and still the guy has something super interesting to say; it's smart and is still electrifying.

– All signal, no noise!

Who are the contemporaries today? Who are the people to tell you you're making art like Blake?! Who are the people today who are working in that way? I mean, I've had the opportunity of hanging out with Genesis P-Orridge. I mean that's a very rare, amazing, extraordinary person. Who is doing that today? Who is the Throbbing Gristle of 2011? It doesn't exist. I was seeing the recent Throbbing Gristle concerts. They look like a bunch of fucking tourist agents. Genesis wasn't really allowed to perform, and the rest of them look like they are sitting with their laptop computers... That is not a show; that is a tourist agency. That's horrible. Even

Throbbing Gristle are not Throbbing Gristle any more. They all became fat and old and boring.

— When you've done something like an installation, or something that is on display, or simply put together a show, do you feel that experience as something cathartic that you just sort of leave behind, or are you very immersed in or attached to the event or the exhibition?

I'm very attached because the things I make are very much part of me. They are extensions of me. I find it very, very, very traumatic to sell a work of art. It's not that I'm not generous... I would rather give away the work of art to somebody I know than sell a work of art to a stranger, even though I have to sell because I need to earn a living. I'm not in a position where I can afford to not sell. The exhibitions are constructed and very carefully planned around the body of work and how everything intersects. You have a grounding of energies, and you're trying to work with male elements, female elements, creative elements, destructive elements that are all in balance within the context of a show. And when you rip that apart and it goes off into the world, I have faith and trust in the things that I have made; that they will still be still able to do whatever it is that they need to do individually. But they will never be as strong as they are in the show where the work was made. Even though I function in a contemporary art market which is about making commodities, I don't see them in those terms at all. Because sometimes, ten years later, I revisit a work of art and I finish it. Just because it's on display doesn't mean it's finished. Sometimes something needs to be added or subtracted in order for that work of art to be finished. Some collectors and galleries go crazy because I decide to finish a work later on. These things are alive, and that is what makes art so interesting. It is alive, it does function, it does have a spirit element, and those spirits are very much alive. We are conjuring spirits. For me the work of art is the materialization of spirit, and the spiritualization of matter. I don't make things; I channel them. I'm a conductor. I'm something that is using my hands to make these things and I'm absolutely not in control of that process. 20 years ago when I was working with something more political, it used to disturb me that I would arrive at conclusions and I would make things that I could not explain rationally. I would make these things but I could not explain how I got there. It used to disturb me sometimes, whereas today it doesn't bother me anymore. I understand that process, and I allow the process to unfold without questioning too much, intellectually.

– Can it perhaps be better understood on an intuitive level?

Absolutely. A lot of people say that you go into an art gallery and it's super boring. And it is. For the most part, contemporary art is extremely boring, extremely over-intellectualized, over-designed, over-finished, over-priced. It's just fancy products, luxury goods, and it gets traded like currency. A lot of artists have played into that, and they are very happy to live in a currency exchange market – and that is why the work is dead. It is absolutely dead. It is too much front brain, cerebral, overly calculated art about art, rational… It's not going to survive because there is no magic, and it's just like making a… It's like IKEA; it's an other IKEA chair. I think there are some artists still that are trying to work in a deeper, more profound way… searching. And most of them are not getting the fame or the recognition of the system, because the work is too complicated. We want to eat processed food and we want to live with processed art. We don't want anything with a little bit of grain and a little bit of texture and a little bit of substance that might turn rotten. It makes people scared. It scares them.

Simeon Coxe III

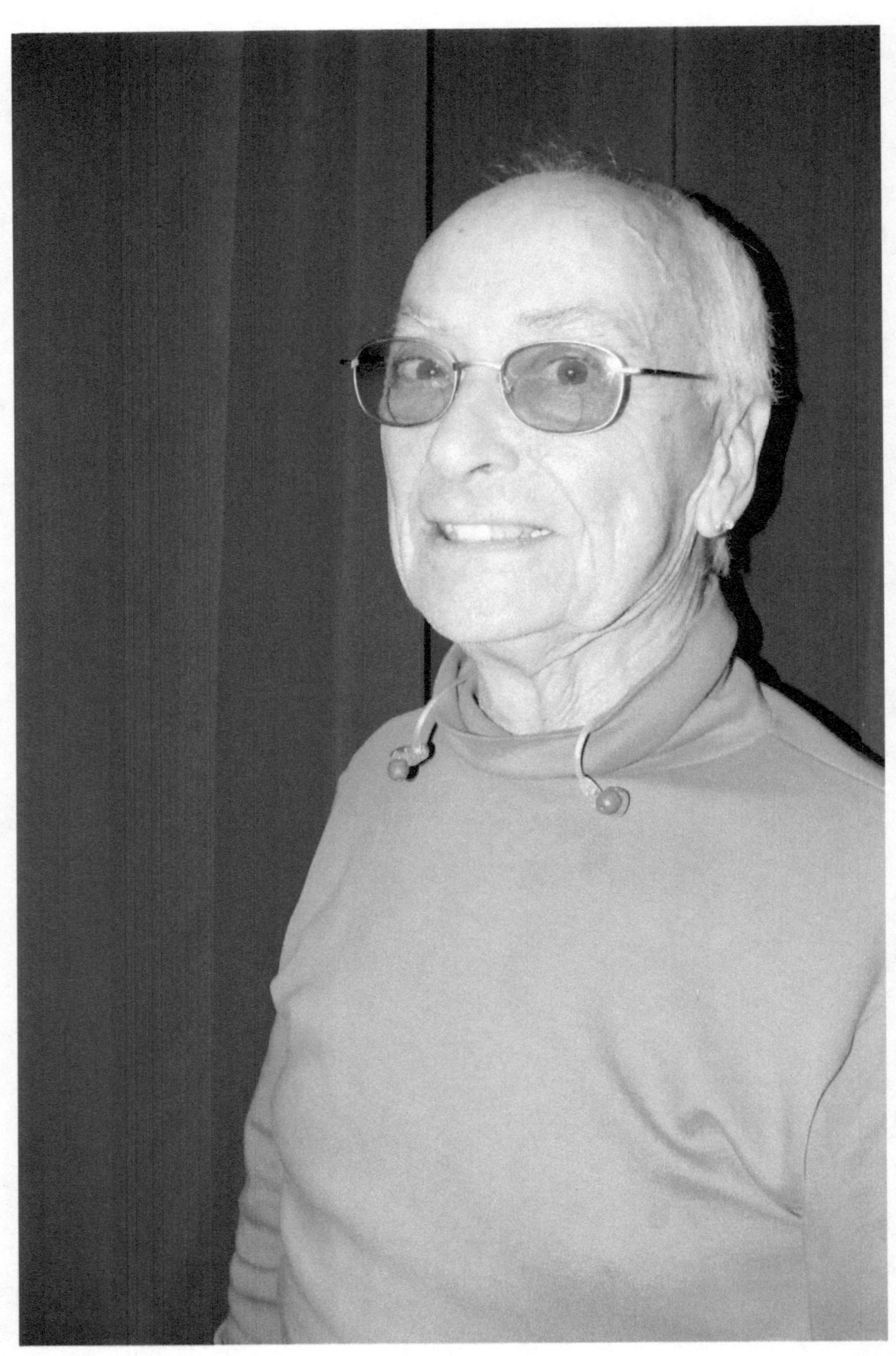

Simeon Coxe III

"I hear Fats Domino in everything I do..."

Want legend? Want demigod? Want a juicy Silver Apple to chew on? Meet Simeon Coxe III, who qualifies for all of that and then some. The band Silver Apples' (originally Coxe and drummer Danny Taylor, who died in 2005) mind-boggling mix of rock, poetry and electronics in the late 1960s transcended everything, and I mean everything. Eerie singing, strange melodies and ultramodern rhythms lovingly hugging electronic oscillations galore from their own gadget called, aptly, "The Simeon." Thus a foundation was chiseled out for German Kraut-explorations, Suicide's suavely brutal synth evergreens, Throbbing Gristle's homemade and existential electronics, Stephen Morris' drumming, Martin Hannett's production values and a million more ripples on the water into which Silver Apples threw the very first gemstone of creation.

Mr Coxe is seemingly as young as then, energized by success and by the respect of both young and old fans alike. What a guy! Not only a sonic pioneer in so many ways, but also a great human being. Yes, he builds his own synths! Yes, he's an accomplished painter! Yes, he broke his neck in a car crash and was paralyzed! Yes, he survived and worked his way back! When Coxe enters the stage and revs up his sonic gadgets and audio-emotional vessels, he moves from nice, well mannered, hard working artist to a vibrating poetic and equally peyotic space person. Still beyond and still ahead after almost 45 years of music- and art making. Who can beat that?

— Could you ever imagine that you'd be here in Stockholm in 2011 in some club with several generations of fans?

The multi-generational thing never occurred to me. I was never looking that far into the future but I always wanted to play in Europe back in the day. I imagine this is what you're talking about. Back in the 1960s and 70s, when Danny (Taylor) and I were the original Silver Apples, we envisioned playing in Europe a lot, and I think that it was going to happen. But when the record label found itself in financial trouble and they started pulling back on the touring and the sponsorship, we just never made it across. But I always envisioned playing Stockholm and the whole Scandinavian area, because we knew there were record sales here. So I always wanted to come.

— If one could sum up the early phase, I would say there was a lot of spontaneity, in the concept and the live stuff and the recordings. It was just really spontaneous sounding music. Has that spirit stuck with you?

Absolutely. Always. I don't have the patience to be a meticulous recording person/musician. I work pretty much from the gut, from the heart, and I kind of just let the mind follow along. I try not to think too much. I find that if I think too much I get in my own way, so I want to record spontaneously: one cut. That's how I do it, because it's more like performing, which I really love to do. That's my main love in life – performing – so that's the way I do it.

— Do you think that there is the possibility of creativity within a perfect structure, a perfect order, or do you think there needs to be some chance element to make things exciting?

I think it has to be according to your own individuality. I know that there are certain artists out there who do beautiful stuff that work on this meticulous, almost engineering kind of level. One that quickly comes to mind is Damon Albarn. I just think he's a marvelous musician, but he is meticulous and precise. Another one I would mention is Geoff Barrow, who can be that way when he records with Portishead, but he can also be spontaneous, as with BEAK›. So there is a guy who works both ways and I'm envious of that. I can only work the one way. I just play, and what happens happens.

— Do you believe that frequency affects emotion?

Probably. I don't understand the science of it. I just know that there are certain levels and also certain pitches that make me feel good, so I tend to gravitate towards them.

— Is that something that you use to make people feel good in a live setting?

Yeah, I think that if it makes me happy, then it must be making somebody else happy – if they are being sensitive to it.

– You've been performing for a long time and in different phases. Do you ever feel that you get high on performing, almost like a psychedelic high?

Every night. I never get bored. Every time I do a song is a new thing. It could be anyone from the ones that have sort of a loose structure, where I can do what I want to pretty much on it, to others that are fairly rigid. I wouldn't say rigid but fairly formally structured, where I know I have to change chords at a certain time and all that kind of stuff, in order to stay true to the melody. I don't even get tired of those because every night, there's just some different little thing that happens that makes it a new song for me. And I feel excited about it as though I'm doing it for the first time.

– I can't really see that happening in a rock context. Your music is loose enough to make it happen.

I deliberately structure my set so that I can have a formal kind of piece and then a loose one. And then a formal one, and then a loose one, and it's kind of like a discipline thing for me to do the formal thing. I don't want to let it get just out-of-control-loose you know, one after another, so I kind of alternate them like that to keep myself in control.

– In terms of a general high or a buzz, have you ever experienced something like extra sensory feelings, or lost yourself on stage?

No. The only time I ever lost myself on stage was fairly recently, actually in May, in China, when they had like seven strobe lights that went on all at once at different rhythms and that threw me into such a feet-off-the-floor strange place that I didn't know if I was passed out or if I was going be sick. I just had to close my eyes and almost stopped playing, and just had some of the oscillators continue to cook until I could feel the strobes were calming down a little bit. And then when I did my encore I got hold of the light guy and said, "turn off the damn strobes, please! Or I'm not going to go back out there," so he shut it off.

– Yeah, that sounds potentially epileptic.

It had that effect. The strobes discombobulated my electrical impulses inside the brain that make me able to think.

— When I've read what you've said about the early phase, you mentioned not being aware of that sort of more scholastic art music, and that that was something that you got caught up with afterwards. Can you see yourself as having integrated any notions or concepts or teachings from that more scholastic vein?

No. You know, I've been interested ever since I learned about the theory of atonal, the theory of dissonance, the theory of arhythmic structures and things like that. I've been interested but only from an amusement or entertainment point of view. I don't like to do it myself. I mean, I love dissonance. Dissonance to me is an amazing tension-relieving kind of tool, and I think that music that doesn't have dissonance gets boring after a while. But that's not because I learned it from some concept that somebody wrote in a book that I studied in school — it's because of the way I feel. I just play music the way I feel it and I don't have any musicology background at all.

— At that time, was there someone around that you could say was an inspiration in this very free-spirited sense, this experimental sense?

In a way, Sun Ra. I used to go to a little club in New York called "Slugs" which was way down on the Lower East Side, in what you would call a bad drug neighborhood, and I remember he played every Thursday night. My girlfriend and I and sometimes some friends used to go down and we'd sometimes be the only people in the whole club, and Sun Ra would just play all night long and I remember just being totally enthralled by what I heard, and by the freedom that he allowed the music to have. He would have musicians standing out on the street corner or in the men's room, standing on a toilet. He'd have a sax player there. You'd go in there to take a leak and there would be a guy playing the sax. His band was just all over the place. He'd go upstairs into the apartments and play out the window, during the set. And I just thought that was marvelous and I'm sure some of that has to have rubbed off. Music doesn't have to be a formal and serious matter. It's from the soul.

— Even given that sort of proto-experimental attitude that you've always had, can you find some other strains, for instance in the music that you've grown up with?

I hear Fats Domino in everything I do...

— Wow... Sun Ra and Fats Domino...

Yes, they are my two heroes. When I was 13, 14, 15 years old, I used to go down to Rampart Street in New Orleans where all of the old artists were all playing in these bars — what they called at the time "race" music, which is now called R'n'B or soul. They weren't like the venues we think of today. They just played in bars. I'd go there, and there'd be Big Joe Turner or Big Mama Thornton or Little Richard or Fats Domino. I mean, you just never knew when you walked in the door who was going be there, and many times I'd be the only white person in the place and nobody cared. Everybody was there for the music. I was 15 years old, underage, but they didn't care. New Orleans is very loose and so I'd stay in the back of the room and just listen to the music in a trance. I grew up with Fats Domino in my veins and I still hear him and the triplet pianos and the way he sings, the way he structures his songs, the simplicity of it all, all through my music, and I shout his name from the hilltop.

— You've always been associated with the East Coast and a sort of harsher sound, but at the same time I can associate your style of singing on the two first albums with an almost West Coast-ish sort of psychedelic rock...

I don't know where that comes from. I'm definitely an East Coast person. I have a country background, and I was born and raised in the South, so there's maybe some bluegrass or some country music in my vocals, but it's not meant to be psychedelic. I have no idea what the word "psychedelic" means.

— I think that the musicians on the West Coast just probably had the same sources of inspiration — blues and early American music. Anyway, early on, you collaborated with a poet on the lyrics?

There were several poets that I worked with. Stanley Warren was one. We worked a lot with the first record. We worked with, I guess, about five or six poets. We put a notice up on the bulletin board in the bar at Max's Kansas City that said, "Rock band would be interested in lyrics. Submit poetry," and gave our phone number. We got dozens of poets who wanted to be involved. Stanley Warren had some nice stuff and there were several other people who had nice things, and we thought

"OK, rather than write our own stuff for the first record, we'll involve these poets. Let's get them in here. Lets make this a group effort." And so that's what we had there on the first record. For the second record we still had a few poems left over from one or two of the other guys but I basically wrote the stuff on the second record. And the third I wrote totally.

— And you continued in that vein, writing your own stuff?

Yeah. I thought it was an interesting idea to have poets submit lyrics, but that was just an idea for the first record. I really like writing my own stuff.

— Can you see a recurring theme, lyrically? Can you see a pattern?

No. What comes out is always a surprise.

— This will to experiment that you have, what would you ascribe it to? Where do you think it comes from?

I'm impatiently intolerant of boredom. I need to have something to tickle my fancy and make me feel challenged. And so I guess that's the root of it. I just can't stand to be bored.

— Itchy pants... Were you encouraged to go into art and creative endeavors as a kid?

Yes, by my grandmother. My parents had no interest whatsoever. There wasn't even a record player in the house. There was no music whatsoever. But my grandmother had an art background. She had studied in Paris when she was a young lady and so forth. So she taught me how to paint when I was quite a young kid and that kind of interest in art stuck with me.

— Except for the itchy pants, the boredom aspect, is there something you can see as a general inspiration for you: a creative source?

Just to be very broad: the human experience, the inter-relationship among all human beings, whether it's a love thing, or a companionship thing or a group thing... I think human beings are fascinating creatures. I'm not one of those people that feels horribly guilty that we're here, that we're destroying the landscape. I don't think we are anymore than an elephant is... So I don't feel any guilt at all. I love being human and I love human beings; I love all things that we do. I'm very happy to be here. Maybe next time I'll come back as a worm? That's still okay. I have been a human and that was cool.

— How would you yourself describe Silver Apples' music to someone who's never ever heard of it?

Electronic pop. If you want to get just simple words. That tells you that it's electronic and that tells you that it's not one of these serious, studied laboratory experiments. These academic approaches to music that I have no interest in whatsoever... So "pop" is a big word for me. I'm proud of it, and "electronic" of course, because that's what I do.

— I assume that bands or young people send you records all the time. Apart from that, do you also try to actively keep up with what's going on in this vein?

I'm not a real student. I don't go to record stores and seek out new stuff. I love it when the musicians come backstage and say, "give it a chance on the road, listen to this." I love that, and I contact them back. So I have an awareness of the new music just because of that, because I'm close to the musicians, having been on the same stage with them. Playing festivals is a real rich thing for me because I get to meet with all these other guys and girls and exchange musical ideas and just move on. So in that sense I'm up on it, but I'm not a student of it.

— I would say that it's not an understatement to say that your work in Silver Apples has been hugely influential on the electronica scene and on so many scenes, from Kraut, Suicide and onwards... What does it feel like, to have played such an instrumental part?

It's a huge honor for me. I feel completely overwhelmed that some of the most beautiful music that I've heard out there has its roots in my little ideas. It's a huge experience. It's humbling. I'm not sure I understand why. But it's there, so I accept it. I'm not going to say "no, no, no, that's not true." I know it's true, because I've talked to enough guys about the way they feel, the way they compose, to know that I have had an influence. But to tell you the truth, I never started off thinking that it would be that way. I was always in awe of other people and wanting to be like them, and wanted to be as good as them and never thought I would ever be, you know. And now I have people telling me that they wish they could be as good as me.

— So apart from that — the joy of being a human being and the joy of having these things projected on you — what else makes you really, really happy?

My little kitty cat, that's one thing. My girlfriend. My boat; a sailing boat. Very simple and direct. I'm not a complicated person. Maybe that is why I'm bored unless I'm being creative; because I'm otherwise a simple person?

— Just one final thing in terms of the recording stuff... Do you actually work with sequencing, computers and MIDI-stuff or is it just the same there: "Hands on"?

No, I do work with the new stuff when I'm recording. When I'm performing, the rhythm tracks, the drum tracks are sequenced and sampled, because Danny died. Rather than get a new drummer and teach the new drummer all of this stuff and then have him being unfairly compared to Danny, I just figured that Danny would be happy that I sampled him. I went through banks of tapes of him practicing in the studio, found all of his sounds, sampled them, categorized them, and now, when I go to make a new song, I can pull Danny's sounds out and figure out what I think he might have done. So it's me working with Danny, the same as I've always done. We used to always work together like that. He would say: "what do you think of this?" and I'd say, "try that," and he would go (drum sounds)... I've always been a little bit involved in his rhythmic structures, so it's all the same. I think that he'd be very happy that I'm sampling him, and that he's out there on the stage with me still.

Vicki Bennett, 2011

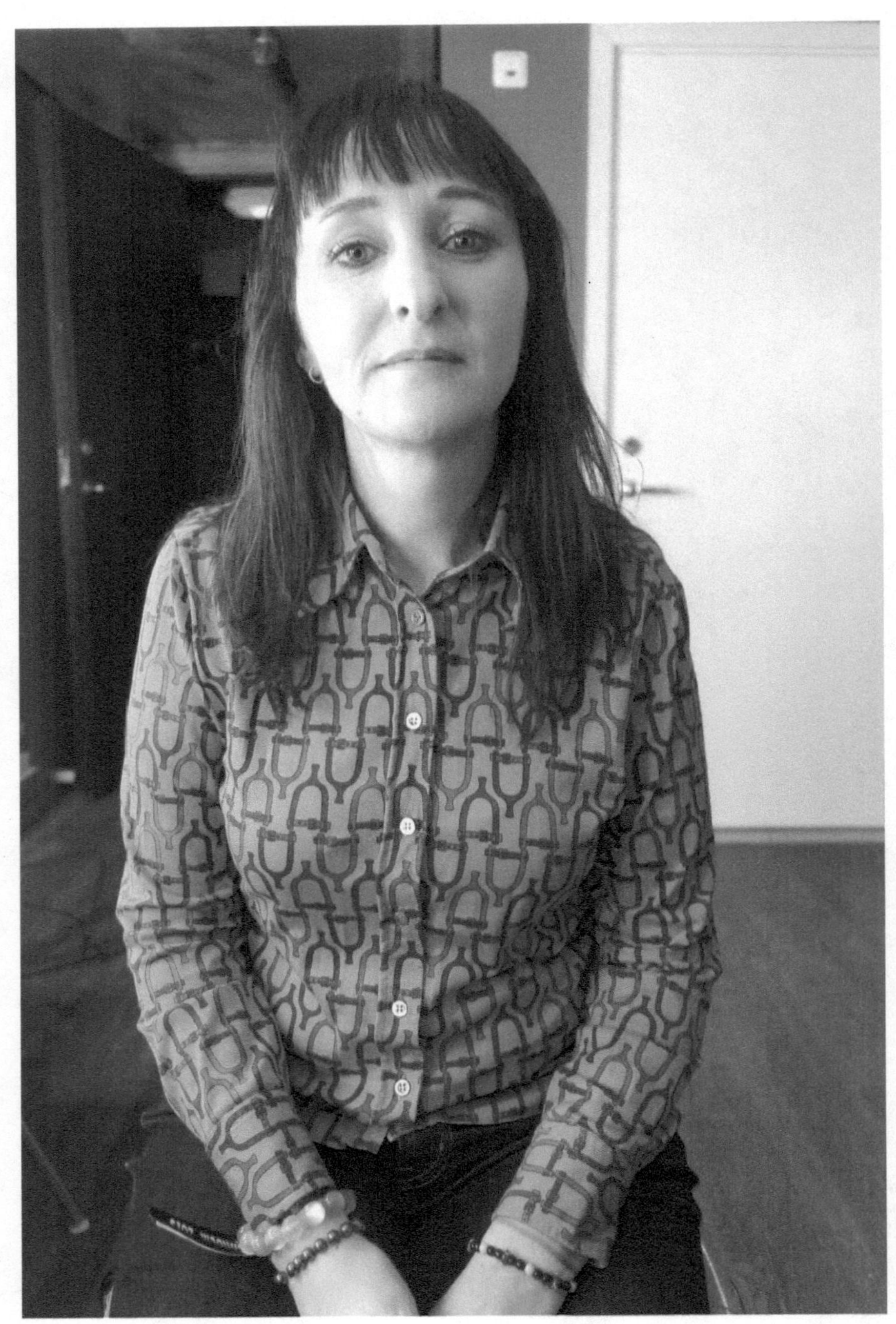

Vicki Bennett / People Like Us

"I think my personality is an integral part of this thing."

I first met British artist Vicki Bennett in London and Brighton in the late 1980s. She was interested in art, psychedelics, magic, networking... Oh, wait! So was I! I therefore immediately took a liking to her. I remember she was getting into video work and music, and in the combination of the two. It didn't surprise me one bit that Vicki bloomed as an exquisite artist merging exactly these two media. Sometimes on their own: in psychedelic sound/music collages and assemblages and remixes and what not, and also in cut-up films, montages, visual rearrangements. But most often actually in that very powerful juxtaposition between music and film in which a new totality is presented after a playful and synaptically challenging remix of already fascinating parts.

Just like me, Vicki early on grew inside the creative greenhouse that was the band Psychic TV, the magical think-tank-order Thee Temple Ov Psychick Youth (TOPY) and, in extension, collaborating with the occultural multi-force that was Genesis P-Orridge (1950-2020). It was an environment cloaked in open-mindedness, experimentation, magical theories, and also in paying homage to the theories and practices of those who had walked before us. Perhaps most significantly British artist Austin Osman Spare (1886-1956), American author William S Burroughs (1914-1997) and British-Canadian artist Brion Gysin (1916-1986). All of them basically serving up a dish that suggested that reality can be broken down into very small common particle denominators, and that should then be heated by chance and random fires, to make for new and unexpected combinations.

Vicki Bennett has continued in that same spirit with her main project People Like Us, and I've just kept admiring her and her work (even to the extent of making a film about her in 2015: "Nothing can turn into a void – An Art Apart: People Like Us." Her work is multidimensional, attractive, thought-provoking, transgressive, poetic and any and all other wonderful adjectives we can think of. People Like Us are not quite like people like us; Vicki's is a very unique ability to pleasantly and humorously tilt any expectations you may have.

I was very happy to finally reconnect with Vicki Bennett in Stockholm in 2011, as she visited with a well-received and cheered performance of film and music. There was a lot to talk about, and the following conversation is what crystallized on that particular evening.

— One thing we can say is that your work is always full of humor and playfulness. But I was wondering if there is something serious in that too.

My idea of success is to be engaging with the audience. The way I choose to do that is through collage, and with sound and moving image, because I figured that is the way you can incorporate several levels into your work. Someone could appreciate it on a very simple level or they could look at it in a very intellectual, complicated level, and they are all right. Everyone is correct in their own assumption. That was the method that I chose for doing my work. But really I want to create a total world that people can step into. I want to create a magical world that engulfs people's imagination in a wondrous way, by using humor as a language, which isn't just English. It is human. Also, the thing about humor is that you can't explain humor. You can't pin it down. It is incomprehensible and so it can't be intellectualized. That is something that is magical as well. I want to create a magical world where humor is a way into that, because people connect through a sense of humor.

— Was that something that dawned upon you slowly or something that hit you like a rock?

I've always been the same. I've always made collages because I don't know how to do things any other way. I am not academically trained. I can't play instruments. I am average with everything I am trying to do except making collages. It is actually by default that I am doing the things I can do and have always done. It is a very intuitive way of working, and also it was a monetary thing. When I first started I was using tools available to me, like records, cassette decks, radio and TV. I recorded things with cassettes, so I was making sound collages. To start with, I saw it as a sort of DJ-ing thing. I wasn't aware of the scope that I later found out about. That you can release things like that and that I have got contemporaries, that there are movements and genres, not only in the last 20 years, but through visual art as well. I did not know any of that. So it has been more like I have gone on this journey, and along the way people have told me things about what it is that I do, and I believe them. It is not really me trying to do anything. I am just ambling along and finding things out along the way.

— There is an analogy to cooking, I think. You don't necessarily have to kill the animal in question yourself, or any animal at all. And you can use basically whatever ingredient to make a dish.

Yeah, it's in the ingredients, or alchemy. I think it is a very natural way of working: to be gathering and processing and transforming what is around you. It's folk art, I think. Making collages and working with found imagery and sound is very much the natural folk art way of working, for they are the tools of the modern times. Whereas before that, people were using instruments and poetry. But they were transforming things as well. Bob Dylan, in Manhattan, was playing a song that was being sung two weeks earlier, just two blocks away. He changed a verse. And that was before concepts of ownership got really entangled with copyright, and it was seen as folk music. Whereas now it's complicated. It's a bit stupid, the way it has got complicated, because it is actually folk art.

— In all of this multifaceted creation, have you ever felt tempted to try to focus on one specific thing? For a longer period of time, I mean. Let's say that you try to decide and work strictly with video, in the same manner, but just work with video for a longer period of time.

In the amount of time I spend a year, I probably do video 80 % of my time and music and sound about 20 %. I can make an album in about three months, whereas making a longer piece of video takes a lot longer because it's a lot more difficult to make a video than it is to make music, as far as I am concerned. I want to make feature films, and I am actually endeavoring to try to get funding to do that at the moment. Because the longest films I have made at the moment have been for my live concerts, which are 45 minutes long. They have a narrative going through them that are like sketches. So actually I am doing a lot of moving image work.

— For a while, you were the only artist with complete access to the BBC archives.

There may have been one other person last year. I was first though. It was crazy, because there's like a million things in the archives. We had 16 weeks to access them; me and one other artist. It was insane. When we got there in the summer, they said that they realized how crazy it was, but as long as we were gone by the end of the year it would be fine. And so we just kept going back. They just let us stay on, and I did make a film out of it, about five minutes long... It was based upon the Festival of Britain. I like world fairs, expos and festivals because they celebrate the goodness and ingenuity of mankind. I also like modernist architecture and that kind of forward thinking. World fairs and expos... they are all about the best and the most forward-thinking things. And so I found a lot of footage from the Festival of Britain. It was in 1951, at The Royal Festival Hall in London, which was a hundred years after the great exhibition at Crystal Palace. The Festival of Britain was about coming out of the war and everything being colorful again. So I found this documentary about a chap called James Gardner, and he was one of the people, three or four people, who had to put together and program a "Festival of Britain." He said that they had no idea what they were doing and they had to do it really fast. I like the approach, and I used him as the talking head in the film. He said that he approached it like a child might. Imagine you are building a castle. He said, "I like to imagine that I could do it and I just try and do it and start..." Just like playing.

— Is that the clip that is on your website, where someone is holding some dancing people?

No, that is a different one. That is the film called "The Remote Control," which is all about controlling things by turning knobs and remotely controlling people. So it has, kind of, got a slightly sinister edge to it, but it's also a self-reflection of you trying to make a film, of you trying to edit a film in the first place. And try to animate these people who are controlling things. All my films have got the same kind of things going on in them but yeah, the James Gardener thing was all about "You just got to try and do it." Don't worry about how you are supposed to do things, because a lot of the time it turns out to be a load of rubbish anyway. Get on with it, you know.

— One thing that strikes me is that not only does the humor play a part in your work, but it is also very, very psychedelic. In your case, has that been just another ingredient or has it been a real inspiration for you? Because it's at the same time a way of looking at things and a way of presenting things, and it is also an esthetic. It must have been important for you.

I am guessing that it has been an integral part of my personality. The artist notices things more than the average person on the street. And I think it has something to do with focusing intensely on things, and then accumulating things in a way that a magpie might go and fly and find a piece of colorful silver foil and put it in their nest. You know, I think that is kind of what I am doing. I am not saying I am like a magpie, but I like to get lots of goodies and put them together, which can make things look a bit like an overload sometime. And I know that what I do is quite dense sometimes. But I don't even notice to be honest. To me it's totally fine but for a lot of people it is too much because the normal way to compose in any medium is you don't mix more than about three elements. Because it's too much for the outsider to take in. Whereas for me, it's normal to do much more than that. And changing direction as well. But it's also a lack of skill. In a traditional sense, everything that I learned to do has just been by accident rather than knowing how to do things properly. So once again it is that trying-things-out ethic which could make things seem psychedelic, because you are actually being quite chaotic. But then I try to keep things in repetition, going through things. It is like the idea of the middle eight in music. Really the middle eight in music is that you have a beginning and an end with anything that you do. I don't have to make a piece of music that is the way you are supposed to do it. You can make the most of not knowing how to do things, which means you can do anything. Which can come across as being a bit chaotic. But I control chaos.

— I was curious also about the work for the radio station WFMU, how does that work? Do you mix that at home and then upload the shows or…?

I have been doing that since 2003. I collage it at home and then I upload it. I can't do it all year around. It is too much. I upload that each week and when the show is actually on the air, we have a live play list with comments and I update "blog-style" every minute, and we are writing the titles in the chat. So it does have a live element, in my presence of being there with the audience. They are commenting and then know that I am actually sitting there while I am doing it. I collage pop with avant-garde because I think all music is pop. I think everything is pop. I don't think one thing is listenable and one thing isn't. I think it is just about the way you introduce things to people. I think you can make people like anything or not like anything. And it is all the same. It's all about education, context and environment.

— Can you remember a distinct point in time when you just decided that "I want to be an artist"? Was there a defining moment in your life, when you said, "this is really what I want to do"?

Yeah, I think when I was about 13 or 14. When I was a child I was always emulating what I wanted to do as an adult. I used to make tapes and I made a radio station which was just tapes. I had a pretend group. I used to collage pictures of me on top of other things, so I was dreaming of all these things that I am doing as an adult. I didn't realize that was what I was doing but I emulated everything that I always dreamed of. You know, like making music. And the video things, I don't know how that happened. That was when I was about 16. It was when I was 13 or 14 that I suddenly realized that you can make those dreams real. So I started thinking, "I am going to really focus on this." I realized that if you actually do keep focusing, then something is going to happen.

— Just keep at it.

Yeah, exactly. And I wanted… I mean, that was essentially the (Psychic TV) "Force the Hand of Chance" album. I was a big Marc Almond fan. That was my way, and listening to him singing "Like a biker in the summer heat…" From the song "Guilt-less." That song is about, "See it and go for it." That really made me think… Yes!

— Those two first Psychic TV albums are so seminal.[1] I think that if it were possible to scan creative people's minds, I would say that those two albums would pop up very often. Instigators of will power, at least for our generation.

Yeah. It really clicked in my head. You don't need many of those moments in life to get going. I always felt that way. Sometimes I go in as a visiting artist at universities and talk, and occasionally I do workshops. I think every now and then that you're going to affect someone, and you will make and impact on them possibly to change their lives. Because when I think about it, it has taken very few people to change my life.

— Another interesting aspect is that when people grow older they really are carrying on in a tradition. When we were younger we could see ourselves as being goo goo-eyed, looking up to certain people. But we are just the same; just keeping on in the same tradition, and it is really remarkable.

Yeah, it is very odd. Last year, I had dinner with Jim Thirlwell and Matt Johnson

---

1 Psychic TV: "Force the Hand of Chance" (Some Bizzare, 1982), and Psychic TV, "Dreams Less Sweet" (Some Bizzare, 1983).

and I was, like, if someone had told me when I was younger that we are equal... I even told Matt Johnson that I used to write to him when I was 14. Very odd.

— That is funny. I had that similar mind-blowing thing when Throbbing Gristle played in Paris 2008. The evening before the concert, Kenneth Anger opened an exhibition of some Crowley paintings. And then after that, I went out to dinner with Gen, Sleazy,[2] David Tibet and Bill Breeze: a great dinner. Then Genesis said, perhaps to confirm his own position as Queen Bee: "I have played with you all." For me that sort of put things and myself in a context, and not only because of the double entendre. All these weird people that I have looked up to so much... I am really part of the gang myself. A phenomenal insight!

It is funny... I met Kenneth Anger last year. There is a festival in Newcastle called the AV Festival. Funnily enough I know the curator. The whole theme was recycling, and I said to her that the first recycling film I ever saw was Anger's "Scorpio Rising." Which is using all the found footage. I said he was the first filmmaker to really use found footage, and she invited Anger because I had said that. Wow, you know! But I was too nervous to speak to him actually.

— We live in a world or a culture where it is possible to appropriate everything: "collage culture," or whatever you want to call it, with sampling and downloading stuff. All of it is basically about a sense of freedom. But it is also a risk. If you work within those parameters, then what is the essence of the creator? Can you pin-point something that you can see is You in your art? Where is Vicki in all of your work?

I think it is way I tie it together. It is a patchwork quilt, and when you stand back from it, you don't see all the parts; you see the whole. I think that I create an atmosphere; it is like the essence. You have got this essence or atmosphere in it that is you. I am always surprised when I hear music or see stuff by people and I can't see the personality. I think my personality is an integral part of this thing. It is just me talking. It is just me. It is me. All these things I am using are just parts of the quilt. And they exist in their own right. The original doesn't die. It still exists. Which is why I find it amazing that people can get annoyed and say that you are doing damage to the original. But I am paying homage to it. Unless you are being negative.

---

2 Peter "Sleazy" Christopherson (1955-2010), a member of Throbbing Gristle, Psychic TV, Coil and other avant garde music constellations.

— But you are not really negative.

No, I am positive. I never use anything that I don't like. It is always paying homage to it. It is a celebration of the content. It is finding ties between things that are disparate and incongruous, showing that everything is actually the same, because I really do believe that. I try to make things humorous, but everyone tells me my work is really dark.

— Oh, really?

Yeah, people get disturbed by it sometimes.

— Maybe it is because we are so jaded?

I am trying to do the light and dark thing, to show that they are the same. Not the same, but they are reflections of the same thing, in the middle, you know. So yeah, I probably answered that question somewhere in there.

— Would you say that you prefer working with stuff in your own confinement or taking it on the road like this, and actually performing it?

I prefer working in confinement. My idea was working in confinement but in collaboration with people who can realize the project. Whether that be other people or artists or producers, distributors, everyone playing a role where it feels real. So I don't work in complete isolation a lot of the time. Not by choice; just because no one is around. But doing gigs and stuff is the way; it is the way that people see things, and as quickly as possible. You know you can have two people or two hundred people see your gig. You can have a lot more people download your stuff — tens of thousands of downloads — but you don't get to be part of the experience. But it is really important because I get all my gigs through the internet. I never ask people for gigs; they come to me. And that is all through the Internet, through Ubuweb or my site and things like that. I did an online album, "Abridged too far," that had 25.000 downloads in the first month... fantastic!

— What is the weirdest thing that has ever happened in a live context like this? People freaking out or...

I have had lots of horror stories. There was a funny one in Norberg. When I played a festival there a couple of years ago and it was mainly noise people. That is when I was still playing stuff off of DVDs. I use a laptop now, but a DVD got stuck. So my gig was actually not ever going to end. It was a bit in in my concert where a robot was singing, "Music alone shall live, music alone shall live. Never to die. We will all die..." and this robot was stuttering over and over. People started to realize it. It was going on and on and on. In the end I just had to press stop. That was the end of the gig and I threw the DVD in to the audience. So that was a really nice experience because everyone thought that was really funny and cheered. I have had loads of other technical horror stories as well. I can't remember any of them actually. More than I care to imagine. I have had strange atmospheres. I work with Ergo Phizmiz who is another collage artist. We made a joint concert last year called "The Keystone Cut-Ups." It is mixing early avant garde film with early comedy to show how important the people in it were to each other. They were both very influential to each other and it was really intense because we had eight weeks to make 45 minutes. Ergo concentrated on the music and I made 45 minutes of film on a dual screen. I and was doing 12 hour a day shifts, seven days a week. It was intense. I was working really intensively with all this footage, particularly with the Marx Brothers. I got this strange feeling with Harpo Marx; I started feeling fixated about Harpo Marx. When we did the concert, it was in a hall just like tonight but bigger but old and grand... And I swear Harpo Marx was there! There was a eerie atmosphere. And he is in that film as well. Everyone said it was very strange. In the end we both turned around and watched him playing the harp and then raised our glasses to him. And I thought, "he is here." I was sure Harpo Marx was there.

— If we get back to the humorous attitude, have you ever considered it to be a kind of defense mechanism?

Yes, because you can put yourself down before anyone else does. Humor is one way of dealing with uncomfortable feelings and taboos, and also confusion. People laugh at things involuntarily because of nervousness. I laugh a lot. I'm a nervous person. But the main reason I use humor is because that's the way I want to connect with other people. I find it difficult to get on with people who don't have a sense of humor. It's a way to get deeper with someone. It's vulnerability that makes you get on with people.

— If a communication is completely straightforward, it's also quite boring.

Yes. You need to get surreal. You need to get off the main path. Surrealism and humor are very similar, in that you can't explain them. They're a parallel way of looking at something.

— When it's time to put something together, like a video for instance, do you have a very clear vision in your mind of what you want to do, or do you look at the material at hand and just go from there?

In the past, I've looked at what's available. With found footage, you only have what they did. You can't work with what they didn't. In the past it's been a case of looking at things instead of looking for things. Just recently, I've been waking up at 5 AM with ideas and just writing them down. My brain's changed the way I work. I think it has to do with that I want to do things for spaces, like installations. That has changed my way of thinking. I think it has to do with that I've realized I can work with the space itself, rather than the screen.

— What's a perfect day like for you?

Having lots of ideas of my own and then seeing other people doing them. A lot of the time it's just either or. A perfect situation for me is to have a communication with the outside world, but also to do work. I love working. I'm on my own a lot of the time. I want to be part of a community but I don't see people that often. That can frustrate me. I know more about the imperfect days. I start wondering if other people have more perfect days than I do. But I don't think they do.

Brian Williams, 2011

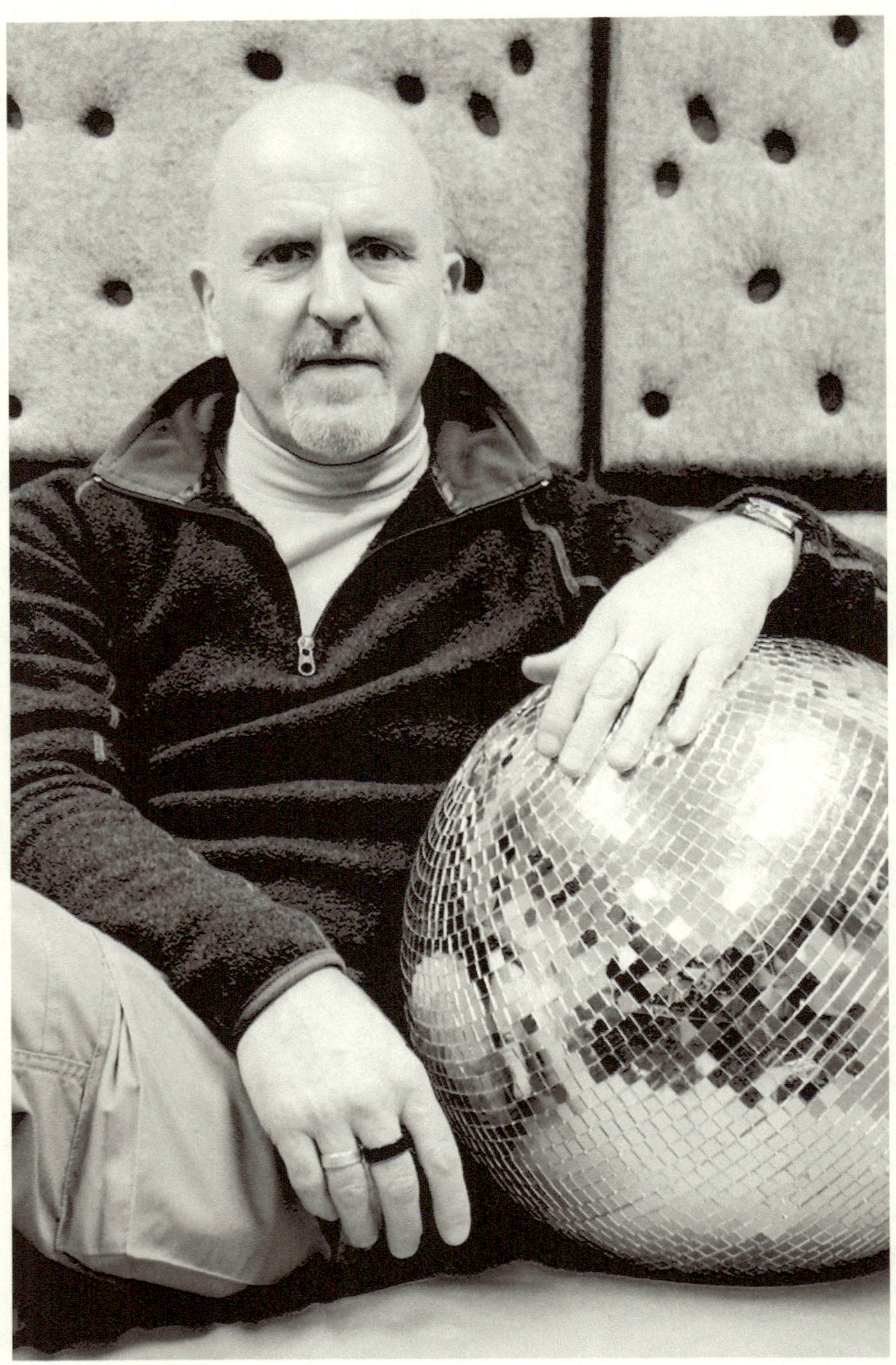

Brian Williams / Lustmord

"I like to create sounds that don't otherwise exist."

Brian Williams is a highly gifted sound person, armed with sensitive ears, ditto fingers, and a creative musical mind. Over the decades he has created a body of work that usually gets tagged "dark ambient." For the lack of a better term, let's stick with that for now. Williams' music is certainly dark, and its strong evocative potential (as in "stirring up inner images, fantasies and daydreams") is there all along too. No wonder he's been busy working on both independent horror films and occasional live performances in odd places (The Church of Satan's 40th birthday bash in Los Angeles 2006, for instance).

After having worked with proto-experimentalist collective SPK in the early 1980s, Brian Williams drifted on to an ambitious productivity under the name/moniker "Lustmord," including many fruitful collaborations (with Jhon Balance of Coil, Jarboe of Swans, and Clock DVA, to mention but a few).

Behind this almost legendary enigma we find the Brian Williams who is also a very normal human being. Williams is a fast talker, funny, and likes to downplay any morose states of mind or sinister agendas. For Williams, it's all about the sound, and about fitting the sounds in question into a context. When that happens, it's all good — albeit dark and, yes, ambient too.

Stockholm was blessed with one of those rare live Lustmord performances in January 2011. On the day before the actual concert, I met Brian Williams at "EMS,"[1] an old but hi-tech studio-cum-hangout for scholastic/electro-acoustic composers. In a way, he was then literally a dark star "hanging out" in this pretty dusty environment. As that's also the title of my favorite Lustmord album — "The Place Where The Dark Stars Hang" — I thought that could be a good way to begin our conversation.

— Where is that place, the actual "place where the dark stars hang"?

---

1 Elektronmusikstudion.

Well, that's an interesting question, I'll give you that. I haven't thought of a deep meaning as to the exact location, because it was never meant to mean anywhere specific. I mean, I don't have anywhere in mind for exactly where that place is. It's just a fact that there is a place; that's what it's about. Pretty much all of my work alludes to things I don't always point any lights on. Sometimes it's deliberately vague, more enigmatic, and also some of the times it's very specific. It's where you go: that's where the place actually is. There's an old concept behind it, and actually all my albums are alluding to each other. They can look back on each other. There are some ideas that I often explore, and mainly I tend to not go too deeply into detail on purpose. Sometimes there is not much detail and sometimes there are a lot of layers of information, but I kind of like it to be your interpretation of the record itself. That album is in that place where your mind takes you when you listen to it. Most of my albums are about creating a space that only exists when the music is playing; quite often a literal space. Well, actually it is a literal space; that's the whole point of what the music is. When the music ends, that place is gone again. And you can enter into it in your own way if you wish.

— You can perceive space in different ways: it could be an emotional space, an audio space or a visual space, for instance. I'm curious, when you concoct the music, when you put that together, do you also get emotionally involved? Do you get images or visions?

No, I don't really get that, because I'm very much about the sound itself. I was going to say "painting with sound." But if you call it that, it sounds really pretentious. You know what I mean. But that's how I approach it. For me, it's always the sound, and actually I fail often. It's a perfectly sensible question, but no, I don't really. I'm always working with the sound, and I'm aware of that some of that sometimes conjures up images in people. But for me, I know it's about the sound. I'm also going back to what I was just saying earlier: the structure of the album is in fact in this journey and this place, because they are always conceived. I always know how my album is going to be. Before I even begin working on it in my head, it already exists. I always work on albums as albums, and there's always a beginning, and you go somewhere, and it brings you back out again.

— The big picture, the concept, is already there in your mind?

Yes, very much so. When I'm working on a project, the actual recording building site is the boring site. I've already planned the house and I actually know how it's going to work and now I have to actually dig the trench. When I'm digging the trench, I'm already thinking about the next phase, and the exciting bit is the planning and the ideas.

— Is that also valid on the detail level, like one structure in the concept, like one specific sound or track? Do you work and rework and rework or is that already clear in your mind?

I don't rework when I record albums and there's nothing left over because I know this is where things will go. In the process of working, something will come up — like another idea — and then things evolve in a different way. But generally speaking, it pretty much follows the plan. Not in a kind of strict plan; it's not strict at all. When I think of these things, it's really interesting planning and having these ideas and then actually doing them. I do enjoy that process but usually in that process I'm already thinking about the next one. That's the bit I really find stimulating.

— I find it very intriguing to hear also, because of all the people I've talked to that are involved in similar kinds of music, I'd say that most of them are very spontaneous, spur of the moment, kind of "try this and try that"... But it's interesting to hear that everything is already there in your mind.

Well, I can imagine doing it the other way myself. I don't have a problem with that, but for me it's the plan that matters. I'm also a bit anal about this. I'm very much a concept kind of guy. Yeah, I like coming up with concepts, that's the bit I really enjoy. The album is always a concept. There are all kinds of really little details in there. I even put in things that are very specific, but it's because the detail is really important to me.

— That leads us onwards to where the concepts come from. Where do you get the inspiration for these details? Where do you think it all comes from, originally?

Well, again, I think inspiration... That's a tricky one. I know I like being around creative people. I like creativity. I find creativity very inspiring. I enjoy the stimulus of being around people who create. That's about as specific as I get for my inspiration actually. As far as where my ideas come from, I honestly can't tell you. I mean obviously I absorb things like we all do on a daily basis. I read a lot, I watch things,

I talk a lot. So they're always bubbling under the surface, these ideas. But as far as specific concepts, I can't say I can point to any specific thing. It's who I am. I don't really think about it.

— My impression of you and your way of working is also that it is a lot of work. There's a lot of discipline, and that you're also sort of fertilizing it with commercial work in that sense. I think my own take on it would be that you're "honing:" you're flexing your creative muscles. Whether it's your brain or something else, you keep it alive and thereby you get benefits.

I enjoy creating. I like to create this stuff; this is why I do it. That's what I very often say. My music is not commercial, and I wish it was, because it'd bring me money and a decent lifestyle and that kind of stuff. But, you know, I do what I do; this is who I am. And it's great that there are some people who are interested in it and who are listening to it. That is very flattering, but this is what I'd do anyway. I can't imagine not doing this. If nobody were listening to it, it would still exist. And I will keep doing it. I mean, I should really get a real job. But this is who I am. I don't really think about it that much; it just is.

— In terms of the movie work and the soundtracks, has it ever happened that the producers have come back and said: "Well, Brian, no, this is too weird"?

Oh sure, it has happened. It's very common.

— How do you adjust?

There have been quite a few times in movies and commercials and little things for TV, that they've come to me because they want "weird and fucked up." "We want something really fucked up and industrial and fucked up and dark. You can do dark, right? Dark!" And then we have this dialogue: "What would you mean by dark? What would you mean by fucked up?" And they go, "It has to be really fucked up!" And then you give them some stuff and they come back and say: "This is so fucked up; this is too fucked up!" "Well we've had this discussion, you wanted it to be really out there so…" And then you give them industrial and you give them some stuff and they say, "This is not industrial! Oh, we were thinking more like Nine Inch Nails." "You didn't say anything about Nine Inch Nails, you said you wanted more avantgarde industrial." This happens quite often. Especially the dark… "We want dark, this is too dark! We can't use this!" Well, for fuck's sake, what do you want?

— Are there any directors that you would like to work with?

I'd love to work with David Lynch, for example. That would be great, but I don't know what he's really doing these days. I don't think he's as interesting as he used to be, unfortunately, but he is an interesting guy. A David Lynch movie would be really enjoyable. I like the way he approaches sound. I think David Fincher is really great. I love Korean and I love Asian directors. David Lynch comes to the immediate mind but actually there are a lot of people doing interesting stuff.

— So it's not like you have a wish list, or your agent has a wish list?

I don't have an agent. I don't have a manager or anything. I saw a movie recently called "Monsters," which I really enjoyed. It wasn't great but it was really good, you know, and after watching it I thought I would really enjoy working on something like that. I just like interesting work, and working with interesting people.

— Was that one of the original reasons for you moving from the UK to Los Angeles? To be closer to the movie world?

If you want to work on movies you have to be there. The first time I went to America was on a tour. I really enjoyed crossing 10.000 miles in six weeks. It was great and as we went further and further West we enjoyed it more, because it's more and more different. It was really interesting because you're European and looking at America from a distance and not being a big fan of it culturally — it's a love-hate kind of thing. Anyway, going over there I realized it's completely different from what I thought it was going be. The "Have a nice day"-stuff which I really hated... When you get there you realize they actually mean it, and it gives you a whole different perspective of what it's really like. And culturally hating things like McDonald's and Coke and advertising and going over there and finding there's stuff like jazz, stuff like blues, a lot of really interesting cultural stuff. Anyway, going over there, I just really liked America, especially the West Coast and California. Arriving in California really felt like coming home. Something I often talk about is growing up in Britain. It's a generalization but it's also true, that things tend to be very negative in Britain. So being in America, being amongst Americans, you feel much more positive about things and doing stuff. I always liked the idea of the ideal world: that it would be nice to live in America. But it was kind of impractical. There were a lot of things getting in the way. It's not an easy country to move to, as far as the barriers they have. They just don't let anybody in. But then I was there on vacation and a friend of mine there, Graeme Revell, was a film composer at the time. He was having some problems with his Mac and I fixed it for him. I was good with that stuff. This was around 1988-89 and he was working on a movie and he was having trouble with some sounds. So when I got back to London I sent him some stuff he could use, which he did, and he really liked what I'd sent him. It was just a few weeks later that he called me up and he said, "You'd be really useful if you were here doing this for me." So he offered me some work there, and I moved to LA to do that. I didn't plan that. Like most things it kind of just happened. I stumbled into it.

— Has the vastness of the space in California has affected you musically?

Well, it's inspiring. We have a big four-wheel drive truck and we love to go off road, miles away, to places that are difficult to go to, miles and miles away from the nearest person. I love the desert; it's just a great place to be. Someone was asking me last year about living in California; how has that changed my work? I don't really think so. It seemed to be like an idea that would change everything. But my music was called dark and stuff before, too. People have responded to my music in just the same way when I'm living in sunny California. It's changed things in the sense that I like what I am now. Los Angeles, where I live, is a great place and it's also like most of the big cities, in that it has plusses and minuses. I like Southern California more than I like living in Los Angeles. I'm happier living in California than I was before I lived in California, as far as being somewhere. So in a sense, it's changed things, as I'm more comfortable now.

— If I wanted to describe your music, the absence of rhythm creates a very slow moving flow feeling, and I was thinking: have you ever thought of that as having almost therapeutic qualities in regard to the times we're living in, which are so fast, rhythmic and fragmented?

Well, yeah, I guess it could do it for some people. It would be nice if it did. But it's a very deliberate approach. My music is what it is. It's kind of ironic, but it exists because it exists. I was feeling a lack of it — of the stuff I wanted to hear that didn't exist — so I had to go and create it myself. Of course the irony is that when you create anything, the last thing you're going to do is listen to it yourself. I'm assuming it's as if I'm reading a book... I'm just not going to read anything that I've written myself. And this has become a style that other people copy, and of course I'm not going to listen to their stuff. The things that I listen to are completely opposite to what I do, which is interesting.

— If we step outside the musical world, can you find any audio memories from childhood that you think have affected you?

Yes, but actually they'd be more synthetic in a sense. When I was really little, there were a few TV shows that were kind of stranger, more electronic. It was something different and, you know, even the tune on it... There was a song called "Telstar," which was great. There was all this singing and people using stranger sounds, and by strange I mean things that aren't real, but synthetic machines. As a kid I wasn't really aware of it. The only thing I'm aware of in the end is that it's just something different and most of the stuff just happened to be electronic. The fact that it was electronic wasn't the factor. The factor was that it sounded different from what you normally hear. That's actually quite good because it's a reflection. It's kind of interesting because I don't do it a lot, but when I'm trying to do it my approach is that I like to create a sound that you don't actually recognize. And over this, I might suggest something too. It might be something that you actually do recognize. But a lot of the time I like my work to have a sound that you can't recognize, even though I have used strings and drums and whatever. Most of my sounds is stuff that I like to think that people can't tell what it really is. People may think they know; they might suggest something, but usually it's not really the case. I like to create sounds that don't otherwise exist.

— Given that you work with music technology in a very cutting edge way, I assume that you're very interested in it. Does that inspire you too? I mean that technological development in itself? Or is it merely a tool?

It's a tool. Or both actually. It's definitely a good question. I always get asked by people who want to do something that I do — what tools do I use, etc? — and the answer is always it doesn't really matter. I'd be happy to tell you, but it doesn't matter what my tools are — it's the ideas. Technology's something that makes things easier but that isn't always a good thing. And a lot of the times I think about when we didn't have this much stuff. Then you would have to use your imagination a little bit more maybe. I think that's the best way to go. But yeah, I have a lot of tools and I love playing around with them. When I moved into using computers for recording and manipulating, that made a huge difference for me, because that's how my brain works. Before that, the things I wanted to do I couldn't quite do and in that sense it has been hugely inspiring. But that's not to say that I wouldn't be doing things anyway. Modern technological tools have definitely helped me going into the direction I wanted to go. But at the same time I don't think it would have stopped me if it didn't exist.

— Have you ever felt tempted to try out any other creative expressions?

I thought I already was.

— In terms of writing or painting or…?

Well, I actually went to an art school for a short while. I was good at art, especially fine art, drawing, and it seemed like a natural kind of direction to go. As I often say, there was a mutual agreement that I should leave. I didn't fit in. I thought it wasn't my place at all. That was really interesting: what art school did for me was stop me doing art. I haven't drawn anything since. I've been doing work for albums and stuff but more like creative, directive stuff. It really took it all out of me. I actually thought for quite a while that art school took it away from me. One thing art school did for me was making me not to want to paint anymore.

— Or maybe it just set you free and focused to work on the sound?

I didn't realize that until many years later. Ironically enough, because I should have realized it much, much sooner. At the same time that was happening, I was in art school and I was getting fed up with all the bullshit and all. This was when punk rock was happening and Throbbing Gristle's first album came out, so I was being drawn to that. And what actually happened, without me realizing it at the time, was that part of my mind became focused on sound as opposed to visuals. I'm dyslectic so writing is always a pain in the ass. I've had fun working with some friends on ideas. Not pretentious work like making movies, but we've had some ideas. I enjoy being around creative people, so there are always ideas and things. Most of my own ideas get focused in the music but there's always these other cool ideas going around.

— In terms of the performances, do you feel an increasing temptation to go on doing shows?

Well, I want to do them. That's the plan. I've been interested in doing live things for a long time. But I really didn't think of them as being a live thing, especially early on, from the technical aspects point of view. And also I didn't think it'd be interesting live, for me, especially early on, because I would have to do something really wild. Also from a technical point of view, and especially early on, the studio became an instrument for me. The idea of actually doing that live was not very practical. It'd be boring, it'd be me tweaking sounds and it's not very interesting. I like the idea of something live but it didn't really occur to me how that would be interesting. So I never really seriously thought about it. And then years later, as technology improved and it became more popular, I thought about maybe doing some of the computer stuff live. Then I realized that more and more people have used laptops in that context. There was a combination of a couple of things. Firstly, I wouldn't pay to go and see myself standing on a stage with a laptop. So why would I actually do it? That's how my thinking has been. Then, quite a few years ago, Kraftwerk were playing in LA. I'm a big fan. I've always loved Kraftwerk. I saw them live, and they are these four guys with a laptop. I love their sound, but just standing there... Maybe I should have realized this before, but... As long as the sound is really good it can be a good show. That's the second part of the answer. Now I just say I can do a live show in a place with a good sound system. Otherwise I'm just not going to do it. I don't want to be fully booked either; I just want to do a few shows here and there, just to keep it interesting; to make it more of an "event." I won't go on a tour because that would be stupid. I mean, if it's not interesting for me, why should I do it? People think of Lustmord as being more like an ambient thing but for me it's not very ambient. There's actually quite a big sound in there and a lot of people don't hear that, because a lot of people don't have really good sound systems. And I've done some visuals for it too. I want people to look at the visuals and have the music do the rest.

— It sounds like it's really going to be like a state of the art show.

Each show is going be a little bit different because I'm kind of improvising. I'm blending elements from different tracks in different ways, depending on how it feels at the time. I go by feeling very much too as I'm working on things, you know. So these live things, I'm doing them by feeling. There's a lot of making up as I go along. I want it to be improvising, but it's not really improvisation because I know exactly what I'm doing. Because first of all that's more interesting for me. And also, there's a chance that it might go wrong. When I'm doing these shows I'm deliberately not rehearsing. I do a kind of run-through so I feel early on if I'm playing this sound, then this is what it's going to be like. I tend to forget, because there are so many of them. It's hard to remember which is which. I want it to be actually live and I want it to have the chance element in there.

— Have you ever felt tempted to be in a band again? To be in that social and creative dynamic?

I love collaborating. I much prefer collaborating. I love being in a room and just throwing ideas around with people. New ideas come up and your ideas get taken to a different place. But as a combination, there are few people I've been lucky to work with. There are a few people I'd actually like to work with but they are always on tour, or they're recording and they have a lot of commitments, so that's tricky. And when you narrow that down now, there's a smaller group of people, including the ones who aren't available but would like to be available. So we include those for a while, but then there's this, "are they in a same town?" That kind of helps, you know. Of course, these days you can collaborate over a distance but it is really nothing if we're not actually in the same room. There's a friend of mine from Limp Bizkit who's interested enough. We've talked about doing some stuff together but he's on tour with them for about a year and a half. And then another friend of mine, Sasha Grey, who is a real porn star. We've talked about doing things together but she's really busy with her career. So there's people we've actually talked to about doing things together but there's always the scheduling thing and it's often more difficult to juggle than you think. And when we're actually in the same place at the same time we think "let's just kick back with a beer," and it's nice to just catch up as friends. And that's a more important thing than work. Sometimes it's nice to just kick back and relax.

— What do you do to kick back and relax? Your ultimate relaxation?

I hang out with my friends. The thing I like the most is to sit around a table with a small group of good friends with a couple of glasses of wine and just have a good laugh. The sense of humor is very important to me. Just good fun, laughing out loud with friends. I watch a lot of movies, and in the evenings we just sit in front of the TV with a movie on. We have a really big TV and a great sound system. The dog loves to be on the sofa and we all just get on the sofa at night. I also like to read. I'm just like the normal people, and at the end of the day it's nice to relax and switch the brain off. Sometimes I watch bad TV, but just not for long because it's fucking annoying. But sometimes you just want to switch off. I go on hikes with my dog too. Nothing too pretentious nor profound.

To watch the documentary films in
Carl Abrahamsson's "An Art Apart" series, please visit:

https://vimeo.com/carlabrahamsson/vod__pages

All the photographs in this book are available for sale.
Please write to: info@trapart.net for more information.

Other books by Carl Abrahamsson:

Temporarily Eternal: Photographs of Genesis P-Orridge 1986-2018 (2021)
The Mega Golem: A Womanual for all Times and Spaces (2021, together with Vanessa Sinclair, Kadmus, Gabriel McCaughry, et al)
The Devil's Footprint (2020)
Genesis Breyer P-Orridge: Sacred Intent – Conversations with Carl Abrahamsson 1986-2019 (2020)
Occulture – The Unseen Forces that Drive Culture Forward (2018)
Reasonances (2014)
Mother, Have A Safe Trip (2013)
Fanzinera: Photographs 1985-1988 (2012)
The Fenris Wolf, volumes 1-10 (as editor, 1989-present day)

In Swedish:

Olika Människor (2007)
Bardo Tibet (2000, together with Max Fredrikson, Henrik Bogdan, Peder Byberg)
Allt var bättre förr men inte länge till (2000)

Also Available from Trapart Books

The Fenris Wolf 10 (2020)

Carl Abrahamsson – Editor's Introduction, Carl Abrahamsson – Onwards to the Source!, Ludwig Klages – On the Essence of Ecstasy, David Beth – Katabasis and Erotognosis, Henrik Dahl – An Introduction to Eroto-Psychedelic Art, Peter Sjöstedt-H – Antichrist Psychonaut: Nietzsche's Psychoactive Drugs, Carl Abrahamsson – Lux Per Nox – The Fenris Wolf As Libidinal Liberator, Jesse Bransford & Max Razdow – Revisiting the Veil of Dreams, Christopher Webster – Beyond the North Wind, Kendell Geers – A Long Boundless Systematized…, Kadmus – Seeking the Three-Headed Saint, Billie Steigerwald – The Chthonic Seed: Reflections of an Ancient Death Gnosis, Fred Andersson – The Gospel According to the Tomb Man, Zaheer Gulamhusein – Sunflower, Charlotte Rodgers – The Riderless Horse…, Craig Slee – The Occult Nature of Cripkult, Damien Patrick Williams – Daoism, Buddhism and Machine Consciousness, Philip H. Farber – Thoughts on the Creation of Memetic Entities, Thomas Bey William Bailey – Memetic Magick, Mitch Horowitz – Is Your Mind a Technology for Utopia?, Ramsey Dukes – I'm Gonna Blow Your Mind, Carl Abrahamsson – Grasping Reality with Gary Lachman, Anders Lundgren – Mike Mignola and the Lovecraft Circle, Peggy Nadramia – So It Was Written, Peggy Nadramia – Addendum to So It Was Written, Nina Antonia – Maya, Jack Stevenson – Häxan/Witchcraft Through the Ages, Andrea Kundry – The Demonic Cultural Legacy of Antonin Artaud, Joan Pope – The Birth of Ideas, Genesis Breyer P-Orridge – Idiosyncratic Use Ov Language…, Vanessa Sinclair – Try To Altar Everything, Claire-Madeline Corso – Cutting Up a New Conversation

The Fenris Wolf 9 (2017)

Vanessa Sinclair & Carl Abrahamsson – Editors' Introduction: Looking back at the crossroads, Katelan Foisy – Invocation: Homage to the spirits of the land/London, Sharron Kraus – Art as Alchemy, Demetrius Lacroix – The Seven Layers of the Vodou Soul, Graham Duff – Sublime Fragments: The Art of John Balance, Ken Henson – The American Occult Revival In My Work, Gary Lachman – Was Freud Afraid of the Occult?, Peter Grey – Fly the Light, Val Denham – Proclaim Present Time Over, Katelan Foisy & Vanessa Sinclair – The Cut In Creation, Claire-Madeline Culkin – Beds, Bodies and Other Books of Common Prayer – A Reading of the, Photography of Nan Goldin, Steven Reisner – On the Dance of the Occult and Unconscious in Freud, Katy Bohinc – The 12th House: Art and the Unconscious, Olga Cox Cameron – When Shall We 3 Meet Again? Psychoanalysis, Art and the Occult: A Clandestine Convergence, Ingo Lambrecht – Wairua: Following shamanic contours in psychoanalytic therapy at a M   ori Mental Health Service in New Zealand, Elliott Edge – An Occult Reading of PAO! Imagining in the Dark with Our Vestigial Shamanism in a Shade, Shadow, Wide, Charlotte Rodgers – Stripped to the Core: Animistic Art Action and Magickal Revelation, Alkistis Dimech – Dynamics of the Occulted Body, Fred Yee – Cut-Up As Egregore, Oracle and Flirtation Device, Robert Ansell – Androgyny, Biology and Latent

Memory in the Work of Austin Osman Spare, Ray O Neill — Double, Double, Toil and Trouble: Psychoanalysis Burn and Surrealism Bubble, Derek M Elmore — Dreams and the Neither-Neither, Julio Mendes Rodrigo — Rebis, the Double Being, Eve Watson — Bowie's Non-Human Effect: Alien/Alienation in The Man Who Fell to Earth (1976) and The Hunger (1983), Carl Abrahamsson — Formulating the Desired: Some similarities between ritual magic and the psychoanalytic process

The Fenris Wolf 8 (2016)

Carl Abrahamsson — Editor's Introduction, Vanessa Sinclair — Polymorphous Perversity and Pandrogeny, Charles Stansfield Jones (Frater Achad) — Alchymia, Tim O'Neill: Black Lodge/White Lodge, Nina Antonia — Bosie & The Beast, Aki Cederberg — Festivals of Spring, Michael Moynihan — Friedrich Hielscher's Vision of the Real Powers, Friedrich Hielscher — The Real Powers, Orryelle Defenestrate Bascule — Ear Horn: Shamanic Perspectives and Multi-Sensory Inversion, Zbigniew Lagos — The Figure of the Polish Magician: Czesław Czynski (1858-1932), Gary Lachman — Rejected Knowledge: A Look At Our Other Way of Knowing, Carl Abrahamsson — Intuition as a State of Grace, Bishop T Omphalos — The Golden Thread: Soteriological Aspects of the Gnostic Catholicism in E.G.C., Kendell Geers — iMagus, Johan Nilsson — Defending Paper Gods: Aleister Crowley and the Reception of Daoism in Early 20th Century Esotericism, Gordan Djurdjevic — The Birth of the New Aeon: Magick and Mysticism of Thelema from the Perspective of Postmodern A/Theology, Tim O'Neill — The Derleth Error, Antti P Balk — Greek Mysteries, Carl Abrahamsson — The Economy of Magic, Stephen Sennitt — The Book of the Sentient Night: 23 Nails, Henrik Dahl — We Ate the Acid: A Note on Psychedelic Imagery, Jason Louv — Robert Anton Wilson's Cosmic Trigger and the Psychedelic Interstellar Future we need, Carey Hodges & Chad Hensley — New Orleans Voodoo: An Oddity Unto Itself, Alexander Nym — Kabbalah references in contemporary culture, Zaheer Gulamhusein — Standing in Line, Carl Abrahamsson — As the Wolf Lies Down to Rest, Vanessa Sinclair & Ingo Lambrecht — Ritual and Psychoanalytical Spaces as Transitional, featuring Sangoma Trance States, Hagen von Julien — Listening to the Voice of Silence: A Contemporary Perspective on the Fraternities Saturni, Erik Davis — Infectious Hoax: Robert Anton Wilson reads H.P. Lovecraft, N — II. Land, Cadmus — Neo-Chthonia, Kadmus — A Fragment of Heart: A contribution to the Mega-Golem, Stojan Nikolic — The One True Church of the Dark Age of Scientism, Miguel Marques — The Labors of Seeing: A Journey Through the Works of Peter Whitehead, Renata Wieczorek — The Conception of Number According to Aleister Crowley, Orryelle Defenestrate Bascule — Fragments of Fact, Derek Seagrief — Conscious ExIt, Kasper Opstrup — By This, That: A spin on Lea Porsager's Spin, and Genesis Breyer P-Orridge — Greyhounds of the future.

The Fenris Wolf 7 (2014)

Carl Abrahamsson — Editor's Introduction, Sara George & Carl Abrahamsson — Fernand Khnopff, Symbolist, Sasha Chaitow — Making the Invisible Visible, Vanessa Sinclair — Psychoanalysis and Dada, Kendell Geers — Tu Marcellus Eris, Stephen Sennitt — Fallen Worlds, Without Shadows, Antony Hequet — Slam Poetry: The Warrior Poet, Antony Hequet — Slam Poetry: The Rebel Poet, Genesis Breyer P-Orridge — Alien Lightning Meat Machine, Genesis Breyer P-Orridge — This Is A Nice Planet, Patrick Lundborg — Psychedelic Philosophy, Henrik Dahl — Visionary Design, Philip

Farber – Higher Magick, Kendell Geers – Painting My Will, Carl Abrahamsson – The Imaginative Libido, Angela Edwards – The Sacred Whore, Vera Nikolich – The Women of the Aeon, Jason Louv – Wilhelm Reich, Kasper Opstrup – To Make It Happen, Peter Grey – A Manifesto of Apocalyptic Witchcraft, Timothy O'Neill – The Gospel of Cosmic Terror, Stephen Sennitt – Sentient Absence, Carl Abrahamsson – Anton LaVey, Magical Innovator, Alexander Nym – Magicians: Evolutionary Agents or Regressive Twats?, Antti P Balk – Thelema, Kjetil Fjell – The Vindication of Thelema, Derek Seagrief – Exploring Past Lives, Sandy Robertson – The Fictional Aleister Crowley, Adam Rostoker – Whence Came the Stranger?, Emory Cranston – A Preface to the Scented Garden, Manon Hedenborg-White – Erotic Submission to the Divine, Carl Abrahamsson – What Remains for the Future?, Frater Achad – Living In the Sunlight, Genesis Breyer P-Orridge – Magick Squares and Future Beats

The Fenris Wolf 6 (2013)

Carl Abrahamsson – Editor's Introduction, Frater Achad – A Litany of Ra, Kendell Geers – Tripping over Darwin's Hangover, Vera Nikolich – Eastern Connections, Carl Abrahamsson – Babalon, Freya Aswynn – On the Influence of Odin, Marita – Runic Magic through the Odinic Dialectic, Aki Cederberg – Afterword: The River of Story, Shri Gurudev Mahendranath – The Londinium Temple Strain, Gary Dickinson – An Orient Pearl, Derek Seagrief – Aleister Crowley's Birth & Death Horoscopes, Tim O'Neill – Shades of Void, Nema – Magickal Healing, Nema – A Greater Feast, Philip Farber – Sacred Smoke, Robert Taylor – Death & the Psychedelic Experience, Michael Horowitz – LSD: the Antidote to Everything, Alexander Nym – Transcendence as an Operative Category..., Carl Abrahamsson – Approaching the Approaching, Renata Wieczorek – The Secret Book of the Tatra Mountains, Sasha Chaitow – Legends of the Fall Retold, Sara George & Carl Abrahamsson – Sulamith Wülfing, Robert C Morgan – Hans Bellmer, Genesis Breyer P-Orridge – Tagged for Life, Carl Abrahamsson – Go Forth and Let Your Brain-halves Procreate, Anders Lundgren – Satanic Cinema is Alive and Well, Anton LaVey – Appendices

The Fenris Wolf 5 (2012)

Carl Abrahamsson – Editor's Introduction, Jason Louv – The Freedom of Imagination Act, Patrick Lundborg – Such Stuff as Dreams are Made of, Gary Lachman – Secret Societies and the Modern World, Tim O'Neill – The War of the Owl and the Pelican, Dianus del Bosco Sacro – The Great Rite, Philip H Farber – Entities in the Brain, Aki Cederberg – At the Well of Initiation, Renata, Wieczorek – The Magical Life of Derek Jarman, Genesis Breyer P-Orridge – A Dark Room of Desire, Genesis Breyer P-Orridge – Kreeme Horne, Ezra Pound – Translator's Postscript, Stephen Ellis – Poems for The Fenris Wolf, Hiram Corso – Mel Lyman, Mel Lyman – Plea for Courage, Gary Dickinson – The Daughter of Astrology, Robert Podgurski – Sigils and Extra Dimensionality, Frater Nigris – Liber Al As-if, Peter Grey – The Abbey Must be Built, Vera Mladenovska Nikolich – A Different Perspective of the Undead, Kevin Slaughter – The Great Satan, Lionel Snell – The Art of Evil, Phenex Apollonius – The Quintessence of Daimonic Ipseity, Phanes Apollonius – Infernal Diabolism in Theory and Practice, Anonymous – Falling with Love: Embracing the Infernal Host, Lana Krieg – Sympathy with the Devil: Faust's Infernal Formula, Carl Abrahamsson – State of the Art: Birthpangs of a Mega-Golem, Carl Abrahamsson – Hounded by the Dogs of Reason

The Fenris Wolf 4 (2011)

Carl Abrahamsson – The whys of yesterday are the why-nots of today, Hermann Hesse – The Execution, Fredrik Söderberg – Black and White Meditations 1-23, Peter Gilmore – Every Man and Woman Is a Star, Peter Grey – Barbarians at the Gates, John Duncan – Hallelujah, Ramsey Dukes – Democracy Is Dying of AIDS, Tim O'Neill – The Technology of Civilization X, Thomas Karlsson – Religion and Science, David Beth – Bloodsongs, Payam Nabarz – Liber Astrum, Hiram Corso – Unveiling the Mysteries of the Process Church, Jean-Pierre Turmel – The Pantheon of Genesis Breyer P-Orridge, Kendell Geers – The Penis Might Ier Than Thes Word, Z'EV – The Calls, Robert Taylor – Dreamachine: The Alchemy of Light, Phil Farber – An Interview with Terence McKenna, Phil Farber – McKenna, Ramachandran and the Orgy, Thomas Bey William Bailey – The Twilight of Psychedelic America?, Ernst Jünger – LSD Again/Nochmals LSD, Baba Rampuri – The Edge of Indian Spirituality, Aki Cederberg – In Search of Magic Mirrors, Carl Abrahamsson – Thelema and Politics, Carl Abrahamsson – Someone's Messing with the Big Picture, Carl Abrahamsson – An Art of High Intent?, Carl Abrahamsson – A Conversation with Kenneth Anger

The Fenris Wolf 1-3 (1989-1993-2011)

Carl Abrahamsson – Editor's Introduction
Carl Abrahamsson – 'Zine und Zeit (2011)

THE FENRIS WOLF 1 (1989)
John Alexander – The Strange Phenomena of the Dream, Helgi Pjeturss – The Nature of Sleep and Dreams, Tim O'Neill – A Dark Storm Rising, Carl Abrahamsson – Inauguration of Kenneth Anger, Carl Abrahamsson – An Interview with Genesis P-Orridge, William S Burroughs – Points of Distinction between Sedative and Consciousness-Expanding Drugs, Carl Abrahamsson – Jayne Mansfield: Satanist, TOPYUS – Television Magick, Anton LaVey – Evangelists vs The New God

THE FENRIS WOLF 2 (1990)
Lionel Snell – The Satan Game, Carl Abrahamsson – In Defence of Satanism, Anton LaVey – The Horns of Dilemma, Genesis P-Orridge – Beyond thee Valley ov Acid, Phauss – Photographs, Jack Stevenson – 15 Voices from God, Jack Stevenson – 18 Fatal Arguments, Tim O'Neill – Art On the Edge of Life, Terence Sellers – To Achieve Death, Stein Jarving – Choice and Process, Tim O'Neill – Under the Sign of Gemini, 93/696 – The Forgotten Ones In Magick, Tim O'Neill – The Mechanics of Maya, Coyote 12 – The Thin Line, Genesis P-Orridge – Thee Only Language Is Light, Jack Stevenson – Porno on Film, Carl Abrahamsson – An Interview with Kenneth Anger

THE FENRIS WOLF 3 (1993)
Jack Stevenson – Vandals, Vikings and Nazis, von Hausswolff & Elggren – Inauguration of two new Kingdoms, Tim O'Neill – A Flame in the Holy Mountain, Frater Tigris – A Preliminary Vision, Carl Abrahamsson – The Demonic Glamour of Cinema, William Heidrick – Some Crowley Sources, Peter H Gilmore – The Rite of Ragnarök, ONA – The Left-Handed Path, Zbigniew Karkowski – The Method Is Science..., Fetish 23 – Demonic Poetry, Ben Kadosh – Lucifer-Hiram, Freya Aswynn – The Northern Magical Tradition, Anton LaVey – Tests, Austin Osman Spare – Anathema of

Zos, Rodney Orpheus – Thelemic Morality, Nemo – Recognizing Pseudo-Satanism, Philip Marsh – Pythagoras, Plato and the Hellenes, Terence Sellers – A Few Acid Writings, Hymenæus Beta – Harry Smith 1923-1991, Andrew M McKenzie – Outofinto, Beatrice Eggers – Nature: Now, Then and Never

Genesis Breyer P-Orridge: Sacred Intent
– Conversations with Carl Abrahamsson 1986-2019

Sacred Intent gathers conversations between artist Genesis Breyer P-Orridge and longtime friend and collaborator, the Swedish author Carl Abrahamsson. From the first 1986 fanzine interview about current projects, over philosophical insights, magical workings, international travels, art theory and gender revolutions, to 2019's thoughts on life and death in the the shadow of battling leukaemia, Sacred Intent is a unique journey in which the art of conversation blooms.

With (in)famous projects like C.O.U.M. Transmissions, Throbbing Gristle, Psychic TV, Thee Temple Ov Psychick Youth (TOPY) and Pandrogeny, Breyer P-Orridge has consistently thwarted preconceived ideas and transformed disciplines such as performance art, music, collage, poetry and social criticism; always cutting up the building blocks to dismantle control structures and authority. But underneath the socially conscious and pathologically rebellious spirit, there has always been a devout respect for a holistic, spiritual, magical worldview – one of "sacred intent."

Sacred Intent is a must read for anyone interested in contemporary art, deconstructed identity, gender evolution, and magical philosophy. The book not only celebrates an intimate friendship, but also the work and ideas of an artist who has never ceased to amaze and provoke. Also included are photographic portraits of Breyer P-Orridge taken by Carl Abrahamsson, transcripts of key lectures, and an interview with Jacqueline "Lady Jaye" Breyer P-Orridge from 2004.

Genesis Breyer P-Orridge: Brion Gysin — His Name Was Master

Brion Gysin (1916–86) has been an incredibly influential artist and iconoclast: his development of the "cut-up" technique with William S. Burroughs has inspired generations of writers, artists and musicians. Gysin was also a skilled networker and revered expat: together with his friend Paul Bowles, he more or less constructed the post-beatnik romanticism for life and magic in Morocco, and was also a protagonist in an international gay culture with inspirational reaches in both America and Europe. Not surprisingly, Gysin has become something of a cult figure.

One of the artists he inspired is Genesis Breyer P-Orridge, who collaborated with both Gysin and Burroughs in the 1970s, during his work with Throbbing Gristle and C.O.U.M. Transmissions. The interviews made by P-Orridge have since become part of a New Wave/Industrial mythos. This volume presents them in their entirety alongside three texts on Gysin by P-Orridge, plus an introduction. This book is an exclusive insight into the mind of a man P-Orridge describes as "a kind of Leonardo da Vinci of the last century," and a fantastic complement to existing biographies and monographs.

Carl Abrahamsson:
Temporarily Eternal — Photographs of Genesis P-Orridge 1986-2018

A photobook with snapshots as well as structured portraits of artist Genesis P-Orridge from 1986 to 2018. A great visual companion to P-Orridge's and Abrahamsson's highly lauded anthology of interviews, *Sacred Intent*, this book is an inspiring journey through the mind and life of someone who never stopped exploring and changing. Also contains an essay by Abrahamsson on P-Orridge's "psychic anarcho-sartorialism."

Carl Abrahamsson: The Devil's Footprint

God proposes the challenge of the millennium: if Satan sorts out the ever growing human mess on Earth, God will lovingly take him back to Heaven as his favorite Archangel. Satan accepts, and sets out on a massive operation to balance out over-population, pollution, corruption, and other severely Satanic headaches — many of which he originally helped create… Easier said than done! Satan's love of the ambitiously mischievous humans is challenged as his own "Team Apocalypse" fervently sets to work. But as the world begins to change quickly and dramatically for the better, a new question arises: can God and his suspicious Archangels really be trusted in this cataclysmic, cosmic undertaking?

Carl Abrahamsson: Mother, Have A Safe Trip

Unearthed plans and designs stemming from radical inventor Nikola Tesla could solve the world's energy problems. These plans suddenly generate a vortex of interest from various powers. Thrown into this maelstrom of international intrigue is Victor Ritterstadt — a soul searching magician with a mysterious and troubled past. From Berlin, over Macedonia, and all the way to Nepal, Ritterstadt sets out on an outer as well as inner quest. Espionage, love, UFOs, magic, telepathy, conspiracies, LSD, and more in this shocking story of a world about to be changed forever…

"It's a thrilling roller coaster ride through psychedelic adventures, juicy romantic interludes, metaphoric dreamscapes, high Himalayan yoga enclaves, telepathic portals, 60's flashbacks, magical constructs, secret government pursuits and many more twists that kept all three of my eyes open. It's a story that you'll definitely want to keep non-stop reading, which I enthusiastically recommend."
— George Douvris, Links by George

"Mother, Have A Safe Trip is a highly entertaining and thought-provoking novel. Chock-full of psychedelia, the book is also a much welcome addition to the far too few fictional works published dealing with psychedelic culture."
— Henrik Dahl, Psychedelic Press

"The dialogues are great. But it's too short. I wanted more."
— Genesis Breyer P-Orridge, Artist

"It's a wonderful read. A lovely book."
— June Newton/Alice Springs, Photographer

Carl Abrahamsson (Ed.): The Mega Golem: A Womanual For All Times and Spaces

An anthology of texts and images constituting the current Corpus of the Mega Golem — the talismanic being/sentience created by Carl Abrahamsson in 2009. With contributions by Carl Abrahamsson, Vanessa Sinclair, Kadmus, Gabriel McCaughry, and others.

Vanessa Sinclair: Switching Mirrors

Switching Mirrors is an amazing collection of cut-ups and mind-expanding poetry by Vanessa Sinclair. Delving into the unconscious and actively utilising the "third mind" as developed by William S Burroughs and Brion Gysin, Sinclair roams through suggestive vistas of magic, witchcraft, dreams, psychoanalysis, sex and sexuality (and more). Causal apprehensions are disrupted by a flow of impressions that open up the mind of the reader. What's behind language and our use of it? What happens when random factors and the unconscious are given free reign in poetic form? Switching Mirrors is what happens.

Vanessa Sinclair (ed.): Rendering Unconscious — Psychoanalytic Perspectives, Politics & Poetry

In times of crisis, one needs to stop and ask, "How did we get here?" Our contemporary chaos is the result of a society built upon pervasive systems of oppression, discrimination and violence that run deeper and reach further than most understand or care to realize. These draconian systems have been fundamental to many aspects of our lives, and we seem to have gradually allowed them more power. However, our foundation is not solid; it is fractured and collapsing — if we allow that. We need to start applying new models of interpretation and analysis to the deep-rooted problems at hand.

Rendering Unconscious brings together international scholars, psychoanalysts, psychologists, philosophers, researchers, writers and poets; reflecting on current events, politics, the state of mental health care, the arts, literature, mythology, and the cultural climate; thoughtfully evaluating this moment of crisis, its implications, wide-ranging effects, and the social structures that have brought us to this point of urgency.

Hate speech, Internet stalking, virtual violence, the horde mentality of the alt-right, systematic racism, the psychology of rioting, the theater of violence, fake news, the power of disability, erotic transference and counter-transference, the economics of libido, Eros and the death drive, fascist narratives, psychoanalytic formation as resistance, surrealism and sexuality, traversing genders, and colonial counterviolence are but a few of the topics addressed in this thought-provoking and inspiring volume.

Contributions by Vanessa Sinclair, Gavriel Reisner, Alison Annunziata, Kendalle Aubra, Gerald Sand, Tanya White-Davis & Anu Kotay, Luce deLire, Jason Haaf, Simon Critchley & Brad Evans, Marc Strauss, Chiara Bottici, Manya Steinkoler, Emma Lieber, Damien Patrick Williams, Shara

Hardeson, Jill Gentile, Angelo Villa, Gabriela Costardi, Jamieson Webster, Sergio Benvenuto, Craig Slee, Álvaro D. Moreira, David Lichtenstein, Julie Fotheringham, John Dall'aglio, Matthew Oyer, Jessica Datema, Olga Cox Cameron, Katie Ebbitt, Juliana Portilho, Trevor Pederson, Elisabeth Punzi & Per-Magnus Johansson, Meredith Friedson, Steven Reisner, Léa Silveira, Patrick Scanlon, Júlio Mendes Rodrigo, Daniel Deweese, Julie Futrell, Gregory J. Stevens, Benjamin Y. Fong, Katy Bohinc, Wayne Wapeemukwa, Patricia Gherovici & Cassandra Seltman, Marie Brown, Buffy Cain, Claire-Madeline Culkin, Andrew Daul, Germ Lynn, Adel Souto, and paul aster stone-tsao.

Sir Edward Bulwer Lytton: Vril — The Power of the Coming Race

Sir Edward Bulwer Lytton's cautionary tale of occult super-powers and advanced subterranean cultures have fascinated readers since 1871. Part early science-fiction, part educational tract, part occult romance, Vril keeps spellbinding readers thanks to its wide range of themes and emotions, as well as its thrilling sense of adventure.

A curious man descends into a mountain through a mine and experiences far more than he bargained for. Deep inside the mountain lies a completely different world. Its inhabitants, the Vril-ya, are human-like but physically superior and philosophically more advanced. They live in harmony made possible by their wisdom but also by the powerful and potentially destructive magical energy they call "Vril."

The impressed yet terrified visitor is allowed to stay and learn more about their ancient and advanced culture, something very few visitors have – it seems that all the previous adventurers have been mercilessly disposed of by the Vril-ya...

This edition includes an introductory essay by Swedish author Carl Abrahamsson.

More information can be found at our web site: www.trapart.net